Accession no.
D0496071

Group Performance

Social interaction is of prime importance in daily life, especially so at work and for the interpersonal professions. *Group Performance* is an invaluable account of the theory, research and practice of work in groups. Its authors, Henk Wilke and Roel Meertens, examine how tasks are performed in groups and how group achievement can be encouraged. They also discuss the best structure for a group in order to achieve optimal results.

Beginning with the performance of the individual, and how this is affected by the presence of others, the authors analyse the role of cognitive and reflective tuning. They then explore how four processes – cognitive, reflective, communicative and structural tuning – operate simultaneously in groups. They also discuss different approaches to leadership in relation to the motivation and coordination of group members.

Group Performance will be of interest to all professionals whose day-to-day work depends on effective communication skills, and to students and researchers in psychology and communication.

Henk A.M. Wilke is Professor of Social and Organisational Psychology at the University of Leiden, and **Roel W. Meertens** is Professor of Social Psychology at the University of Amsterdam.

International Series on Comunication Skills
Edited by Owen Hargie
*Head of the Department of Communication
University of Ulster*

Group Performance

Henk A.M. Wilke and Roel W. Meertens

LIBRARY
ACC. No. _DEPT._
0100958
CLASS N
34   WIL
WITHDRAWN
UNIVERSITY
COLLEGE CHESTER

·1040716

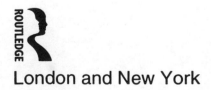

ROUTLEDGE

London and New York

First published 1994
by Routledge
11 New Fetter Lane, London EC4P 4EE

Simultaneously published in the USA and Canada
by Routledge
29 West 35th Street,New York, NY 10001

© 1994 Henk A.M. Wilke and Roel W. Meertens

Typeset in Times by LaserScript, Mitcham, Surrey
Printed and bound in Great Britain by
Mackays of Chatham PLC, Chatham, Kent.

All rights reserved. No part of this book may be reprinted
or reproduced or utilized in any form or by any electronic,
mechanical, or other means, now known or hereafter
invented, including photocopying and recording, or in any
information storage or retrieval system, without permission
in writing from the publishers.

British Library Cataloguing in Publication Data
A catalogue record for this book is available from the British Library.

Library of Congress Cataloging in Publication Data
Wilke, H.A.M.
  Group performance/Henk A.M. Wilke and Roel W. Meertens.
  p. cm. – (International series on communication skills)
  Includes bibliographical references and index.
  1. Social groups. 2. Social interaction. 3. Interpersonal
  communication. I. Meertens, R.W., 1943– . II. Title.
  III. Series.
  HM131.W4668   1994
  302 – dc20   93-17211
                                                                  CIP

Contents

Figures

Editorial introduction

INTERNATIONAL SERIES ON COMMUNICATION SKILLS

In recent years increasing attention has been devoted to the analysis of social interaction in terms of the communicative competence of the participants. In particular, the conceptualisation of interpersonal communication as skilled performance has resulted in a veritable flood of empirical, scientific and descriptive publications regarding the nature of interpersonal skills. However, these publications have been disseminated over a wide spectrum of discipline areas including psychology, communication, sociology, education, business, and counselling. As a result, there is a clear need for a new series of books designed specifically to draw together this material, from disparate sources, into a meaningful evaluation and analysis of a range of identified communication skill areas.

Each book in this series contains a blend of theory, research and practice pertaining to a particular area of communication. However, the emphasis throughout the series is upon the practical application of communication skills to social interaction *per se*. The books are written by authors of international repute, chosen for their knowledge of, and publications in, the specific topic under consideration. As such, this series will make a significant contribution to the rapidly expanding field of interpersonal communication.

The books in the series therefore represent a major addition to the literature, and will be of interest to students and researchers in communication, psychology and other disciplines. They will also prove valuable to the vast range of people in the 'interpersonal professions' (doctors, nurses, therapists, managers, etc.) whose day-to-day work so depends upon effective communication.

Taken as a whole, this series represents an encyclopedia of information regarding our current knowledge of communication skills. It is certainly the most comprehensive attempt to date to chart the existing state of this field of study. As such it is both a privilege and a pleasure to have been involved in the conception and execution of this series.

GROUP PERFORMANCE

Few topics have generated greater interest within the social sciences or produced as much research as that of the study of group dynamics. The reasons for this are many and varied. Given the prevalence of groups to all of our lives, it is hardly surprising that the subject of group performance has for decades greatly exercised the minds of psychologists, sociologists and communicologists. In essence, groups serve five important and related functions. They help us to achieve desired goals and fulfil specific needs; give us a sense of identity; enable us to interact with others whom we perceive to be similar; offer us a feeling of belonging and acceptance; and allow us more potential to influence others. Most of us have to interact in a wide range of groups in order to satisfy all of these functions and this very fact means that a knowledge of group dynamics can be both illuminating and beneficial.

On occasions, we have to decide whether to work with others or operate alone. What factors influence such decisions? What is it about certain types of people and certain types of groups that make them mutually attractive? Once we have joined a group, how and in what ways, can we influence its performance? How does it in turn influence our behaviour? What features of groups help determine success or failure in terms of performance? These are just some of the issues addressed by Wilke and Meertens in this text. They illustrate how the effects of the presence of others has been studied by social psychologists for over 100 years. During this period a voluminous number of papers, articles, book chapters and books have been devoted to this topic. Drawing together all of the separate elements from this wide and varied data bank on groups is clearly a difficult task. The publication of this text is therefore of considerable value, in that it brings together into a meaningful whole many of the sometimes diverse elements associated with this area. There is exhaustive referencing throughout, with lucid expositions of central experimental studies and extensive use of primary sources to chart a thorough map of the area of group performance.

Within this volume, Wilke and Meertens begin with an analysis of the performance of the individual in a social context, illustrating how the understanding of group performance necessitates the integrated study of individuals, the task being undertaken and the overall group effort *per se*. They therefore provide a rich tapestry of all of the separate strands which determine the performance of groups as a whole and of each group member individually. This includes a study of social facilitation and inhibition; social comparison and loafing; influence, conformity, conflict and polarisation; goal, task and reward structures; task and profit interdependency; innovation, brainstorming, groupthink and decision-making; together with an in-depth consideration of the nature, functions and outcomes of types of leader and leadership patterns. In this sense, the coverage of the topic of group performance in this text is exhaustive. The authors, Henk Wilke from the University of Leiden and Roel Meertens from the University of Amsterdam, have a breadth and depth of knowledge of research, theory and practice in the area of group performance and have published widely in this field.

Overall, the content of this book provides an informed and informative account of research, theory and practice in the field of group performance. As the authors point out and demonstrate, the contents of the book are directly relevant to numerous settings. The ability to understand and indeed influence the performance of groups is central to effective functioning in many situations, and so the information presented herein should be of considerable benefit to a wide range of professionals. Since this is an area of study which is of widespread interest, the information presented will be of relevance, and benefit, to academics in many contexts. Furthermore, the broad sweep of theoretical perspectives and wealth of research material covered results in a fine balance of academic and applied perspectives on the study of group performance. In this way the book is, in every sense, comprehensive.

Owen Hargie
Professor and Head of the Department of Communication
University of Ulster

Preface

Performing task groups have become the cornerstone of modern society. The achievements of nations, sciences and organizations for example depend to a large extent on the performance of people working in groups. And, even when people are working alone, their individual performance is quite often directly or indirectly affected by evaluating others.

Although we think that the insights presented in this book are of interest to anyone involved in group processes, our main emphasis is on a social psychological analysis of group performance. A large number of ideas have been generated concerning the way individuals perform in groups. The plausibility of these ideas has been demonstrated by means of experimental studies. These ideas can also be applied to groups in natural settings, such as specific work groups in profit and non-profit organizations. This cannot be done in an automatic way however, since in real life group-specific tasks, specific persons, specific constraints and specific rules of conduct are involved. We argue nevertheless, that the ideas about group performance presented in this book may serve as an analytical and predictive framework for task groups in practice.

The structure of this book is quite simple. In the first chapter, we explain that the individual task-performer confronted with a task, cognitively processes the task, and through reflection before, during and after performance, considers the possible behavioural outcomes. In chapter 2 the main emphasis is on the way individual task performance is affected by the presence of others, for example an experimenter in the role of supervisor and/or other evaluating group members. In chapter 3 we argue that cognitive tuning takes place in groups, though in chapter 4 we stress that group members also reflect upon possible behavioural outcomes during task performance. Whereas cognitive and reflective processes occur during individual task performance, communicative tuning takes place only in groups. The consequences of communicative tuning are sketched in chapter 5.

Communicative tuning pertains to the organization of both the group task and the group. The above-mentioned cognitive, reflective and communicative processes in groups lead to a collective description of the task as well as the performing group. Agreement on a collective description of task and group implies prescription, a set of rules about how individual group members should contribute to the collective task. Chapter 6 deals explicitly with these prescriptive consequences of group processes by explaining structural tuning in groups.

Lastly, in chapter 7, an important aspect of structural tuning, namely leadership, is explained. It is shown that cognitive, reflective and communicative tuning are important in understanding leaderships in groups.

H.A.M. Wilke and R.W. Meertens
Leiden, Amsterdam

Acknowledgements

The present book may be considered a group product. In the abstract, this book has been made possible by the contributions of our many colleagues who have developed ideas and investigated group processes.

More concretely, in designing this book we collaborated with and were greatly supported by Laura Sweeney, who improved the text and corrected many mistakes in our Dutch-English; by Cora Jongsma and Maja Metselaar, who helped us greatly in preparing this text, and by Mary Senechal, who provided many editorial comments. Although we take full responsibility for the text, we want to thank all of the persons mentioned above for their efforts to make this book possible.

Permission to reprint Figures is gratefully acknowledged from the following: B. Brehmer and Elsevier Science Publishers for Figure 3.3 from Brehmer, B. (1988), *The Development of Social Judgement Theory*, in B. Brehmer and R.B. Joyce (eds.), *Human Judgement, the SJT View*, Amsterdam: North-Holland; Houghton Mifflin Company and the Free Press, a Division of Macmillan Inc., for Figure 5.1 from Janis, Irving L. (1982), *Groupthink: Psychological Studies of Policy Decisions and Fiascoes*, Second Edition, Boston: Houghton Mifflin; G. Heider for Figure 6.4 from Heider, F. (1958), *The Psychology of Interpersonal Relations* (fourth printing 1965), New York: Wiley.

H.A.M. Wilke and R.W. Meertens

Chapter 1

The individual performer

A task is a set of rules about why, when and how goals and subsequent activities may lead to a product. The product – a constructed house or a solved problem, for example – can be the result of the performance of a single individual and the result of members of a group as well.

For two reasons we have chosen to start this book on group performance with an explanation of how an individual performer applies a set of rules in order to achieve a product. First, to show that a task is in the 'eye of the beholder', which means that task performance may be considered as a consequence of cognitive and reflective representations before, during and after task performance, and not as something outside and remote from the task performer. Cognitive processes taking place more or less automatically refer to the architecture of the memory, which is conceived as a connectionistic representation. It is more or less hierarchically organized. Reflective processes are also cognitive, but we have selected this term to emphasize that task performers deliberately set goals and monitor their performance during and after task performance – that is, reflective processes are less automatic but more conscious.

Second, these processes apply to individual performance and to group performance. Of course, group performance is more complicated, since in the case of group performance, group members have to exchange, to communicate their representations about their task. Moreover, in groups members face another problem, that is, the problem of how to structure their interaction.

As we will explain later, group performance may be considered as a consequence of cognitive, reflective, communicative and structural processes. To anticipate the performance of groups, in this first chapter we will focus on the cognitive and reflective processes in the individual task performer.

TASK APPROACH

What is a task? It is a set of rules that must be followed to accomplish a goal. Building a house, assembling a jigsaw puzzle, learning foreign words, all of these activities involve different goals: a house built, a jigsaw puzzle assembled and retention of foreign words. The requirements of different tasks also vary. Building a house involves many organizational and labour activities, assembling a jigsaw puzzle requires spatial insight, and learning foreign words requires the performance of retention exercises. In order to deal with these tasks, the task performer has to engage in certain activities.

Not all tasks require the same set of activities. Building a house requires different activities from learning a foreign language, for example. One of the most convincing general descriptions of tasks is that put forward by Miller, Gallanter and Pribram (1960). They describe a task as a minisystem which has a sensing, a testing and an effecting function. Basically, it works like a thermostat. As one knows, a thermostat measures what the actual temperature of a room is; this is the sensing part. Moreover, a thermostat has been set on an ideal temperature. The second function is testing whether the actual temperature of the room agrees with the ideal temperature. If there is inconsistency – for example, the actual temperature is 18°C, but the ideal temperature is 20°C – then the thermostat gives a signal to the furnace so that consistency between ideal and actual temperature will be realized, that is, effecting takes place as long as there is inconsistency between the ideal and actual temperature. This minisystem, containing a sensing, a testing and an effecting function, is a cybernetic control system. The basic unit is the negative feedback loop. This feedback loop is termed negative because its function is to negate or reduce any deviation (or inconsistency) between goal and information, in this case the desired temperature and the actual temperature of the room.

Human tasks may also be considered as cybernetic systems. For example, ham- mering a nail into a board involves STE or sensing, testing and effecting: a carpenter measures, or senses, how far the nail has been hammered into the board; tests to establish whether the actual position of the nail agrees with the ideal position; and effects hammering as long as there is inconsistency between the actual and the ideal (goal) position of the nail.

As another example of a task, consider a woman (or a man) putting on make-up in front of a mirror. If she has sufficient time, she will continue this task for as long as she remains dissatisfied. In terms of the foregoing, this task may be represented as follows. The 'goal' is the 'ideal' image she has of herself. The first information she receives from the mirror falls short of her ideal image. She perceives a discrepancy between her ideal image and the incoming information (her current face). Subsequently she develops activities, such as adding or removing eye shadow, lipstick or powder, which are performed to establish consistency between her goal (the ideal face) and the information reflected in the mirror (her current face). She stops these activities at the moment a new comparison (test) between her current face (information) and the ideal face indicates that the previous inconsistency between the ideal and the current face has been removed. Her task is now completed.

Complex tasks consist of several minisystems, each having a sensing, a testing and an effecting function. Tasks may differ in the degree to which they are

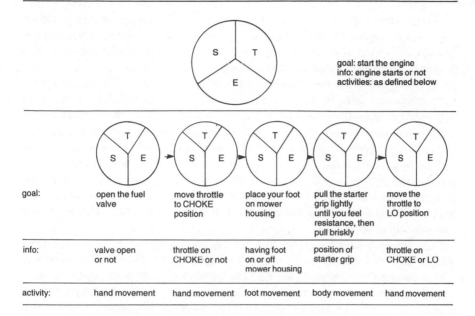

goal: start the engine
info: engine starts or not
activities: as defined below

goal:	open the fuel valve	move throttle to CHOKE position	place your foot on mower housing	pull the starter grip lightly until you feel resistance, then pull briskly	move the throttle to LO position
info:	valve open or not	throttle on CHOKE or not	having foot on or off mower housing	position of starter grip	throttle on CHOKE or LO
activity:	hand movement	hand movement	foot movement	body movement	hand movement

Figure 1.1 Sequential task performance

hierarchically organized and in the extent to which they require sequential processing. To demonstrate the hierarchical and sequential organization of a task, in Figure 1.1 we have presented a grass-mowing task. The goal at the top of Figure 1.1 is hierarchically higher than the subordinate goals, which are represented below it as five minisystems. Or to put it differently, the supergoal (starting the engine) steers the five subordinate goals. An essential element is that subordinate goals may be considered the activities of the supergoal, i.e. from the point of view of the supergoal, turning the valve, moving the throttle, etc. are activities. Figure 1.1 also demonstrates that the five activities implied by the minisystem have to be performed in a given sequence. Thus, sequential interdependence is involved: another sequence is not likely to promote the supergoal of starting the engine. Many tasks are hierarchically and sequentially organized – the tasks involved in making a car, building a house and making a coat for example.

COGNITIVE TASK PERFORMANCE

In the previous section we proceeded as if task performance were a result of automatic task processing by a person who is programmed like a robot: the person has only to perform certain sequential activities to make the lawn-mower run. This approach may have a certain appeal. However, it implies certain cognitive capacities on the part of the performer that make it possible for the task to be performed.

In the present section we will not be able to sketch a complete representation of how a performer engages in his or her task, since our present knowledge is insufficient on this point. Instead, we offer a number of clues about the complex way task performance may come into being.

We start with what may be called the cognitive approach. Several cognitive approaches (e.g. Schank, 1982, on scripts; Fiske and Taylor, 1991, on cognitive schemata; Rosch, 1978, on categorization; Wolters, 1988, on connectionism) may be distinguished. In the following we have chosen to describe the connectionistic view, since this view seems to be the most comprehensive to date. As we will show later on, this view is rather silent on what goals a task performer sets, how a task performer engages in a task, how a task performer monitors task progress, and when a task performer stops engaging in a task. However, these aspects will be addressed when we deal with self-reflective task performance in the subsequent section.

The connectionistic view of task performance emphasizes that learning is storage of new information in memory. It is assumed (Shiffrin, 1975; Wolters, 1988) that the memory consists of a great number of associated representations that are hierarchically ordered. On the lowest level there are representations of elementary physical characteristics (such as lines and colours), and on higher levels of organization more general and more abstract representations, such as concepts, words and schematic representations, are available. Elaboration of information takes place through the activation of representations in the memory which correspond with the presented information. When that information is no longer available the representations in memory are no longer activated. In that case these representations fall back to inactivity. Representations that get more attention are more strongly activated. The latter representations are more likely to be associated with other representations in memory, which may lead to a modification of the representations in memory and the establishment of new representations. From this viewpoint, memory is a system that can exist in one of several states, and it is more or less hierarchically organized.

In the connectionistic view the learning of tasks is nothing other than the storage of information. That the memory is an automatic by-product of information processing is demonstrated in experiments which show that incidental learning, that is, learning by subjects who do not know that their memory will be checked later on, is as effective as intentional learning. Storage of new information activates existing representations. This implies that the storage of new information simultaneously leads to the retrieval of older information. Information processing refers not only to the specific stimuli (words, lines, etc.) but also to the context, for example, the sequence of the stimuli. Forgetting or unsuccessful remembering may occur in two circumstances: when the information presented is not strong enough to activate the focal representations from memory, and when the information presented activates not only relevant but also irrelevant representations from memory. An interesting consequence of this view is that stored information always remains in memory. Forgetting is merely a retrieval problem. Stored information may be inaccessible when correct retrieval information is not strong enough and when irrelevant representations are triggered and overpower relevant ones.

Retrieval of information from memory is a rather complex process. Norman and Bobrow (1979) describe remembering as follows. The process starts by specifying what has to be remembered. This specification can be more or less complete. The next step is the retrieval of what Norman and Bobrow call 'memory records', which are activated memory representations. The search process stops when a 'memory record' that is similar to the retrieval specification is located. If this does not occur, then the 'record' is used to revise the retrieval information specification after which other 'memory records' are retrieved. This cyclic process (see Wolters, 1988) is continued until the requested information is found, or appears to be unfindable.

The connectionistic view is a rather general view on the organization of knowledge in memory, that is, it was not specifically developed to describe task performance. Concerning task performance, Johnson and Johnson (1991) have argued that concrete tasks may be considered task knowledge structures. Just like other cognitive representations, task knowledge structures are learned and stored in memory; for example, the task knowledge structures of designing a living-room layout form a cognitive representation in memory. Some connections between representations are more probable, i.e. some representations are more associated than others, and task knowledge structures are hierarchically built up. A temporal ordering of representations is also part of the task knowledge structure.

In our opinion, an interesting aspect of the connectionistic view is that it is less deterministic than the task approach, since it is assumed that a task performer responds to a task on the basis of his or her own learned representations, that during task performance other representations may become activated and that these associations may change as a consequence of activation. In the connectionistic view, in the beginning of the performance of a complex task (as depicted in Figure 1.1) several loosely coupled complex representations are activated. However, after repeated performance, that is, after successive activation of hierarchically ordered representations, the associations between the five representations in Figure 1.1 may become so strong that these operations take place in an automatic way. This means that through learning, any initially complex task may be reduced to what will be experienced psychologically as a simple task.

In other words, the task approach, as presented above, sketches a well-established abstract representation which has been built up in the past by repeated activation. By learning – that is, through activation – the connections between representation are strengthened, modified and extended. STE minisystems can be combined until a high-order and systematic description of the steps involved in a task may be given. Thus, it may be posited that generally a task may be learned by bottom-up processing, that is, through the activation of sensory representations which may become associated with high-level – more abstract – representations. However, once a hierarchically structured set of representations has been learned, a task may be viewed from a top-down perspective, that is, a set of task cues may trigger the whole architecture of the task (see Figure 1.1) and the high-level representations (and their associations) may steer further processing of the task.

SELF-REFLECTIVE TASK PERFORMANCE

The task approach implies that the task performer sets certain goals. However, it is not specified why certain goals and subgoals (=activation) are chosen. Also, the ideas presented in the section on connectionistic task performance overemphasize the passivity of the task performer: it seems as if task performers are subjected to incoming information that activates representations and that these representations, which are hierarchically organized, steer the behaviour of the task performers in a way that suggests that task performers are acting without awareness of what they are doing. In contrast with these ideas, it may be argued that task performers may consider their own behaviour from a distance; in other words they may take their own behaviour and environment as an object of scrutiny and decision making, because they are able to reflect upon their own behaviour and their own environment.

In this view the task performer is not entirely subjected either to 'external' and inherent task properties or to internal connectionistic processing. Reflexivity refers to the process of an entity acting back upon itself. Mead (1934) and Cooley (1902) showed that reflexivity in human beings is rooted in the social process, particularly the process of taking the role of the other and seeing oneself from the other's perspective. As a result of this process, the organism develops an awareness of self. The individual (the self) comes to be both the knower and the object of knowledge. Awareness of self implies these two related aspects. First, there is the self as an object of knowledge. This self may be considered a cognitive representation in self. Second, there is the self as a knower. This means that the self has consciousness about how the self as a cognitive representation is organized and how this internal cognitive representation relates to external contingencies, such as tasks. The concept of self-reflection we want to introduce here implies both aspects. Self-reflection is necessary, because it is assumed that the self has to deal with its social and physical environment. It cannot deal with the environment if it has no awareness of its own internal representation and of the possible consequences of the environment for the self. The difference between this and the purely cognitive view is that it is argued here that the human organism is not a passive product of activities, but that the self shapes its own activation in an active way. In order to be able to assess what the future self will be, i.e. what a future internal representation of self will look like, the self has to know the current internal representation and has to assess the consequences of external contingencies for self. Why is it necessary that the self has an awareness of self in relation to the external environment? We assume that the self is motivated to strive for a positively evaluated representation of self, because it seeks to maintain and to enhance its identity (see further Rijsman, 1983).

We now have the necessary ingredients of self-reflection: (1) the self strives for a positively evaluated representation of self; and (2) in order to assess whether a positively evaluated representation of self will be realized, the self has to be aware of both the current representation of self and the consequences of environmental contingencies for a future representation of self.

More concretely, in our account of task performance we assume that the performer strives for a positively evaluated representation of self. Since positive evaluation of self largely stems from the esteem of others (that, in turn, has positive consequences for self), we argue that task performance is influenced by the anticipation of evaluation by others (see further chapter 2). A positive evaluation of self may also be directly experienced, for example, if the self compares its own performance at moment t_1 with performance at t_0. In that case a social orientation is also at stake: self slipping into the shoes of other. Moreover, we assume that the task performer has a representation of self (e.g. its own capabilities) and a representation of the task at hand, and that both are used during and after task performance to assess whether a positively evaluated outcome for self may be expected.

In cognitive social psychology (for excellent reviews, see Hewstone, 1989; Fiske and Taylor, 1991), several implications of the self-reflective view have been explained. Since these insights are partly relevant to our understanding of task performance, we shall briefly elucidate the more important ones in the following.

1 *Integration and differentiation.* Forming or having formed a representation of self implies that it is established which cognitions or attributions are part of self and which cognitions are not conceived as part of self. For example, a person may consider herself as diligent and intelligent and not as lazy and stupid. Another way to put this is to say that the self has formed a scheme of attributions ascribed to self, and that some attributes are defined as belonging, being part of self or being integrated into self, whereas other attributes are considered to be not-self, i.e. are differentiated from self. So, the self as a representation of self or self-categorization (see Turner, 1991) may be considered a system of attributions in which some attributes are integrated into self, whereas other ones are differentiated from self.

2 *Homogeneity of integrated and heterogeneity of differentiated cognitions.* Attributes related to self are more interrelated and form a more uniform or more homogeneous bundle of attributes or cognitions than attributes not related to self, which are perceived as more heterogeneous.

3 *Self-favouritism.* During the formation of self-representations and also in the product, i.e. the definition of self in itself, there is a tendency to prefer positive over negative attributes. This tendency to put oneself in a favourable light, or to accentuate one's positive attributes, has been labelled the self-serving bias.

4 *Hierarchical organization of cognitions.* Like the representation of a task, self may be considered as hierarchically organized: some attributes are more important, are more closely connected with the 'core' of self, than other attributes. For example, a person may consider intelligence a more essential part of self than diligence, i.e. some attributes connected with self may be

more dominant than other ones.

5 *Social comparison.* In the process of self-definition, comparison with others plays a role. For example, describing oneself as intelligent or diligent may take place because one has experienced – has activated – seeing oneself as more intelligent and more diligent than other people.

6 *Hierarchical self-definition.* In (4) we argued that the representation of self is hierarchically organized and in (5) that the representation of self includes comparison with others. From (4) and (5) it follows that the self may be defined at several hierarchical levels of organization. The self may define herself as a person at the lowest level of organization and as different from other people. The self may also define herself as being a member of a group, an ingroup, and not belonging to another (out)group, i.e. inter-group comparison is at stake and in that case the representation of self coincides with, or is part of, the representation of the ingroup as different from the outgroup.

7 *Hierarchical comparison.* In (1) we posited that some attributes are more strongly integrated into self, whereas other ones are more strongly differentiated. In (3) we argued that attributes related to self are more positively evaluated than attributes not related to or differentiated from self. In (6) we suggested that the self may define herself, *inter alia*, in relation to another person (i.e. she may engage in interpersonal comparison), or she may define herself as connected with the ingroup and not with the outgroup (i.e. she may engage in inter-group comparison).

Now, we state that in interpersonal and inter-group comparison integration and differentiation take place in a way that favours self. This implies that if the self engages in interpersonal comparison, it is inclined to favour itself. If the self considers itself as part of an ingroup, it is inclined to favour the ingroup over the outgroup. Conversely, the self will select comparison with others (interpersonal comparison) and will seek membership in groups (inter-group comparison) in a way that gives rise to a positively evaluated self-representation.

Without going into detail (see Tajfel, 1978; Turner, 1991) we note that this implication of self-reflection has received wide support. In the domain of inter-personal comparison it has been shown that (a) if subjects were led to compare themselves with another person, they accentuated their positive attributes; and (b) subjects who were asked to allocate financial outcomes to self and others favoured themselves. In the realm of inter-group comparison it has been found that (a) ingroup members were evaluated more positively than outgroup members; and (b) ingroup favouritism occurred when subjects were asked to allocate financial outcomes to either ingroup or outgroup members, i.e. they favoured the ingroup at the expense of the outgroup. Conversely, in interpersonal comparison the persons selected for comparison are those who are likely to contribute to a positive evaluation of self. Moreover, one wants to join (reference) groups that are likely to contribute to a positively evaluated self.

8 *Private–public self.* Attributes or cognitions serve not only private purposes, namely those involving the private self, but also public purposes. This latter part

of self is referred to as the public self. For example, a person may consider herself intelligent (private self), but may not show this because she is expected to behave in a modest way, that is, self-presentational concerns may play a role. From the foregoing it should be clear that the self-reflective view supplements the cognitive view. Implications 1 (integration and differentiation), 2 (homogeneity of integrated and heterogeneity of differentiated cognitions), 4 (hierarchical organization of cognitions), 5 (social comparison) and 6 (hierarchical self-definition) describe the self as a cognitive representation. Implications 3 (self-favouritism), 7 (hierarchical comparison) and 8 (private–public self) emphasize that the self as a cognitive representation is sensitive to the consequences of its cognitive representation, in that self evaluates, or reflects upon, the outcomes that are involved.

In the following we will elucidate some of the implications of the self-reflective view for the task performer, who is assumed to make active assessments before, during and after task performance.

Engagement

It may be assumed that before engaging in a task, the task performer makes an estimation of the expected consequences, or to put it differently: a task performer selects those tasks which optimize expected utility or expected satisfaction. Mitchell and Beach (1990) argue that specific problem-solving strategies are selected according to the so-called 'profitability' test, and the research carried out by Christensen-Szalanski (1978, 1980) indicates that problem solvers are likely to select strategies by weighing their costs in terms of time invested and gains involved. She predicts that more time is invested and more elaborate strategies are selected as the gains, in terms of, say, money to be earned, increase. Less time and fewer alternative strategies are selected as the costs, in terms of, say, solution time, increase. So it is predicted that when the rewards for solving a problem are rather low and the expected costs high, problem solvers will not start to elaborate on the problem but instead restrict themselves to guessing at the correct solution. Conversely, when the expected costs are low but the gains high, problem solvers will spend more time and select rather elaborate problem-solving strategies.

To illustrate, Christensen-Szalanski (1980) gave subjects an opportunity to select problem-solving strategies. Male business students were presented with stock exchange scenarios and told that an investor believed that his gains from stocks on the stock exchange would depend on whether the banks raised the lending rate (probability 7 per cent), kept the lending rate constant (probability 31 per cent) or decreased the lending rate (probability 62 per cent). Thereafter subjects were told what the expected pay-offs would be if the lending rate became lower, higher or remained the same. For example, subjects were told that if the lending rate were lower there would be a 71 per cent chance of earning $27,000, a 23 per cent chance of earning $16,000 and a 6 per cent chance of earning $25,000. Subjects could select a strategy from a list of seven alternatives, ranging from 'accurately calculate all three possible states of the world', with states of the world referring to higher, lower and constant lending rates, via 'round [estimate] and calculate the two most likely states of the world', to 'guess'. The problem-solving strategies thus ranged from very complex to rather simple. In one of the experiments subjects could earn 10, 25, 150, 350 or 500 points for the various problems they had to solve. These were the experimental conditions. In general it was found that the subjects used significantly more elaborate or complex strategies to solve the problems associated with higher rewards. So increasing profits increases the probability that one will make a thorough analysis of the problem, i.e. it increases the likelihood that one will endure the costs of a thorough analysis of the problem at hand. It should be noted that the 'profitability test' refers to the tendency of people to engage in tasks for which the expected profits, or gains minus costs, are higher – a formulation which comes close to the formulations of many models of choice (e.g. Fishbein and Ajzen, 1975).

A similar view has been proposed by McClelland in his theory of achievement motivation (see McClelland, 1961; Atkinson and Feather, 1966; West and Wicklund, 1980). The theory proposes that any task evokes an approach motivation (a motivation to prefer a task) and an avoidance motivation (a motivation to avoid a task). In a simplified version of this theory it is assumed that a person's inclination to select a specific task or difficulty level is affected by three factors: a personality trait that involves avoidance and achievement motivation; expectations of failure and success at the task and the incentive value of failure and success at the task.

The personality trait is measured by the Thematic Association Test (TAT). This test (Murray, 1943) requires the person to examine a number of pictures – such as two men in a factory working on a machine, or a young boy sitting at a desk – and to create a story about the picture. Subsequently, an analyst judges the story for failure and achievement themes and the person is then given a score for avoidance or failure and a score for achievement motivation. The test is a projective test. An example of an achievement theme is the men in the factory working on the machine in order to gain promotion in their firm. An example of a failure theme is the young boy sitting at the desk pretending to do his homework. To estimate a person's motivation to engage in a specific task, two equations have to be derived. Approach motivation is higher as the product of achievement motivation (as measured by the TAT), expectation of success and incentive for success is greater. Likewise, avoidance motivation is higher as the product of failure motivation (as measured by the TAT), expectation of failure and incentive for failure is greater. In general, this theory of motivation is strongly supported. West and Wicklund (1980) state that the theory is quite able to predict the level of difficulty chosen for a certain task. Two studies illustrate this.

Hamilton (1974) selected a number of high school males on the basis of their scores on personality measures. Half of his subjects had higher achievement scores and lower fear of failure scores than the other subjects, who scored lower on achievement but higher on fear of failure. Each subject was faced with an apparatus. The apparatus was composed of a peg about 12 in. tall, 10 large rings to be pitched in the direction of the peg, and a 'throwing field' marked off at intervals between 1 and 18 ft from the target. To establish the subject's probability of success, each subject was given a good number of chances to throw rings from the various possible distances. Once this probability of success was clear to the subject, the subject was given 10 'free throws' with no directions about the appropriate distance. The average distance selected was the main dependent variable. The results indicated that achievement-oriented subjects (as measured by the TAT) selected distances associated with a moderate probability of success (40 per cent) whereas failure-oriented subjects selected large distances for which the average probability of success was 10 per cent.

These results were in agreement with the earlier findings of Moulton (1965). Moulton's subjects were achievement-oriented and failure-oriented boys. First they had to perform an anagram task of medium difficulty. Thereafter, they received bogus feedback about their performance. Half of the boys were told that they had succeeded on the previous task, while the other half received the feedback that they had failed. Subsequently, subjects could select a new task from a group of tasks of varying difficulty. It appeared that achievement-oriented boys selected hard tasks after previous success and easy tasks after failure. The failure-oriented boys showed the reverse behaviour: following failure they selected hard tasks and after success they selected easy tasks. These results were in support of the theory: achievement-oriented boys selected a task which they considered of medium difficulty; however, failure-oriented boys avoided the task they believed to be of medium difficulty, instead choosing the most extreme available tasks. In sum, the above-presented ideas and findings suggest that – when requested – achievement-oriented people select tasks of medium difficulty, whereas failure-oriented subjects select tasks at one or the other extreme of difficulty, i.e. tasks at which they can easily succeed or tasks at which success is highly improbable. Failure-oriented people who have chosen easy tasks are likely to succeed, but their success can easily be discounted by attributing their task performance to easy task conditions. Failure-oriented subjects who have selected the hard tasks are likely to fail. And that failure may also be discounted, because hard tasks were involved. So it may be suggested that a performer selects tasks (or achieves goals) by taking into account the future consequences of task failure and task success – a highly reflective process indeed.

Assessment during task performance

That reflectivity plays a role not only before task performance but also during task performance is proposed by Scheier and Carver (1988) (see also Carver and Scheier, 1990). They suggest that the task performer monitors task performance. During task performance one reflects upon the correspondence between what one is doing and what one is intending to do. Intentions, of course, are similar to what we referred to as setting goals. In other words, during task performance task performers reflect upon whether the processing of the task is taking place as expected.

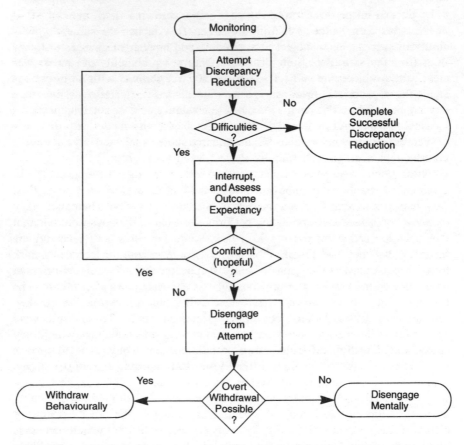

Figure 1.2 Self-reflecting and self-monitoring (adapted from Scheier and Carver, 1988)

Figure 1.2 displays the basic elements of Scheier and Carver's model. Note that the task process starts with what we have labelled sensing, testing and effecting, but what is here called 'attempt discrepancy reduction'. However, on top of what was proposed earlier, it is now assumed that self monitors the processing. When the task processing proceeds as planned, that is, when no difficulties arise, the task may be completed as intended. When task performers perceive that they cannot reach their goals (difficulties?), the task is interrupted. What task performers will do when the outcomes are unfavourable depends on whether they feel confident that the goal can be reached. When they feel confident enough, the sensing/testing/effecting operations (i.e. attempts to reduce discrepancy) may be repeated. If not, then task performers withdraw from task performance.

Three aspects of Figure 1.2 are of importance: monitoring, the role of confidence and the consequences of the monitoring. Monitoring or self-regulation refers to self-reflective activity, and it is assumed that the person checks on whether task performance is taking place as intended. Scheier and Carver (1988) illustrate this with the example of an assembly-line worker who performs a series of six operations on each unit that passes his work station. Simply getting the work done is not sufficient. He must complete the operations before the next unit arrives at the work station. In that circumstance, Scheier and Carver propose, the expectancy–assessment loop must evaluate progress with respect to a standard (goal) that is much more stringent than the one based only on progress.

The degree of confidence a task performer feels about his or her ability to complete a task determines whether the task performer will continue a task in spite of experienced difficulties. Scheier and Carver (1988) have shown that highly confident subjects who were faced with failure on a previous task were more reluctant to proceed on a similar subsequent task than less confident subjects.

Lastly, what a task performer will do after meeting difficulties depends on the degree of confidence that has been built up in the past. When the task performer repeatedly experiences failure, his or her self-confidence – that is, the degree to which a task performer feels competent to solve the task at hand – decreases, and consequently the tendency to withdraw from the task becomes greater. Scheier and Carver (1988) specify two responses in that case: actual and mental disengagement. Mental disengagement takes place when, for some reason or another (e.g. the presence of evaluating others), it is not possible to withdraw. When actual withdrawal is not possible the task performer may engage in task-irrelevant thinking, daydreaming and pretending.

Attribution after task performance

Several versions of attribution theory (e.g. Hewstone, 1989) indicate that people are able to reflect on the consequences of their task performance, suggesting that after task performance one makes inferences about the causes of a certain result (e.g. success or failure). Two conspicuous versions of the theory will be presented here.

In Figure 1.3 a recent view (Hewstone and Jaspars, 1987) of Kelley's attribution theory (Kelley, 1967) is presented. A task performer may attribute task performance to several causes: to the stimulus or task, to self and to circumstances. To give an example, a task performer who succeeds may attribute his success to the task at hand (the task was easy or hard), to himself (I was competent) or to the circumstances (the weather was nice, or I was very energetic at the time), respectively. To decide which cause was responsible, one needs extra information. According to Hewstone and Jaspars, the task performer needs two pieces of information, – namely, information about consistency and consensus – and the combination of these two pieces of information determines which attribution (to the task or stimulus, to persons or to circumstances) will be made. Consistency refers to information about whether a result (e.g. success or failure) occurred frequently (consistency is high) or infrequently (consistency is low) after repeated task performance. For example, when a task performer

		KELLEY	WEINER	
Consistency	Consensus	Attribution to	Attributional dimensions	Attribution to
High	High	Stimulus (Task)	Stable/external/ beyond control	Task difficulty
High	Low	Person	Stable/internal/ beyond control	Ability
Low	High	Circumstances not related to person	Instable/external/ beyond control	Chance
Low	Low	Circumstances related to person	Instable/internal	Effort

Figure 1.3 Kelley's and Weiner's attributional analyses (in Siero, 1987)

succeeds repeatedly at the same task, consistency may be assumed to be high in comparison with when a task performer succeeds only from time to time. Consensus refers to information about what others were doing. When others have achieved the same results – for example, when others have also succeeded – then there is high consensus. When other performers have not achieved the same result – for example, all others failed where one person has succeeded – low consensus is inferred.

Kelley's predictions of the specific cause that will be inferred from the available information are presented in the left part of Figure 1.3. A specific result (e.g. success) is attributed to the task when the person always succeeds at this task (high consistency) and when others also do so (high consensus). When the person always succeeds but others do not, task performance will be attributed to the person; in other words, with high consistency and low consensus the task performer may be considered the cause of the effect.

The second conspicuous attribution theory is that proposed by Weiner (e.g. 1986). As Figure 1.3 shows, Weiner's classification system is somewhat more refined than the one presented by Kelley. Weiner (1986) makes a distinction between several more specific causes: task difficulty, ability of the person, chance and effort. Also, Weiner assumes that task performers need extra information when deciding which cause was responsible for a certain result. Where Kelley (see Hewstone and Jaspars, 1987) primarily makes a distinction between consensus and consistency information, Weiner proposes three dimensions: whether the result is stable in time, which is more or less equivalent to high consistency versus low consistency; whether the result (e.g. success) can be attributed to the person or rather to some outside instance or circumstance (i.e. internal or external); and whether the task behaviour was under the control of the person.

Research results indicate that persons presented with information of relevance to these attributional dimensions make attributions as predicted. For example, when a task performer consistently receives one type of feedback about his or her task performance (stable) and learns that other persons obtained results which differ from his or her own results (internal), an ability attribution is made. Kelley's theory (see Hewstone and Jaspars, 1987) also makes quite accurate predictions, suggesting that people can make causal inferences about the consequences of their behaviour because they reflect upon the outcomes after task performance.

Recently, two rather different criticisms have been raised against the attributional approach. The first is that it appears from many studies that attributors are not so rational in making attributions as presumably supposed by Weiner and by Kelley. For example, Stevens and Jones (1976), who provided their subjects with bogus feedback about their performance, found that subjects who received success feedback attributed their results to personal factors like ability and effort, whereas subjects who received failure feedback attributed their results to the difficulty of the task or to bad luck. This tendency on the part of an actor to take credit for success and deny responsibility for failure has been coined in the literature the 'self-serving bias', a bias which appears to be quite strong when there is no critical evaluating spectator available who can falsify this self-presentational behaviour.

A second criticism is the work on actor-observer differences. Both Kelley and Weiner assume that a brief description of a work situation leads actors to make the same causal attributions as observers. Jones and Nisbett (1972), however, have shown that different attributions are made by actors as compared with observers. Actors have more information and focus their attention more on the situational factors involved. As a consequence (e.g. Bar-Tal and Frieze, 1976), actors attribute their performance on an achievement-related task more to the external factor of task difficulty, whereas observers are more likely to attribute the outcome to the internal factor of effort.

The foregoing might suggest that attributional analysis has a direct effect on performance. However, it should be noted that in most attribution studies effects on subsequent performance have rarely been investigated, so it may not be concluded that attributions always affect subsequent performance. This is especially not so when the result (success or failure) is unexpected (e.g. Jones and Davis, 1965). For example, when one expects success but receives failure feedback, one may search for a cause to which the unexpected result may be attributed. Given that these self-generated causes are self-serving, as discussed above, self-serving attributions may explain why higher aspirational goals are chosen that is, why more difficult goals are selected after success, and why the previous aspiration level will be maintained after failure feedback, as Zander (1968) found. It could very well be that, after unexpected success, people will be inclined to attribute their unexpected success to their own ability and therefore see reason to choose a higher aspiration level for the future. However, unexpected failure is very likely to be ascribed to external circumstances beyond a person's control, and therefore after failure persons might have no reason to revise their aspiration level, which might explain why people are inclined to maintain their previous aspiration level after failure.

CONCLUSIONS AND SUMMARY

In this introductory chapter we have dealt with the inherent properties of tasks, which may be conceived as STE hierarchically coupled minisystems. We have also focused on cognitive and self-reflective processes taking place in the individual task performer. We have argued that cognitive and self-reflective processes supplement the approach to tasks as described in 'task approach'. The cognitive view explains why individual performers build up a hierarchically organized representation of a task. The self-reflective view makes plausible which goals are set and when an individual performer decides to end task performance.

Of course, this is a book on group performance. As we will see later on, performance in groups is also determined by cognitive and self-reflective processing. In addition, communication about the task representations of individual group members and the structuring of intra-group relations will be of importance for our understanding of group performance.

Chapter 2

Individual task performance under social conditions

Consider the following problem: A man bought a horse for £60 and sold it for £70. He bought it back for £80 and sold it for £90. How much money did he make in this transaction? According to Steiner (1972) the way an individual performs a task depends primarily on two elements, namely task demands and human resources, the latter referring to the individual's ability to perform the task at hand. In the following we will examine these two elements and indicate how they are related to potential and actual performance.

Task demands are the resources required to perform a task. In order to solve the horse-trading problem, one has to split the problem into two negotiations, namely one in which £70 is compared with £60 and another in which £90 is compared with £80. One has to realize that in both instances a gain of £10 is made and that the two gains add up to £20.

Human resources include all the knowledge, abilities, skills and tools that enable the individual attempting to solve a problem to engage in cognitive and reflective processing (see chapter 1). In the case of the horse-trading problem, an individual may or may not possess the analytical and computational resources needed to meet the task demands. Thus, whereas task demands specify the kinds and amounts of resources that are needed, human resources specify whether the individual or the group possesses these resources.

The potential productivity of an individual or a group refers to the extent to which the available human resources suffice to meet the task demands. When an individual or group possesses all the skills necessary to solve the horse-trading problem, then this individual or group has greater potential productivity than a group or an individual lacking some of the human resources required to meet the task demands.

Suppose now that we have an individual whose potential productivity is high, because he or she possesses the human resources necessary to meet the task requirements. Does this guarantee a high actual level of performance? From daily life we may observe that high potential productivity may not always be realized in actual performance. In our example an individual may be able to distinguish between two negotiations. However, the positions of seller and buyer may be mistaken and the individual may end up with an incorrect answer, or may make some unexpected computational errors, or may make the right computations but nervously write down the wrong answer. In these cases actual productivity – actual performance – fails to equal potential productivity: the individual possesses the human resources needed to perform the task, but something goes wrong during the enactment process (the actual steps taken by the individual when confronted with the task). In a similar way, actual performance may exceed potential performance. This is the case, for example, when an incompetent person, whose resources are insufficient to meet the task demands, makes the wrong computations, which nevertheless lead to the right answer. In the latter case process gains are involved.

The above reasoning suggests the following relation between actual performance, potential performance and process gains and losses (see also Steiner, 1972):

$$\text{actual performance} \quad = \quad \text{potential performance} \quad \pm \quad \begin{array}{c} \text{process} \\ \text{gains/losses} \end{array}$$

This reasoning implies that potential performance amounts to a person's ability to meet the task demands, i.e. his or her human resources for meeting the task requirements, or to put it differently, his or her ability to take the steps necessary for solving the problem. Process gains and losses refer to gains and losses which may be undergone during the enactment process, which in turn involves both cognitive processing and reflective processing as explained in chapter 1.

In this chapter we will focus on how individual task performance is affected by the presence of others, whereas in chapter 3 we will describe how interacting group members perform a group task.

TASK PERFORMANCE IN THE PRESENCE OF OTHERS

How the presence of others affects an individual's task performance was one of the earliest research interests in social psychology. As early as 1897 Triplett observed that cyclists rode faster when racing together than when racing alone. In the years that followed, numerous experiments were carried out in which the effect of the presence of others was investigated in a wide variety of task domains. Some studies showed performance improvement as a result of the presence of others (social facilitation), others performance impairment (social inhibition). Probably because of a lack of theoretical progress, the interest in social facilitation and inhibition (SFI) research suddenly dropped in the late 1930s. The issue was neglected until Zajonc (1965) published an article which represented a major theoretical breakthrough in understanding social facilitation and inhibition phenomena. Zajonc's work inspired social psychologists to resume the study of the effects of the presence of others on task performance, and since then social facilitation and inhibition has once again constituted a lively research area in social psychology.

Early social facilitation and inhibition (SFI) studies

SFI has traditionally been investigated in two broad categories of social situation: audience presence and coaction. The first type of study deals with the question of how the presence of a passive audience influences individual performance. Coaction studies focus on the question of how the presence of someone else performing the same task affects an individual's task performance. In both research areas, the results seem contradictory. For instance, Travis (1925) found that when working in front of an audience compared to working alone, well-trained subjects clearly performed better on an eye–hand coordination task. An opposite audience effect was reported by Pessin (1933). He found that subjects needed fewer trials to learn a list of nonsense syllables when practising alone than when facing an audience. However, when subjects were later asked to recall the list of syllables, their performance was better with than without an audience. Similar patterns of results were found in coaction studies. Sometimes coaction seemed to facilitate performance (e.g. Triplett, 1897), particularly the 'quantitative' aspects of performance, while in other studies the quality of performance was impaired in coaction settings (e.g. Gates and Allee, 1933).

Zajonc's explanation of the ambiguous SFI results

In his classic article, Zajonc (1965) noted a distinct regularity in SFI research which had thus far been only tacitly understood. Furthermore, Zajonc proposed a set of ideas which could account for the observed results. Zajonc suggested that the presence of others led to improved performance (social facilitation) if subjects worked on easy, well-learned tasks. However, the presence of others led to impaired performance (social inhibition) if subjects were engaged in difficult tasks which were not (yet) well-learned. This simple distinction between easy and difficult tasks could account for many seemingly conflicting results of audience as well as coaction studies. It explains for instance the above-mentioned results of Triplett (1897), Travis (1925), Pessin (1933) and Gates and Allee (1933).

Zajonc not only observed these regularities, but also proposed a theoretical explanation for them. Zajonc's crucial suggestion is that audiences enhance the emission of *dominant* responses. A dominant response is described as the response which prevails, that is, which takes precedence in a subject's response repertoire in a given stimulus situation. In easy tasks, Zajonc argues, the correct responses are dominant, and therefore audiences facilitate performance on easy tasks, such as pedalling a bicycle. However, in complex tasks (like reasoning or learning), the wrong answers tend to be dominant, and therefore audiences give rise to performance deterioration on such difficult tasks.

Why do audiences elicit dominant responses? According to Zajonc, audiences create arousal in subjects, i.e. enhance their general drive level or activation level. In Zajonc's view, the mere physical presence of others (conspecifics) suffices to induce arousal in subjects. The presence of others leads to an innate response of some sort of preparedness, a readiness to respond to whatever unexpected action the other might undertake (Zajonc, 1980). Furthermore, according to Zajonc, enhanced drive or arousal leads to an increased emission of dominant responses, a notion Zajonc derives from Hull-Spence drive theory (cf. Spence, 1956; Zajonc and Nieuwenhuyse, 1964). Since dominant responses tend to be correct in easy tasks, performance on easy tasks will be facilitated. Performance on difficult tasks, where dominant responses tend to be incorrect, will be impaired.

Two principal methods have been employed to show social facilitation and social inhibition effects (see Geen and Bushman, 1989). Zajonc and Sales (1966) created response hierarchies through manipulation of the amount of practice subjects were allowed. In the well-learned responses condition, response hierarchies were better established than in the less well-learned responses condition, because more practice had been allowed. This differential learning was followed by measurement of the frequency of occurrence of each response to ambiguous stimulus conditions, with subjects responding either before an audience or alone. Zajonc and Sales found that the tendency for well-learned responses to be elicited more frequently than less well-learned responses was stronger among subjects who worked in the presence of an audience than among subjects who worked alone. According to Geen and Bushman the distinction between well-learned and less well-learned responses refers to differential habit strength or the availability of dominant responses.

For well-learned responses a stronger habit strength is established, or to put it differently, for well-learned responses the pattern of responses is better established than for less well-learned responses. The second method of demonstrating SFI effects also makes use of the idea of habit strength hierarchies, but in this case it is assumed that these hierarchies are reflected in differing levels of performance across variations in a task. An example is the experiment reported by Geen (1983) in which subjects study lists of paired words made up of items with either a high (difficult list) or a low degree (easy list) interresponse competition. Learning took place in two conditions. In the observer condition, the subject was told that an observer would evaluate his or her performance. In the alone condition no observer was present. It turned out that subjects who worked in the presence of an evaluating observer made more errors on the difficult list than subjects who worked alone, but fewer errors on the easy list.

The notion of habit strength (or dominant responses) fits in rather well with the connectionistic view discussed in chapter 1. The two above-described experimental paradigms can be understood when it is taken into account that associations are learned through activation. The method employed by Zajonc and Sales (1966) compared the effect of response hierarchies which had been either more (well-learned responses condition) or less (less well-established responses condition) established or activated in the past. The method employed by Geen (1983) reflects the learning of response hierarchies while previous associations either were (difficult list) or were not (easy list) counteracted by rivalling or competing activations.

Zajonc's explanation seemed to account for many of the observed effects in the SFI literature. Furthermore, his article inspired social psychologists to disagree with him. In anticipation of the following section, it should be noted that they all more or less accepted Zajonc's ideas about the establishment of dominant response hierarchies, but disagreed with him about the theoretical explanation for the effect of the presence of others (see Glaser, 1982, and Geen and Bushman, 1989, for critical reviews). In the subsequent literature, alternative explanations for the relationship between presence of others and arousal, and for the relationship between arousal and task performance, were suggested, and in fact some entirely different models were proposed. Below, a brief outline of some of these alternatives is presented.

Alternative explanations of SFI

Cottrell (1968, 1972) was among the first to criticize Zajonc's approach. He suggested an alternative explanation for the connection between the presence of others and arousal. In Cottrell's view, increased arousal constitutes a learned response to the presence of others, not an innate one. Subjects tend to be aroused by audiences because they have learned to associate the presence of others with performance evaluation, which is in turn linked to positive or negative outcomes. Thus audiences produce 'evaluation apprehension', which enhances drive (or arousal). The mere physical presence of others is not sufficient to elicit arousal and the concomitant increased emission of dominant responses.

Several experiments yielded support for Cottrell's view (e.g. Henchy and Glass, 1968; Paulus and Murdoch, 1971). The former experiment may serve as an example. Henchy and Glass assigned subjects to one of four conditions: 'Alone'; 'Expert Together' (i.e. task performance in the presence of two others who were explicitly introduced as experts); 'Non-expert Together' (i.e. task performance in the presence of two non-experts); and 'Alone Recorded' (in which the subject performed the task alone, but was filmed for later evaluation by experts). As predicted by Cottrell's approach, facilitation of dominant (well-learned) responses only occurred in the Expert Together and Alone Recorded conditions, while task performance in the Non-expert Together condition was similar to that in the Alone condition. These results thus seem to demonstrate that some concern about being evaluated is necessary for the enhanced emission of dominant responses.

Another explanation of why audiences are arousing was suggested by Sanders, Baron and Moore (1978; see also Sanders, 1981). In their view, the simple physical presence of others serves as a distracting stimulus (for example, because of noises or gestures, anticipated approving or disapproving reactions or the tendency to make social comparisons). The presence of others leads to increased drive because it brings about, 'a response conflict between attending to the task at hand and attending to the distracting stimuli' (Sanders, 1981, p. 233). Two distinct effects of the presence of others on task performance may then be noted. First, distraction as such always leads to an impairment of performance, on both complex *and* simple tasks, because attending to the distracting stimuli (the audience) detracts from attention to the task. Second, the drive increment evoked by the distraction–response conflict facilitates performance on simple tasks and hinders performance on complex tasks because – as in Zajonc's view – increased drive results in the enhanced emission of dominant responses. Thus, the presence of others always inhibits performance on complex tasks, and facilitates performance on simple tasks only when the positive effect of the drive increment outweighs the negative effect of distraction. Support for the distraction hypothesis (for other studies in natural settings, see Geen and Bushman, 1989) was found in a study by Strube, Miles and Finch (1981), who investigated the behaviour of joggers. Results of an initial study indicated that the presence of an attentive spectator, but not that of an inattentive spectator, produced faster running relative to a no-spectator condition. In a second study it was established that joggers who reported more distraction also ran faster.

While the respective theories put forward by Cottrell and Sanders pertain mainly to why the presence of others elicits arousal in individuals, Manstead and Semin's (1980) approach focuses on the information-processing aspects of SFI phenomena. In Zajonc's theory, the distinction between simple and complex tasks plays a central role. This distinction, however, appears to be an uneasy one, because there is no solid theoretical basis for an independent assessment of which tasks are easy and which are difficult (or, for that matter, for the a priori assessment of which responses are dominant). Manstead and Semin suggest an elegant alternative by referring to Shiffrin and Schneider's (1977) two-process ('automatic' versus 'controlled') theory of human information processing. Automatic, routinely processed tasks tend to be characterized by suboptimal performance. The presence of an evaluative audience leads subjects to devote more attention to automatic task sequences, which generally results in improved performance. In more complex tasks, namely tasks which require cognitively controlled processing, the presence of an evaluative audience tends to impair performance, because the audience places further attentional demands upon the individual, which leaves less attention available for the already demanding task requirements. This explanation of SFI phenomena substantially modifies Zajonc's model in that it avoids the somewhat strained assumption of arousal-induced emission of 'dominant' responses by introducing a more advanced information-processing perspective on activation level and on the (competitive) allocation of attention, a perspective which we already encountered in chapter 1 when we dealt with the distinction between simple and complex tasks as approached from a connectionistic view.

A cognitive-motivational model of group influences on individual performance

The social facilitation literature of the past decades presents a wide range of views and theories, the most influential of which were described in the previous

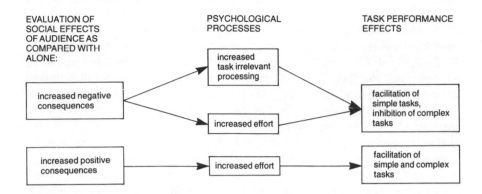

EVALUATION OF
SOCIAL EFFECTS
OF AUDIENCE AS
COMPARED WITH
ALONE:

PSYCHOLOGICAL
PROCESSES

TASK PERFORMANCE
EFFECTS

Figure 2.1 A cognitive-motivational model of SFI effects (adapted from Paulus, 1983)

section. This area of research would benefit from a more comprehensive theoretical model which incorporated the most valuable ideas of the approaches outlined above. Such an integrative model has been proposed by Paulus (1983). A slightly modified version of this model is described below in some detail.

In Paulus's model three steps can be distinguished: (1) the presence of others generally increases (but sometimes decreases) the potential social consequences of an individual's performance; (2) variations in social consequences affect the individual's psychological processes; (3) these psychological processes have specific effects on individual task performance. Our adapted version of Paulus's model is schematically represented in Figure 2.1. Step by step, we shall describe the propositions put forward by Paulus.

In terms of the model, the presence of others generally implies an enhancement of the social consequences of performing well or poorly. In this respect, Paulus adopts the viewpoint of Cottrell (1968), who suggested that the presence of others is associated with performance evaluation, which is in turn linked to positive or negative outcomes. According to Paulus, in some coaction settings (such as being a member of a rope-pulling team) the social consequences of individual performance may be reduced because the success or failure of the group cannot be easily attributed to one particular individual. However, the typical audience situation entails increased focus on the individual's performance, and hence, social consequences will be enhanced. Therefore, diminished social consequences do not form part of the model presented in Figure 2.1.

Paulus made a distinction between negative and positive social consequences. Negative consequences are associated with the prospect of failing, that is, with the possibility that the individual's accomplishments may not meet the standards set by the audience. Negative consequences include, for instance, embarrassment, disapproval and contempt. Conversely, the prospect of success in the presence of others may enhance potential positive consequences, such as approval or admiration.

As can be seen in Figure 2.1, increased negative consequences affect the individual's psychological processes. First, negative consequences give rise to an increase in task-irrelevant processing. In the definition of Paulus, task-irrelevant processing is described as the focusing of attention on factors other than the task at hand. For example, the individual may begin to worry about whether he or she is able to perform well, or may start looking for signs of disapproval. This concept of task-irrelevant processing is quite similar to the distraction effect posited by Sanders, Baron and Moore (1978; Sanders, 1981). Second, negative consequences elicit increased effort. Negative consequences enhance the motivation to perform well because they mean an increase in the costs of failing. Third, in the model proposed by Paulus, arousal is introduced as a separate effect of increased negative consequences. As a slight modification of Paulus's model, we suggest that arousal is a psychological state that tends to accompany task-irrelevant processing; for example, arousal is associated with the subject's worrying about failing and the consequent negative evaluations. In fact, in the original model arousal always coincides with task-irrelevant processing. Therefore, we have not included arousal in our version of the model (see also Glaser, 1982, on the problematic concept of arousal).

What is the combined effect of increased task-irrelevant processing and increased effort on the performance of simple tasks? Paulus suggests that performance on simple tasks will be facilitated. When an individual is working alone on a simple, routine task, performance tends to be suboptimal because of a low expenditure of effort (cf. Kahneman, 1973; see also Manstead and Semin, 1980). In such situations individuals may not try very hard because simple tasks are generally not very challenging or inspiring. When others watch, the potential negative consequences of poor performance are enhanced, and effort therefore increases, which facilitates performance. Although the model predicts that task-irrelevant processing also increases, this need not hinder performance on easy tasks because these tasks do not require the individual's full attention.

In the case of complex tasks, however, the combined effect of increased task-irrelevant processing and increased effort is an inhibition of task performance. Working alone on a complex task, such as solving a difficult problem, already requires considerable effort from the individual. The presence of others may lead to enhanced effort, but the performance gains resulting from this will generally be smaller than in the case of simple tasks. Furthermore, increased task-irrelevant processing is much more harmful for complex tasks than for simple tasks since a complex task demands the individual's undivided attention, and therefore any attention paid to non-task factors (e.g. worrying) leads to poorer task performance (cf. Manstead and Semin, 1980). Thus, the net result of increased task-irrelevant processing and increased effort is an impairment of performance on complex tasks.

An example may illustrate the latter process. Consider a boy of average intelligence who, sitting alone in his room, tries to solve the horse-trading problem. As there is little time pressure, he can carefully select the appropriate steps for solving the problem. He takes his time, and in a few minutes he comes up with the correct solution. Now consider the same boy trying to solve the horse-trading problem while his older brother, known to make sarcastic remarks about his younger brother's incompetence, looks over his shoulder. The boy increases his effort. But, since he is worried that he will be criticized for working too slowly, he nervously picks the wrong numbers and finally reaches the wrong solution, i.e. his preoccupation with the prospect of being negatively evaluated (task-irrelevant processing) impairs his performance.

The presence of others may also increase the positive consequences of individual task performance. Successful performance may elicit approval from others, increased liking or material rewards. According to the model, increased positive consequences lead to increased effort, simply because there is more at stake. Trying harder results in facilitation of performance on both simple and complex tasks. Suboptimal performance on simple tasks is easily improved by working harder. And even in the case of complex tasks the additional effort induced by potential positive outcomes is expected to lead to improved performance. An example of the latter is the situation in which a highly skilled piano player gives a musical performance in the presence of others. Increased potential positive outcomes (applause, admiration) would motivate the pianist to play better than when playing alone.

In most task performance situations, the presence of others entails the enhancement of both positive and negative consequences, although the one or the other may be more salient. Such differences may result from characteristics of the situation and/or the audience. In our view it is also important to consider the implications of task difficulty for the salience of positive and negative consequences. Since success is more likely to be attained on simple tasks than on difficult tasks, it may be argued that simple tasks are more often accompanied by potential positive consequences, whereas complex tasks more often evoke potential negative consequences. As a result of this differential salience of positive and negative consequences, the probability that audiences will facilitate performance on simple tasks and inhibit performance on complex tasks is further enhanced.

Paulus's model provides an elegant explanation of social facilitation and inhibition. The model is an eclectic one in that it incorporates the theoretical notions of many important researchers in the field (Cottrell, 1968; Sanders *et al.*, 1978; Manstead and Semin, 1980). The basic structure of Paulus's explanation can be formulated in terms of process gains and losses (Steiner, 1972).

With regard to process gains and losses, Stroebe and Frey (1982) made a distinction between 'motivation' and 'coordination'. The positive effect of increased effort posited in Paulus's model may be interpreted as a motivation gain. The negative effect of increased task-irrelevant processing may be viewed as coordination loss. Although Stroebe and Frey focused on interpersonal coordination losses, in individual task performance the typical effect of task-irrelevant processing (e.g. worrying) is that *intra*personal coordination deteriorates (e.g. the individual gets mixed up).

The effect of the presence of others can be expressed as:

individual productivity in the presence of others	=	individual productivity when working alone	+	motivation gain	−	coordination loss

What the model of Paulus amounts to is that the net result of motivation gains and coordination losses is decisively different for simple and complex tasks.

Since the effect of coordination losses on simple tasks is generally negligible, while the motivation gains may be substantial, actual productivity on simple tasks comes closer to the individual's potential productivity when he or she is in the presence of others as compared with working alone. Conversely, on complex tasks negative effects of coordination losses on productivity in general outweigh the positive effects of motivation gains. Therefore, individual productivity on a complex task comes closer to potential productivity when the individual works alone as compared with in the presence of others.

CHOICE OF A COMPARISON OTHER

In the previous section we addressed the question of how individual task performance is affected by the mere presence and coacting of others. It was shown that evaluation apprehension on the part of task performers is rather important in influencing task performance, because subjects take the positive and negative consequences of the comparison with others into account (see Figure 2.1). In these studies the others were introduced by the experimenter. However, in real life one quite often selects one's own comparison other. Choice of a comparison other is the topic of this section.

Social comparison

Festinger's social comparison theory (Festinger, 1954) assumes that self wants to establish how able self is. Self does this by collecting information about how its own task performance relates to the performance of other. The other's task performance can be of interest for two related reasons. First, to see how well one has performed the task itself. For example, did I give the correct solutions? The performance of the other might give information about how to perform the task in the future. Second, to see how well one performed in comparison with the other, for example, did I score higher or lower than other? These two related reasons have also been labelled informational versus normative dependence; that is, self may turn to the other to gather information about how task performance may be improved and self may try to discover its status, i.e. how well self performed in comparison with the other (see Jones and Gerard, 1967).

This distinction has also been labelled 'task' and 'group' set (Thibaut and Strickland, 1956). Information about another's task behaviour may give insight into one's own task behaviour (how should the task be performed?) and how one's own task performance relates to the task performance of the other, for example, do I perform better or worse than the other?

In a recent study, Butler (1992) found support for the idea that concern for the task and concern for status or for one's relative ability may be evoked by task instructions. While introducing a divergent thinking task which required sixth-grade children (11-year-olds) to create pictures from a page of empty circles, she gave two different instructions. In the 'mastery' condition she focused the children's attention on the task itself by suggesting, 'that a task was developed which can help you express your imagination, and develop new ways of looking at everyday things'. In the 'ability' condition she focused the children's attention on their relative ability, by suggesting that studies have shown that children who do well on this test are more creative than those who do poorly. After this, the children worked for fifteen minutes.

It was shown that when children could spend time at a table containing information about the task itself ('Ideas that 6th graders have for drawings based on circles') or at another table containing information about their relative ability ('My creative ability relative to other 6th graders'), the children in the ability condition spent more time at the table where relative ability information could be acquired, whereas those in the 'mastery' condition spent more time at the table containing information about the task itself. Moreover, children who received 'mastery' instructions outperformed children who received 'relative ability' instructions, the latter being more concerned about ego-related factors such as relative ability and the desire to outperform others, cognitive activities that presumably inhibited task performance.

As for people performing tasks, Festinger's social comparison theory makes two assumptions. First, self will be inclined to compare with persons of similar ability. Festinger reasoned that if a person's performance is greatly discrepant from that of other persons, then all self knows is that its own performance is unique and that such information as far as task performance is concerned does not offer prospects for task improvement. If, in contrast, similar ability others are available, self knows that its own possibilities for action are identical or very similar. Second, since having more ability is culturally preferable, self will select superior others for comparison. Together, these two tendencies are expected to result in a tendency to select a somewhat more able other for comparison.

The rank-order paradigm

In earlier research the basic question was, 'Who will be selected to compare with?' An example is a study by Wheeler (1966), who had subjects work at a task and then presented them with rank-order information on their performance. All subjects were led to believe that they themselves received the middle rank out of five or seven ranks. Thereafter subjects were given the opportunity to select one other group member whose exact score they could find out. It was shown that when the range of exact scores was known, subjects had a preference for similars over dissimilars, that is, they more often wanted to know the exact scores of others who were closer in rank than of others whose ranks were further away. Moreover, they had a greater preference for seeing scores from persons above than from persons below. Both tendencies – similarity and upwardness – resulted in a high frequency of preferences to see the score of the nearest higher-ranked person.

The interval paradigm

A similar conclusion may be drawn from the 'interval paradigm'. As in the rank-order paradigm, in the interval paradigm subjects work first at a task. However, in the interval paradigm they receive the exact scores of four or six others. Their own score is the middle score. After that, subjects have to anticipate a similar collective task and the question is then who they select to work with at that task. Again it turned out (see Wilke, Kuyper and Lewis, 1983) that subjects selected a partner whose score was more similar and that upward choices were preferred over downward choices.

In a second experiment employing the interval paradigm a subject could also select a partner with an identical score. The results showed that persons having a identical score were chosen most often, suggesting that the similarity tendency is stronger than the upward tendency.

Further evidence for the strength of the similarity tendency comes from a study by Wheeler (1966). Wheeler noted that the tendency to make an upward choice seems to lead to a paradoxical situation: if subjects select someone who is superior, then subjects themselves experience their own ability as inferior. Further evidence selected by Wheeler (1966) might give a clue: he found that 75 per cent of the subjects who did prefer to see the exact score of a nearest higher other (in the rank-order paradigm) considered themselves similar to the chosen person (see also Gastorf, Suls and Lawhon, 1978).

So it seems that the choice of a partner to work with is mainly based on similarity. This does not mean that the processes behind the choice of a similar other are clear. Miller and Suls (1977) report a number of studies in which the nature of the subsequent task was specified. Subjects were either facing future cooperation or future competition. It was shown that with future cooperation a very superior other, and with future competition a very inferior other, was selected, suggesting that subjects were trying to achieve a high collective out-come on a cooperative task or to beat the other, on a competitive subsequent task. These are, of course, utilitarian reasons associated with the reflective view explained in the previous chapter. So one might conclude that the preference to select similar others in the above-described studies was a consequence of the fact that subjects were uncertain about the nature of the future task: because they were uncertain about whether they would be exposed to a cooperative interaction (which should lead to the selection of a superior other) or to a competitive interaction (which should lead to the selection of an inferior other), they made a compromise by selecting a person who was best to cooperate with in case of cooperation and whom they had a chance to beat in case of competition.

In the interval paradigm studies reported above, subjects received their own score and the scores of other group members whilst only one ability dimension was at stake. What happens if one has to select a partner for a two-dimensional task?

De Vries (1988) did a number of experiments in which subjects had to perform a task involving two dimensions, namely alertness and creativity. Thereafter, four conditions were induced. Subjects learned that they had scored either High on both dimensions (HH), Low on one of the dimensions and High on the other one (LH and HL respectively) or Low on both dimensions (LL). Lastly, subjects were asked to sketch the profile of a co-worker. Most interesting were the results for the LH and HL conditions. It turned out that in these conditions a complementary partner was preferred. For example, LH subjects sketched a profile of an HL partner, and the reverse. Subjects in the HH and LL conditions had a preference for a similar other. Other experimental results reported by de Vries suggest that the choice of a complementary other was made more often when cooperation than when competition was anticipated, again implying that the nature of expected outcomes had a strong effect.

We started this section by stating that quite often one selects one's own comparison other. The research by Butler (1992) showed that two motives may be distinguished, namely, mastery of the task (the search for information about the task itself), and relative ability or status comparison (the search for information about how one's own performance compares with the performance of others). The results of the three paradigms – the rank-order paradigm, the interval paradigm for one dimension, and the interval paradigm for two dimensions of comparison – were explained. In none of these paradigms could subjects obtain direct information about the task itself. So we may safely assume that in these paradigms the motive of comparison of relative abilities was stronger than the mastery motive.

Festinger's theory of social comparison (Festinger, 1954) predicts that when ability is at issue a similar other will be chosen. Besides this pressure towards uniformity, a culturally determined upward drive would operate. Even if one is willing to believe that in the three paradigms the relative ability motivation was stronger, we may, however, arrive at another explanation than that derived from Festinger's theory. We argue that one selects a partner and one wants to see their score for self-serving reasons (see chapter 1): one selects a partner who will provide one with higher outcomes. If future possible outcomes are not specified, in the rank-order paradigm and in the interval paradigm one indeed selects a similar other. However, when anticipating cooperation, one selects a superior, and anticipating competition one selects an inferior partner. In both cases one presumably guarantees optimal personal outcomes for oneself. Research employing the interval paradigm with two dimensions supports this line of reasoning: the tendency to make a complementary choice turns out to be much stronger under cooperative interdependency than under competitive interdependency conditions.

SOCIAL LOAFING

'Many hands make light work' is a well-known recipe for group performance. Steiner (1976) remarks that the recipe for group success is quite simple: each group member should do as much as that member can while maintaining the necessary coordination with the other group members. However, although this recipe is simple, adhering to it may not be.

This was observed by Ringelmann, who carried out his research between 1882 and 1887 (see Kravitz and Martin, 1986). Ringelmann was a professor of agricultural engineering at the French National Institute of Agronomy who investigated the relative efficiency of work carried out by horses, oxen, men and machines in various agricultural applications. He had young men pull a rope, either alone or in groups of two, three or eight members. He measured the momentary force exerted, by means of a recording dynamometer. When subjects worked alone, they pulled with an average force of 63 kgs. But two men did not pull with a force of 126 kgs, three with a force of 189 kgs and so on. The two-person group had an average pull of only 118 kgs (a loss of 8 kgs), while three-person groups pulled with an average of 160 kgs (a loss of 29 kgs) and the eight-person group exerted a force of 256 kgs below its potential. Thus the productivity loss increases with group size. This inverse relationship between the number of people in the group and individual performance is termed the *Ringelmann effect*.

Productivity losses

Why does individual performance decrease as group size increases? Ringelmann explains this result in terms of coordination losses, stating that the result is 'due to lack of simultaneity of the muscular contractions of the individuals' (see Kravitz and Martin, 1986). According to Steiner (1972, 1976) actual group productivity is not equal to potential productivity because losses due to faulty processes must be taken into account.

Stroebe and Frey (1982) are more explicit in this respect. They point out that the productivity losses of the Ringelmann group may be ascribed to at least two sorts of losses:

1 *Motivation losses*, i.e. the tendency to let the others do the work while taking advantage of the circumstances that one's own contribution is not identifiable and that one shares in the total group product, which makes it profitable for each of the group members not to contribute fully. Incidentally, this type of motivation loss is also at the base of many public choice problems. For example, for each of us it is most attractive to let others pay the taxes or to let others work to ensure an unpolluted environment, because while doing so one profits in two ways: one withholds one's contributions to the public good and one profits from the public good – in the form of the welfare state or the clean air – when it is provided. In the area of public good this motivation loss is dubbed the 'free-rider effect': it is in

anybody's interest not to contribute to a public good, but if all do so, one is worse off than if all had contributed. It should be noted that the idea of motivation losses corresponds with the so-called 'social effects' in Paulus's (1983) model of social facilitation and that the free-rider effect seems to imply that decreased negative consequences are involved.

2 *Coordination losses*, e.g. the Ringelmann group members might not have pulled in the same direction, and even if they had, they might not have exerted their potential force at the same moment.

Extending Steiner's original approximation of group performance (see the introduction to this chapter), we are now in a position to be more specific, i.e.

group productivity	=	potential productivity	±	motivation losses/gains	±	coordination losses/gains

And indeed, from the results of subsequent experimental studies (e.g. Ingham, Levinger, Graves and Peckham, 1974) in which an attempt was made to distinguish between the two kinds of productivity losses, it appears that besides coordination losses, motivation losses also play an important role in rope-pulling groups.

Productivity losses have also been demonstrated in the performance of other tasks such as shouting, pumping air and brainstorming (cf. Jackson and Harkins, 1985; see also the following section). In a study on social loafing – an Americanized version of the Ringelmann effect – Latané, Williams and Harkins (1979) tried to disentangle productivity loss into two components, namely motivation and coordination losses. They asked subjects to cheer as loudly as they could, and then measured performance by a sound-level meter (in dynes per cm^2). Subjects wore headphones so they could not hear each other. Each subject was asked to shout by himself, in actual groups of two or six, and in pseudo-groups of two or six. In the pseudo-groups subjects were led to believe that others shouted with them, but in fact they were shouting alone, which prevented coordination losses. By inference, motivation losses could be estimated. The productivity was 82 per cent of capacity in two-person pseudo-groups and 74 per cent in six-person pseudo-groups, indicating 18 per cent and 26 per cent motivation losses respectively. The productivity was 66 per cent in actual two-person groups and 36 per cent in actual six-person groups, indicating 34 per cent and 64 per cent productivity losses. Coordination losses can be inferred by subtracting the productivity of the pseudo-groups from the productivity of the actual groups: 16 per cent in two-person groups and 38 per cent in six-person groups. These results demonstrate that about half of the productivity losses may be ascribed to motivation and the other half to coordination losses, suggesting that actual productivity in real groups is equal to the potential productivity of group members minus coordination and motivation losses.

The subsequent question is how these losses may be prevented. Recent research (e.g. Jackson and Harkins, 1985) suggests that when participants believe they can evaluate their contribution through comparison with the contributions of others, the Ringelmann effect disappears, i.e. group productivity is then equal to the potential productivity of group members.

A number of studies have investigated other conditions in which social loafing may be counteracted. One important condition of the occurrence of social loafing is the identifiability of individual effort expenditure. Kerr and Bruun (1981, 1983) found support for the 'hide-in-the-crowd' explanation, which holds that anonymity increases with group size, which decreases productivity, but when group members' contributions can be identified social loafing tends to be weaker.

A recent field experiment demonstrated the way in which identifiability affects individual performance. Williams, Nida, Baca and Latané (1989) carried out a study with members of the Ohio State University swim team. Four comparable teams of four men each were created by matching for ability and speed, based on the coach's estimate of each swimmer's time for a 100 m lap. Two of the four teams were randomly assigned to the 'low identifiable' condition, the other two to the 'high identifiable' condition. Identifiability referred to the knowledge, public and private, of an individual's lap time. Within each of the identifiability conditions, swimmers competed for individual and team prizes. Each swimmer raced a total of 400 m in four events: two 100 m 'individual' free-style races and one lap in each of two 400 m free-style relays. The results indicated that when swimmers' times were highly identifiable, they swam faster in the relay event. In the low identifiable condition, the opposite occurred. Swimmers swam faster in the individual event than in the relay event, suggesting that social loafing is inhibited when individual efforts are identifiable.

Harkins and Petty (1982) reported that group members were less likely to loaf when they perceived the task to be challenging or when they perceived their own contribution to group action to be unique. Zaccaro (1984) found that social loafing did not occur in groups with a high commitment to task performance. In contrast, social loafing did occur in groups with a low level of task commitment, in which intra-group pressures to maximize individual effort were either entirely absent or could not be effectively applied.

Social facilitation and social loafing: self-efficacy

As Latané et al. (1979) have shown, two types of losses may be incurred as a result of social loafing: coordination losses and motivation losses due to the need for group members to coordinate their efforts. Coordination losses can only partly explain why performance in groups in which individual contributions cannot be evaluated separately is worse than performance in coacting groups in which individual contributions can be identified. On the other hand, there is the social facilitation literature. In the social facilitation literature, interpersonal coordination does not play a role, since it is only individual performance that is investigated, either alone or in comparison with another performer (coaction).

Recently, Sanna (1992) has explicitly addressed the question of how the social facilitation literature relates to the loafing literature. Since interpersonal coordination losses cannot play a role in social facilitation settings and can only partly explain social loafing, he focuses on motivational consequences.

He took as his basis self-efficacy theory, as formulated by Bandura (1986). Bandura made a distinction between two related expectancies: efficacy expectancy, that is, a performer's belief that he or she is able to perform the requisite behaviour; and outcome expectancy, the performer's belief that a given behaviour will lead to a given outcome. To illustrate, Bandura gives the example of a high jumper: 'The expectation that one can jump 6 feet is an efficacy judgment; the social recognition, applause, trophies and self-satisfaction anticipated for such a performance constitute outcome judgments' (Bandura, 1986, p. 240). Sanna argues that the performance of a simple task creates high efficacy, whereas the performance of a complex task induces low efficacy. Moreover, outcome expectancy is affected by whether one has to act alone, together with one other person who serves as a comparison other (coaction), or collectively, that is, when one's own contribution cannot be distinguished from the contributions of others. Since the achievements of a performer acting alone or in collective circumstances are not to be compared with the performance of others, Sanna proposed that outcome expectancy in coaction conditions in which evaluation or the comparison with another is explicitly induced will be greater.

Sanna noticed that in the social facilitation literature, subjects' performance in an alone condition is quite often compared with the performance of subjects in a coaction condition, whereas in the social loafing literature, subjects are either working in coaction conditions in which individual performance can be compared or in collective conditions in which subjects can hide in the crowd. Moreover, he reasoned that in previous studies high efficacy had been induced either by exposing subjects to easy tasks or by providing subjects with feedback that they had performed in a capable way, which led to better performance as compared with that of low-efficacy subjects, presumably because high-efficacy subjects expected to be evaluated in a positive way, i.e. expected a higher outcome than low-efficacy subjects, who expected a low outcome. Further on he argued that in the alone and (collective) social loafing conditions, outcome did not matter as much as it had in coaction conditions in which a subject's performance was explicitly evaluated in comparison with the performance of a coactor.

Lastly, he expected that the effect of efficacy on the quality of performance would be more pronounced for subjects in the coaction condition, since evaluation is more salient in the coaction condition than in the alone or social loafing conditions; in other words, because the outcome in the coaction condition is more relevant than in the alone and collective conditions, outcome expectancy in the coaction condition was expected to be greater.

In order to demonstrate the plausibility of his application of self-efficacy theory, Sanna (1992) conducted two experiments. In the first experiment subjects had to perform a vigilance task in which they were asked to detect as many signals as possible. Bogus efficacy feedback was provided. In the high-efficacy condition subjects were told that they had scored in the 80th percentile according

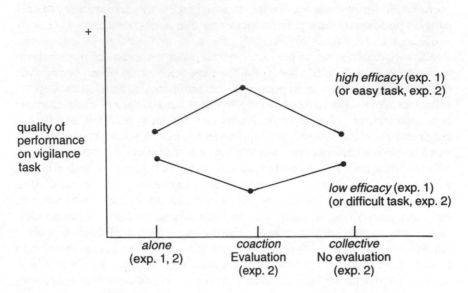

Figure 2.2 Efficacy expectancy, outcome expectancy and performance (adapted from Sanna, 1992)

to established norms for the task, i.e. they had scored high; in the low-efficacy condition subjects were told that they had scored low, i.e. in the 20th percentile. Outcome expectancy was induced by giving subjects the impression that their performance was observed by the experimenter ('alone'), that it would be compared with the performance of one other participant ('coaction'), or that the experimenter would evaluate the joint performance of the subject and his or her partner ('collective'). Two predictions were made:

- The social facilitation prediction was that in the high-efficacy conditions, 'coaction' subjects would perform better (i.e. they would make fewer vigilance task errors) than 'alone' subjects. The reverse was predicted for the low-efficacy conditions, that is, 'coaction' subjects would perform worse than 'alone' subjects.
- The social loafing prediction was that in the high-efficacy conditions, 'collective' subjects would perform worse than 'coaction' subjects, whereas in the low-efficacy conditions, 'collective' subjects would perform better than 'coaction' subjects.

In Figure 2.2 the results of the 2 (efficacy: high, low) × 3 (outcome: alone, coaction, collective) factorial design are depicted. The results indicated that the high-efficacy subjects performed better (as compared with before feedback about their capability) than the low-efficacy subjects. Moreover, the expected statistical interaction between efficacy and outcome was observed. In accordance with the social facilitation hypothesis, we see that in the high-efficacy condition 'alone' subjects performed worse than 'coaction' subjects, whereas in the low-efficacy condition the reverse was the case.

The social loafing hypothesis also received support: in the low-efficacy condition 'collective' subjects performed worse, whereas in the high-efficacy condition 'collective' subjects performed better than subjects in the 'coaction' condition.

In the second experiment efficacy expectancies and outcome expectancies were again varied. Efficacy expectancies were varied by exposing subjects to either easy (high expectancy) or difficult (low expectancy) tasks. It was expected that subjects who had to perform easy tasks would spontaneously develop a high sense of efficacy, whereas subjects exposed to more difficult tasks were expected to develop a low sense of efficacy. Outcome expectancy was also varied in another way as compared with the first experiment. In the second experiment three levels of evaluation were induced. Subjects were evaluated as single individuals (alone, low outcome), in comparison with a coactor who worked at the same task (evaluation, high outcome) or as a pair with one other subject who worked at another task (no evaluation, low outcome). In Figure 2.2 we have also reported the results for these six conditions. It turned out that subjects performed better on easy tasks than on difficult tasks. In this experiment there was also a statistical interaction that supported both the social facilitation hypothesis and the social loafing hypothesis. The social facilitation hypothesis appeared to be supported because in easy task conditions subjects in the (coaction) evaluation condition performed better than the subjects performing alone, while the reverse took place in the more difficult task conditions, that is, subjects who acted alone performed better than coacting/evaluated subjects. The social loafing hypothesis was supported because in the easy task condition coacting/evaluated subjects performed better than non-evaluated subjects who worked at another task, whereas in the difficult task conditions the reverse pattern of results was observed.

So it may be concluded that the two experiments, which differed considerably in their operationalizations of efficacy and outcome, provided consistent results in that the social facilitation hypothesis and the social loafing hypothesis were corroborated. To show how self-efficacy theory might explain these results, Sanna (1992) reported the results of path analyses for the two experiments. Since the results of these two analyses were similar, in Figure 2.3 we have reported the most important (significant multiple) correlations. For simplicity's sake we have numbered the arrows.

It should be noted that Sanna's proposal (Sanna, 1992; see Figure 2.3) is rather similar to the explanation of Paulus (1983; see Figure 2.1). Whereas Paulus refers to negative and positive consequences, Sanna is more explicit in emphasizing the importance of self-efficacy. Having to perform easy tasks or knowing that one is capable of doing the task does lead to better performance, either via self-efficacy expectancy (arrows 1 and 3 in Figure 2.3) or directly (arrow 2 in Figure 2.3). As for the interaction between efficacy and outcome, the proposals made by Paulus (1983) and Sanna (1992) are more or less identical. Paulus postulates that

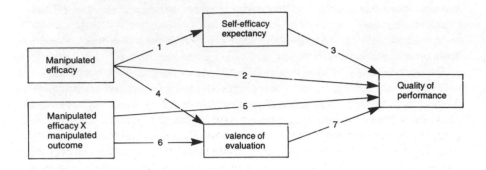

Figure 2.3 Self-efficacy: simplified version of two path analyses (adapted from Sanna, 1992)

high-efficacy subjects anticipate positive consequences, whereas low-efficacy subjects anticipate negative consequences. Moreover, he postulates that the anticipation of being evaluated may amplify these consequences. Sanna postulates that high-efficacy subjects, who expect to be evaluated more positively, are more motivated to perform well when they are to be evaluated than when they are not. Conversely, low-efficacy subjects, who expect to be evaluated more negatively, are more motivated to perform well when they do not anticipate explicit evaluation.

In sum, with respect to the comparison between social facilitation and social loafing, the following may be concluded: (1) An interpersonal coordination-loss interpretation of social loafing is logically and empirically relevant; (2) Theory (Paulus, 1983; Sanna, 1992) and empirical evidence (Sanna, 1992) suggest that these phenomena, with the exception of the coordination losses associated with social loafing or free-riding in groups, may be explained by one integrated theory. Self-efficacy theory (Sanna, 1992) provides the most elaborate proposal to date.

Brainstorming

'Brainstorming' is a group technique originally launched by Osborn (1957), having as its aim the improvement of group productivity. To facilitate productivity, members of groups receive instructions before they start to generate ideas about a certain topic within a certain time interval. They are encouraged to generate as many ideas as possible, but are not allowed to evaluate or be critical of their own or others' expressed ideas, although they may offer ideas that build upon a previously expressed idea. Sorting out of ideas is to be done later. Osborn claimed that groups which follow these instructions generate more ideas, and that the (subsequently assessed) quality of these ideas is also superior. However, the empirical evidence does not support this claim.

McGrath is quite explicit in this respect: 'Individuals working separately generate many more, and more creative (as rated by judges) ideas than do groups' (McGrath, 1984, p. 131). This conclusion has been corroborated in a recent meta-analysis, or comparison, of the results of twenty separate studies (Mullen, Johnson and Salas, 1991).

Quantitative productivity was established by measuring the number of non-redundant ideas generated, and qualitative productivity was measured in terms of the perceived quality of the ideas as rated in some way by judges. Mullen and his co-workers made a distinction between two different types of brainstorming groups: real brainstorming groups, the standard face-to-face interacting groups receiving the standard brainstorming instructions; and variant brainstorming groups, some variant on that basic theme (e.g. group members interacting in some unusual or controlled way).

Two different types of nominal groups (in which subjects act alone) were distinguished: alone nominal groups, the standard nominal group in which individuals perform the task individually without interaction; and together nominal groups, groups who sit together during individual performance. To test whether brainstorming groups indeed do worse than nominal groups, Mullen et al. (1991) compared the productivity of real brainstorming groups with that of together and alone groups. It turned out that quantitative and qualitative production losses did occur in brainstorming groups as compared with nominal groups. In addition to type of group Mullen et al. also measured the effects of other factors, such as group size, the presence of an authoritative observer or experimenter, and the medium by which group members are requested to express their ideas (vocalizing versus writing down). It turned out that production losses in brainstorming groups were largest (a) when the size of the brainstorming group was largest; (b) when an experimenter was present; (c) when brainstorming group members vocalized their contributions (rather than writing them down); and (d) when the point of comparison was a nominal group of individuals who were truly alone, rather than a nominal group of individuals performing together.

In a similar vein, Mullen et al. (1991) suggest that practitioners who want to employ this technique – in spite of the general failure of brainstorming techniques to enhance either the quantity or the quality of performance – would be wise (a) to use smaller groups; (b) not to introduce an authoritative observer; and (c) to let brainstorming group members write down their ideas, in order to minimize productivity losses.

Bond and Van Leeuwen (1991) have criticized the meta-analysis performed by Mullen et al. (1991), and their reanalysis of the same twenty studies shows that two factors did contribute to production losses in brainstorming groups: group size and type of nominal group (together versus alone). Response mode (vocalized versus written) and the presence of an authoritative outsider (experimenter present versus absent) had no effect.

Diehl and Stroebe (1987; see also Stroebe and Diehl, 1991) have made a more thorough effort to explain why production losses occur in brainstorming groups.

They identify three distinct explanations. We will deal with these explanations, together with the corresponding empirical evidence, in the following.

Free-riders

The free-rider explanation (see also Stroebe and Frey, 1982, and the previous section on social loafing) suggests that in brainstorming groups members expect that their individual ideas will be pooled, whereas in nominal groups it is believed that each person will be directly credited for any idea proposed. The fact that individual contributions are pooled in brainstorming groups leads to a temptation to free-ride, that is, to let the others do the work, a motivation loss which is unlikely in nominal groups where each person's contribution remains visible.

To investigate the plausibility of this explanation, Diehl and Stroebe (1987) instructed nominal and brainstorming groups to expect either *individual* assessment or *pooled* assessment. The results indicated that assessment indeed had an effect: there was greater productivity among subjects who had been led to expect individual as opposed to pooled assessment. However, the explained variance – a statistic that reflects the impact of the effect – was only 8 per cent. Most of the variance (80 per cent) was explained by type of group: brainstorming groups produced less than nominal groups. Having discarded the idea that the free-rider explanation was a very important one, Diehl and Stroebe tested another hypothesis.

Evaluation apprehension

The evaluation apprehension explanation proposes that in brainstorming groups – despite the instruction not to evaluate the ideas that are put forward – the fear of negative evaluations from other group members prevents subjects from presenting their ideas, an explanation which is consistent with the social facilitation literature (Cottrell, 1972, and Sanna, 1992; presumably the tasks given to brainstorming groups are difficult ones that lead to negative self-efficacy). In the study by Diehl and Stroebe (1987) nominal and brainstorming groups either worked as usual or were videotaped ostensibly for the purpose of presentation to a social psychology class which was attended by most of the subjects. Moreover, pooled and individual assessment instructions were provided in this experiment. It appeared that type of group again explained most of the variance (70 per cent): nominal groups outperformed brainstorming groups. Moreover, the expectation of evaluation reduced group productivity. From their study Diehl and Stroebe concluded that, 'although assessment expectations and evaluation apprehension have been shown to affect brainstorming productivity and can thus be assumed to contribute to productivity loss in brainstorming groups, their impact has been minor when compared to that of type of group' (Diehl and Stroebe, 1987, p. 505). Having discarded the idea that assessment and evaluation apprehension are crucial to explaining productivity losses in brainstorming groups, Diehl and Stroebe investigated the production blocking explanation.

Production blocking

The production blocking explanation proposes that the most important cause of the inferiority of real groups is the rule of etiquette that only one group member may speak at a time, which induces non-participation by other group members, who may possibly forget their ideas or be prevented from developing new ideas. The production blocking explanation has also been investigated by Diehl and Stroebe (1987). They reasoned that because production blocking cannot be eliminated in real brainstorming groups, its role can only be examined by introducing blocking in individual sessions. Four subjects worked in individual rooms, and in front of each subject was a display of four lights, each light belonging to one specific group member. As soon as one person started to speak, a voice-activated sensor switched his or her light on green. The green light switched off when the person did not say anything for 1.5 seconds. In the meantime all other lights were red. The investigators constructed five conditions. Three experimental conditions were realized, and in addition the usual real group and nominal group conditions were run.

In condition 1 (blocking, communication) subjects could hear the ideas of other subjects, which was not possible in condition 2 (blocking, no communication). In condition 3 (no blocking, no communication) subjects were informed about the function of the lights, but they were encouraged to disregard these lights and talk whenever they wanted to do so.

The results indicated that quantitative production in the conditions with blocking (real groups, condition 1 and condition 2) was less than that in the two conditions without blocking (condition 3, nominal groups), suggesting that blocking is a major factor explaining production losses in brainstorming groups. While discussing the practical implications of the result that blocking was associated with production losses in brainstorming groups, Diehl and Stroebe remark: 'Because blocking slows down the generation of ideas in groups, it might be more effective to ask subjects first to develop their ideas in individual sessions and next have these ideas discussed and evaluated in a group session. The task of the group would then consist of evaluation rather than production of ideas' (Diehl and Stroebe, 1987, p. 508).

It should be noted that these recommendations are already part of another technique, namely the Nominal Group Technique (NGT; see Delbecq, Van de Ven and Gustafson, 1975; Van de Ven, 1974). NGT involves a two-stage process. Individuals work separately in a generation stage and thereafter work as an interacting group in an evaluation (choosing) stage. This technique has been employed for the generation and evaluation of ideas (as in brainstorming), of goals to be set and of decisions to be made.

Thus, brainstorming tasks are usually additive and difficult tasks (see preceding section), and it appears that with increasing group size, fewer ideas are produced, a finding which is consistent with the social loafing literature explained in an earlier section. It is not easy to explain why brainstorming groups are less productive than individuals acting alone. The free-rider explanation and the evaluation apprehension explanation have received some support, i.e. the motivation to let others work to provide the group product and the fear of negative evaluation by others do reduce group productivity, and these factors constitute motivation losses. However, the most prominent reason why production losses occur in brainstorming groups seems to be the rule that as long as one member speaks other group members have to listen, i.e. blocking. According to Diehl and Stroebe (1987) blocking also leads to motivation losses, since by the coordination rule of only one speaker at a time, other group members may forget, or be discouraged from presenting, their ideas. From that perspective it may be argued that the blocking rule itself creates too much coordination, which presumably is detrimental to the motivation of group members to produce new ideas.

Extra evidence in support of the blocking hypothesis is provided by a study of Valacich, Dennis and Connolly (forthcoming), who employed an interesting new technique. They studied nominal and real groups of various sizes, but subjects used the Electronic Brainstorming System (EBS). In a two-tiered workroom containing individual work stations connected via a local network, subjects meet. The network allows for the formation of subgroups of any size up to twenty-four. Each group member types a brief comment in response to a theme-question, and then sends the file to a shared pool, getting in return another, randomly drawn file containing the theme-question and any comment it may have already elicited. The participant appends a further comment, returns the file to the pool, receives another randomly drawn file, and so on, until the session is terminated.

Typed comments are not identified as to sender, and group members are dispersed around the room. Individuals in nominal groups used a version of EBS designed for single users in which no file sharing took place. Subjects were requested to generate as many ideas as possible. The tasks were brainstorming tasks, for example, to generate as many ideas as possible about the consequences of the introduction of a new organization policy.

In one of their experiments (Experiment 1) the investigators compared real and nominal groups of different sizes, namely groups consisting of 3, 6, 9, 12, 15 and 18 persons. The results indicated that for groups of 3 and 6 it did not matter whether they were nominal or real. However, groups of 9, 12, 15 and 18 members performed better under real than under nominal conditions. This latter result runs, of course, counter to what has been found in previous research. In prior research it was found that individuals working alone generate more, and more creative, ideas than real groups (McGrath, 1984). Valacich et al. (forthcoming) ascribe the superiority of real groups to the EBS technique, in which group members are not blocked, that is, are not inclined to wait for an opportunity to contribute but are able to produce new ideas right away.

CONCLUSIONS AND SUMMARY

In this chapter we focused on individual performance in groups. Whereas in the social facilitation (and inhibition) literature individual performance is investigated either alone or in comparison with one other worker under easy and more difficult task conditions, in the social loafing literature individual performance is observed in coaction circumstances in which individual performance may be identified and compared, or in collectives in which this is not the case, under easy or more difficult task conditions. The results can be explained and integrated in terms of the models proposed by Paulus (1983) and Sanna (1992), who emphasize the following:

(a) Having to perform easy tasks leads to the expectation of a more positive evaluation (positive consequences) than having to perform more difficult tasks.
(b) In the social facilitation conditions (alone versus audience or coaction) and the social loafing conditions (coaction versus collective) the expectation of being evaluated (i.e. evaluation apprehension) tends to enhance the expectations mentioned in (a).

Brainstorming is a technique for investigating whether nominal groups (summed individual performances) perform better or worse than real groups. Several explanations seem to account for the disappointing result that nominal groups are superior to real groups.

Besides the free-rider explanation, the evaluation apprehension explanation has received empirical support. The evaluation apprehension explanation is, of course, strongly related to the dominant explanation of social facilitation and social loafing, which concerns the enhancement of negative or positive consequences depending on whether or not one feels evaluated. However, since task difficulty has not been investigated explicitly in brainstorming studies, further integration of the brainstorming literature with the SFI and social loafing literature will have to wait for further evidence.

The most important explanation of the inferiority of real groups as compared with nominal groups is that the production of ideas is frustrated when group members have to wait for others to express their ideas. If this blocking is removed – for example, by introducing an Electronic Brainstorming System – then real groups perform better than nominal groups. So Osborn's (1957) original idea that individuals perform better in groups than alone is correct after all, provided that blocking does not occur.

Chapter 3

Cognitive tuning

Let's start by repeating what we have said about the individual task performer. (1) An individual task performer builds up an individual, more or less hierarchically ordered cognitive representation of the task, which may be assumed to be triggered or activated by the 'objective' task properties at hand. (2) An individual task performer also reflects upon task engagement and monitors how the task is progressing and when the task may be completed.

How is a task performed by individuals who are members of a group that has to perform a task? Contrary to individual task performance, group performance involves two additional related problems. The first problem is that group members have to build up a collective representation of the task and agree about whether to engage in the task (or not); and if the group decides to engage in the task, group members have to agree how the task should be executed. The second problem is that several people are involved, which evokes the question of how the group as such should be organized so that the task may be completed.

To give an example, suppose group members have individually thought about the horse-trading problem (as the Nominal Group Technique recommends, see chapter 2), and subsequently are requested to provide a group solution. Here the group faces two related problems. The first is how to determine what the group task entails. What is necessary therefore is that group members start to communicate about how each individual perceives the horse-trading problem and which solutions are available. This part of the problem is more complicated in this case than in the case of individual task performance, because now several individuals are involved; these individuals have to develop a common perspective on the cognitive and reflective processing of the task. The second problem concerns how communication in the group should be organized in a way that will allow the group to achieve its goal in an efficient way. For example, if group members start to communicate simultaneously so that everyone speaks and no one listens, the group task cannot be solved. In sum, group performance involves the development of a collective view of both the task and the group.

In order to solve these related (task and group organization) problems, group members have to communicate. The nature of their communication has the character of mutual influencing: through the process of mutual influencing a common perspective on how the group task may be solved and how the group should be organized is created. The products of this mutual influencing are a mutually agreed task structure and a mutually agreed group structure, i.e. consensus about how the subparts of the task are related to one another and consensus about the way the group members relate to one another. These products have both descriptive and prescriptive implications. As for the group task, a collective description or definition of the task may be reached. Moreover, this description has consequences for how the task should be performed, since it prescribes how the task should be performed. As for the group structure, a collective cognitive representation or definition of how the group members relate is evoked by mutual influence, and this representation is the descriptive aspect of group structure. By implication, this consensual description has behavioural consequences for how the group members should act, that is, an agreed group structure prescribes how group members should relate to one another in the future.

CONFLICTS

Through communication group members may become aware that they do not share a collective representation about the problem to be solved. When it is difficult to come to a collective set of representations because contradicting representations are expressed, a cognitive intra-group conflict is said to exist. Such a cognitive conflict may have to do with higher-order representations. For example, what is the ultimate goal of the task?

A cognitive intra-group conflict may also refer to a lower-level representation concerning how to perform the task or the specific task procedures to be executed in order to perform the task. Cognitive intra-group conflicts arise mainly from group members' previous experiences. For example, some of the group members may have learned to approach problems like the horse-trading problem analytically, whereas other group members may want to deal with it in a more global sense.

Communication is also necessary for the more reflective task processes. As you may remember, one of the most important problems in the area of reflective processing is establishing whether engagement in a task would be profitable or not. A consensual estimation of whether it is worthwhile to engage in a task may be difficult to attain for two reasons.

First, group members may have different representations about what course of affairs will provide the highest expected outcomes for the group. If that is the case, then we still assume that the cognitive intra-group disagreement has a primarily cognitive origin and we refer to an intra-group cognitive conflict: group members maintain differential judgements, discrepant judgements that may be resolved through communication. To give an example that is related to what we said in chapter 1 about the difference between group members who score low and high on achievement motivation: in group gambling tasks highly achievement-motivated group members may prefer tasks which involve a moderate chance of moderate outcomes, whereas less achievement-motivated group members may prefer gambling tasks involving either low outcomes with a high expectation of success or high outcomes with a low expectation of success. As a consequence, group members who are low and high on achievement motivation may differ in their appraisal of acceptable levels of risk.

Second, group members may differ in their interests. In that case we do not speak of a cognitive conflict, but of a conflict of interests. To illustrate, when more and less achievement-oriented group members are very strongly motivated to make their own judgement the group judgement, for example because they have committed themselves strongly to their a priori judgement, we have a conflict of interests. In this circumstance, by accepting goals with a moderate probability of success and a moderate outcome, less achievement-motivated group members may feel that they have lost, whereas highly achievement-motivated group members might feel that they have won, the contest about which targets to set. A more pronounced example of a conflict of interests within a group arises when some group members may profit from the choice of a certain task, whereas other members may lose by it.

So we may distinguish between two kinds of mutual influencing: communication about cognitions is meant to reduce cognitive ambiguity or cognitive conflict, which is greater to the degree that group members' representations and reflections differ. It should be noted that many group problem-solving tasks involve this type of conflict. On the other hand we may have mutual influencing which is meant to bridge differential interests of group members, and this communication involves bargaining. As we have suggested above, this distinction between cognitive communication and bargaining is not always entirely clear. A cognitive conflict may give rise to a conflict of interests, and a conflict of interests may quite often be framed as a cognitive conflict, for example because group members are reluctant to show that a conflict of interests is involved.

These two types of conflict may also be involved when group members have difficulty agreeing on a specific group structure. A cognitive conflict is involved when group members disagree about the preferred group structure. For example, some members may prefer that a leader be chosen who controls the communication process, whereas other group members may prefer a more egalitarian structure in which every group member has his or her say. A conflict of interests is involved when some members prefer a specific group structure because they may profit from it, whereas other group members are afraid that they will lose as a result of it. For example, group structure involving a leader may be preferred by group members who hope to become the prospective leader and opposed by group members who are afraid of being excluded from the mutual influencing process by a prospective leader who may take decisions on behalf of all without taking notice of the other group members' preferences.

After this abstract analysis, we will end this introduction to group performance with an example that summarizes what we have explained thus far. Suppose we have a four-person group that has decided to build a house. Each of the

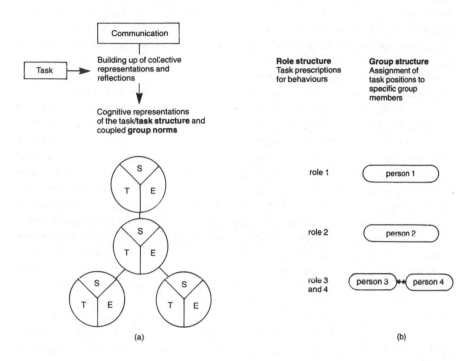

Figure 3.1 Collective task structure and group structure

participants has individual representations of what a house should look like and how the actual house-building should be done. What is necessary therefore is that they exchange these representations. Each of them communicates what the house is to look like and how further steps should be taken to build it. After some time they may decide to build a wooden house with a concrete basement. This decision may be considered the supergoal of the group. Now they have to start to reflect upon how this supergoal can be reached. Through mutual influencing they may distinguish a collective representation involving three levels (see Figure 3.1): (1) the designing of the house and maintenance of contact with the municipal officials who have to consent to the building; (2) the supervision of the building; and (3) the actual building of the basement and the wooden house. In the left column of Figure 3.1 we have depicted these three levels of the task structure. Note that the collective representation of the task is inspired by the task and agreed upon through mutual influencing. We see also the now well-known sensing, testing and effecting functions at each level and that the effecting function at a higher hierarchical level serves as an input for the nearest lower hierarchical level of the organization of the group task. Note also that the three

LIBRARY, UNIVERSITY COLLEGE CHESTER

collective task levels not only function as a description of the group task, but also have implications for how the task should be performed, that is, descriptive and prescriptive aspects are involved.

Mutual influencing concerns discussions not only about how the group task should be organized, but also about how the four-person group should be organized and how each of the four members should behave. The organization of the group is presented in the right part of Figure 3.1. We see that person 1 has been made responsible for the designing of the house, person 2 for the supervision during building, and persons 3 and 4 for the actual building of the house. This is not only a collectively agreed representation of the four-person group (description), but this representation also implies prescriptions about the behaviour of each of the four persons and of the group at large. Thus, a collective task structure and a group structure are arrived at through communication, which implies mutual influencing when there is initial disagreement about how the group task should be organized. Mutual influencing is also necessary when the four persons differ in their ideas about how each of them should contribute to this rather complex task. Their disagreements about the group task and structure amount to a cognitive conflict when they hold different cognitive representations. When they have different preferences because their interests are perceived as opposed – for example, each of the group members wants to act at the lowest level (actual building of the house) and not at the highest level (designing the house) – we speak of a conflict of interests.

It should be noted that in the case of a cognitive conflict and/or a conflict of interests, groups will not endlessly communicate until their disagreements entirely disappear. The reason for limited mutual influencing is that communication in itself is costly, and these costs are weighed against the prospective rewards of the further consensus that may be reached by further communication. Thus reflection also plays a role during mutual influencing (or communication) in that group members make appraisals about whether it is profitable to engage in or to abandon further communication.

In the following, we start with the cognitive tuning of task groups. It should be noted that this aspect of task-tuned groups is part of the total functioning of task groups and that a role is also played by reflective and communicative aspects, which we will deal with in the subsequent chapters.

COGNITIVE TUNING

Cognitive tuning arises when the representations that group members have built up in the past do not appear to be in agreement with one another. The classic study on the autokinetic effect (Sherif, 1936) provides an example of (a) how individuals build up cognitive representations; and (b) how individual representations may be changed as a consequence of social activation, i.e. through the influence of other group members.

If a person in a completely dark room is presented with a small stable point of light, the subjective impression is that the light is moving erratically. This seeming movement is called the autokinetic effect and is caused by eye movements and several central nervous processes. In one of his studies, Sherif (1936) presented individual subjects with such a light a hundred times for two seconds, and each time the subject had to report orally to the experimenter the distance which he saw it move. The results showed that in the absence of an objective range and an externally given standard, each subject formed his own range (e.g. between 2 and 6 in.) and his own reference point (e.g. 4 in.). The range and reference point differed between subjects, but were stable within subjects for several days. As such, this result seems to indicate that subjects build up stable representations. One may wonder, however, whether the stable reference point selected (e.g. 4 in.) was a response directed towards the experimenter, or an indication of a stable 'frame of reference' in the memory of subjects, as Sherif has stressed, or both. Of more importance are the results after the individual sessions.

After these initial individual sessions, Sherif placed two or three subjects together, instructing them to give their estimates of the light movement in turn. Over several consecutive group sessions, the estimates showed a funnel pattern, converging nearly around the (geometric) mean of the individually given responses. These responses remained the same afterwards, when subjects had to give their estimates alone, without the presence of others. In later research the influence of the common reference point remained evident after a month and even after a year (Sherif and Sherif, 1969). When, in other conditions, subjects did not start individually but in groups of two or three, the funnel effect was even stronger than when subjects had formed individual norms beforehand. Sherif stresses two points: the effect shows a gradual temporal pattern, not a sudden shift, and most subjects did not fully realize to what extent they were influenced by the answers of the other group members.

The results obtained by Sherif and later researchers can be summarized in a conceptual scheme developed by Holzkamp (1972). In Figure 3.2. the person is confronted with an external stimulus (S), to which he or she reacts with a covert internal response (Rc.1). The person is also confronted with the overt response of another, supposedly responding to the same S, which forms a second stimulus (SO). The person reacts with a second covert internal response (Rc.2), which in turn influences Rc.1. The modified Rc.1 leads finally to an external overt verbal response (Ro). The arrow from S to SO indicates that the person assumes that the other refers to the same stimulus. Having the impression of responding to the same stimulus is a general necessary condition for any successful communication situation, which Rommetveit (1974) called 'a shared social reality'. Indeed, if subjects are informed beforehand that the movement of the light is a subjective optical illusion, then the convergence or conformity in judgement during the group sessions has been shown to be drastically reduced (Sperling, in Asch, 1952; Alexander, Zucker and Brody, 1970). According to Campbell (1961) and Holzkamp (1972) the robustness of the initial internal response Rc.1 is mainly dependent on the strength or the lack of ambiguity of the original stimulus. In other words, robustness, referring to the tendency of a stimulus to activate

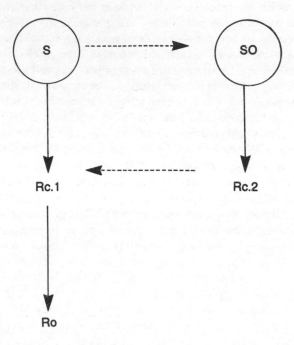

Figure 3.2 The social influence process (adapted from Holzkamp, 1972)

clear-cut representations in the memory of the perceiver, depends on the distinc-
tiveness of the original stimulus. If a perceiver is more able to associate a
clear-cut representation with the stimulus, the perceiver is inclined to make a
judgement with greater confidence and is also more resistant to changing that
judgement. In a similar way, the robustness of the internal response Rc.2 is
dependent on the perceived competence and motivation of the other, and as we
shall discuss later on, on the sheer number of others and their mutual agreement
or disagreement. The integration of the original Rc.1 and Rc.2 into a new Rc.1
can be conceived of as a process of integrating the two original responses into a
final one, with weights according to their initial robustness.

In the description so far, we have focused on one perceiver, while in the Sherif
situation there are two or three perceivers who may influence one other. Mutual
influencing is elegantly described in J.R.P. French's (1956) formal theory of
social power. He does not use the concept 'robustness' or 'weight' but instead
uses the concept of 'force'. The theory departs from three postulates. The first
states that, 'for any given discrepancy of opinion between A and B, the strength
of the resultant force which an inducer A can exert on an inducee B, in the
direction of agreeing with A's opinion, is proportional to the strength of the bases
of power of A over B', e.g. to the extent that A is considered to be more

competent than B. The second postulate is that, 'the strength of the force which an inducer A exerts on an inducee B, in the direction of agreeing with A's opinion, is proportional to the size of the discrepancy between their opinions'. The third postulate is that in one unit of time, 'each person who is being influenced will change his opinion until he reaches the equilibrium point where the resultant force (of the forces induced by other members at the beginning of the unit and the resisting force corresponding to his own resistance to change) is equal to zero' (J.R.P. French, 1956, pp. 184–5). We will discuss the bases of power in postulate 1 extensively in chapter 7; in the Sherif situation they correspond with the robustness of the initial internal response Rc.1 and Rc.2 in Figure 3.2. Ultimately, after mutual influencing over time, A and B reach a final stable equilibrium point, which in the Sherif situation happens to be the (geometric) mean of the initial internal responses Rc.1. If this point is reached, the cognitive conflict for A and B between their Rc.1 and Rc.2 is resolved and a collective judgement is established. Because such a common description serves as a common prescription for the future, we call it a group norm.

How persistent is a group norm?

It has been demonstrated experimentally that a group norm may last for several generations of group members. Jacobs and Campbell (1961) placed four-person groups in the Sherif situation. Initially, three persons were confederates instructed to give extremely large estimates. After a number of trials the judgements of the fourth, 'naive' subject approached these judgements, so that what may be called 'an arbitrary group norm' had been established. After thirty trials one of the confederates was replaced by a new naive subject, whose judgements again rapidly approached the estimates of the other three. In this way new generations were introduced repeatedly. During the fourth generation all confederates had been replaced by naive subjects and in the fifth generation the first naive subject was replaced by a new one. This went on through twelve generations. The results showed a persistence of the original group norm and a very gradual decrease of the initial group norm over generations. In a comparable experiment, MacNeil and Sherif (1976) varied the degree of arbitrariness of the norm in the first generations. It appeared that a moderately arbitrary norm survived much longer than an extreme norm. Montgomery, Hinkle and Enzie (1976) showed that the decline of the norm was slower if the subjects had highly authoritarian personalities than if they were low on authoritarianism. Zucker (1977) demonstrated how the degree of institutionalization of the context affects the persistence of group norms. In a first condition subjects had to respond simply as individuals. In a second condition they had to respond as members of a model organization. In a third condition they had to respond as low-status members of an organization. It appeared that the persistence of group norms was stronger the greater the degree of institutionalization, i.e. rising from condition one to condition three.

Cognitive conflict and the subsequent formation of a group norm is not restricted to the autokinetic effect. Comparable results have been reported for cutaneous perceptions of temperature, estimates of size, estimates of numbers and aesthetic judgements (Sherif and Sherif, 1969). It should be noted that in performing these tasks, group members were quite unaware of the presence of a conflict and the way it had been resolved.

Differences in perspective and cognitive conflict

The cognitive conflict created by the autokinetic illusion may be called 'one-dimensional'. It concerns disagreement on one dimension, that is, the distance through which the light is seen to move, which is used and shared by the subjects. More complicated cognitive conflicts arise if group members differ in their point of view because they consider different aspects of the stimulus in forming their judgements. These cognitive conflicts are called 'multi-dimensional' and have been studied mainly by the researchers who developed Social Judgment Theory (see, for example, Brehmer, 1976; Brehmer and Joyce, 1988; Hammond, 1965). This theory is an elaboration of Brunswick's (1952) lens model of perception and cognition as depicted in Figure 3.3(a).

According to the lens model, the human environment consists of objects and events of which the real state, i.e. the inherent properties, can only be inferred from observation. The objects themselves are called 'criteria' or 'distal variables'. A criterion may, however, give rise to a number of observable stimuli, called 'proximal cues' or 'surface variables'. The connections between the criterion and these proximal cues are probabilistic in nature. To give an example: when physicians see a patient with an internal disease, they do not observe the disease itself (the criterion or distal variable); they can observe only a number of symptoms (proximal cues). Their task is to combine and weigh the cues in order to make inferences which result in a diagnostic judgement. The lens model connects two systems: the task system and the cognitive system. The task system consists of the relations between the criterion and the cues. The cognitive system consists of the relations between the cues and the judgement. The relation between cues and judgement is also probabilistic in nature. In Social Judgment Theory the task system and the cognitive system are described in terms of the same concepts, which are statistical, because the relations within the two systems are basically probabilistic.

The relations between the unobservable distal state, the observable cues and the judgement together form what Hammond (e.g. Hammond, Stewart, Brehmer and Steinmann, 1975) has named a 'zone of ambiguity'. Ambiguity has at least four causes. (1) Within the task system cues differ in the strength or importance of their relation with the criterion. The relation can vary from nearly perfect to almost non-existent. Judges forming a cognitive representation weight in a subjective way the relation between cues and criterion. These weights may or may not correspond with the actual importance of the relations between the cues and

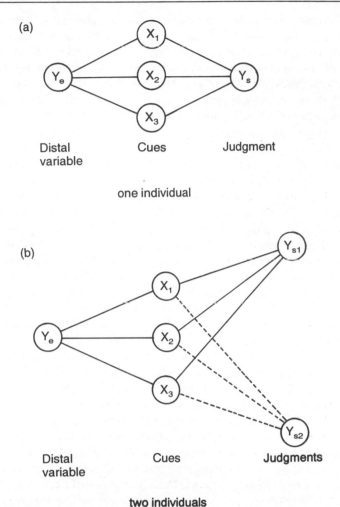

(a)

Distal
variable

Cues

Judgment

one individual

(b)

Distal
variable

Cues

Judgments

two individuals

Figure 3.3 Brunswick's lens model (Brehmer, 1988)

the distal variable. (2) The functional relation between criterion and cues may have a variety of forms; for example, the relation may be linear and positive, linear and negative, or curvilinear. The relation between cues and judgements may also assume various forms, which may correspond more or less with the forms in the task system. (3) Cues may be organized in different ways, for example in an additive or configural way within the task system, and they may be integrated in different ways in the cognitive system. (4) Finally, task systems may vary in their predictability, that is, the relation between the total set of cues and the criterion may vary from very weak to very strong. Judges, on the other hand, may vary between relying on particular cues or any combination of cues in a more or less consistent way in the process of forming their judgements.

Brunswick's original lens model concerned perception of the physical environment. The model has been extended to clinical judgement in medicine and clinical psychology by Hammond (1955). In later research it was extended even further to policy formation. Examples are its applications to value judgements about alternatives in regional planning, which involved the conflicting goals of economic growth and pollution of the environment, and judgements about the relative importance of several academic planning areas, such as research emphasis and instructional methods (Hammond, Rohrbaugh, Mumpower and Adelman, 1977). More important for our purposes is a second extension of the lens model involving two (or more) judges (Hammond, 1965), as depicted in Figure 3.3(b). In the case of two judges, three systems are involved: the task system, the cognitive system of the first judge and the cognitive system of the second judge. The cognitive representations of the task system formed by the two judges may be different; if the representations differ, a cognitive conflict exists between them. The difference may arise from the use of different cues, or from use of the same cues in a different way, for example by assigning different weights, by using different functional forms or by applying different rules to combine the cues in the formation of their representation. These differences are called different 'judgment policies' in Social Judgment Theory.

The research paradigm for studying interpersonal cognitive conflicts in the laboratory situation involves two stages (Hammond, 1965). The first stage is a training stage. Subjects are presented with different task systems and trained to develop different judgement policies. In a study by Hammond, Todd, Wilkins and Mitchell (1966), subjects were required to learn to estimate the criterion of the level of democratization in a number of nations on the basis of two proximal cues: the extent to which free elections exist in the nation and the extent to which state control is a factor in the government. One subject learned to depend heavily on the state control variable, which was linearly related to the criterion level, and learned not to depend on the free elections variable, which was non-linearly related to the criterion. The reverse task system was presented to the second subject. So, through training, the subjects acquired different cognitive representations of their task. The second stage in the paradigm is the conflict stage. Subjects are brought together and presented with a common task system consisting of a number of new nations. They are not informed of the fact that they harbour different representations. In each trial subjects have to study the cue values, to make individual judgements of the level of democratization in a nation (the criterion), to exchange their judgements and in case of disagreement to discuss the matter in order to reach a joint judgement. Afterwards they are informed of the correct criterion value, which depends on both cues together.

If subjects learn that their judgements differ, they experience a cognitive conflict, which they have to resolve. Brehmer (1976) has reviewed a number of studies using this paradigm. By and large the results indicate that the amount of disagreement between subjects showed little or no reduction over twenty trials. However, the structure of the disagreement changed. At the beginning of the second stage disagreement did arise because the subjects used different judgement policies in a well-learned and consistent way. In the course of their interaction, subjects reduced systematic differences between their policies by changing them. In order to reach agreement, each of the subjects decreased the relative weight given to the learned cue and increased the weight given to the other, non-learned cue. To retain consistent representations the decrease and the increase should occur at the same rate. The results showed a strong tendency for subjects to decrease the learned weight faster than they increased the other weight, with inconsistency of judgement as a result. As a consequence, the inconsistent policies at the end of the conflict stage produced nearly the same amount of disagreement and conflict as had existed at the beginning of this stage.

Brehmer (1976) distinguishes two mains reasons for subjects to change their judgement policies. The policy may be changed in order to advance judgemental accuracy, that is, to reduce the discrepancy between the judgement and the value of the criterion according to the feedback. A policy may also be changed in order to reduce interpersonal cognitive conflict, that is, to reduce the difference between the judgements of the two subjects. Which reason is more important? In the conflict stage in the studies discussed so far, both cues were equally valid. However, in another series of studies (see Brehmer, 1976) only one cue was valid, while the other was completely invalid. As a consequence, in the conflict stage one subject had an optimal judgement policy and the other subject had a useless, invalid policy. The results showed that subjects with an invalid policy changed their policy far more than subjects with a valid policy. So, an important reason to change policies appears to be the advancement of accuracy or task adaptation and not the reduction of interpersonal cognitive conflict.

Later laboratory studies and field studies (see, for example, Brehmer, 1976; Brehmer and Joyce, 1988) have shown that diverse formal and structural task characteristics, for example, the number, metric level and interrelations of cues, their functional relation to the criterion and the underlying organizational principle, determine the judgement policies formed by subjects. These policies, in turn, determine the amount and structure of disagreement or cognitive conflict between persons involved. It may be extremely difficult to solve these cognitive conflicts in existing task groups outside the laboratory, because adequate feedback is often lacking. To overcome cognitive conflicts, social judgement theorists have developed a variety of elaborated intervention strategies to promote conflict resolution (e.g. Brehmer and Joyce, 1988; Cook and Hammond, 1982; Hammond *et al.* 1977). The intervention strategy usually involves a computerized step-by-step procedure for listing and exchanging ideas about the relationship between proximal cues and judgements about distal variables. First, group members are invited to make individual judgements. Thereafter, their judgements and differential policies are exchanged. Lastly, the group is invited to reach a collective policy.

According to Cook and Hammond (1982) the results of this intervention strategy, which obliges group members to think systematically about their policies, are quite impressive, suggesting that this technique is a powerful instrument for reducing cognitive conflict.

PRESSURES TOWARDS UNIFORMITY

In Sherif's autokinetic situation, subjects had no clear representation available to help them judge the distance moved by the stimulus. The results indicate that subjects who had to guess in the individual sessions did build up an individual representation, whereas in the collective session the organization of the individual representation was highly facilitated by the responses of other group members. In terms of Figure 3.2, subjects were initially exposed to an S that triggered, or activated, no clear representations, i.e. Rc.1.

A further question is what will occur if people have a clear Rc.1, while they are exposed to a divergent SO communication from other group members. In that case it is plausible to expect that the subject will be aware that there exists divergence between Rc.1 and SO, that is, a more salient conflict of cognitions arises compared with that which was the case in Sherif's autokinetic situation.

Such a salient conflict in a group is uncomfortable for several reasons. First of all, quite often group members have to strive for a common representation in order to take action. For example, for a team to build a house it is necessary to agree upon what the house should look like. Festinger (1950) calls this motive 'group locomotion': if group locomotion is important, the divergent opinions about how a group should make progress are uncomfortable.

The second and third reasons are interrelated. On the one hand, a discrepancy between the members' own Rc.1 and the SOs communicated by other group members may lead people to doubt whether their own initial representation is valid. Festinger (1954) calls this motive 'reality testing': others may help the self to form a more valid representation. Festinger argues that, in this case, the self is quite likely to turn to similar others to establish what a better representation would be. Related to this, and this was already anticipated in chapter 1 where we explained that self may define itself in a hierarchical way, is that one may define oneself as a member of a group, and being a member of a group would mean that one's own opinion should coincide with the opinions of other group members. Then, learning that one's own opinion differs from the opinion of other group members leads to doubts about whether one has built up a valid representation and whether one is part of the group, i.e. whether one is an acceptable group member (see also Turner, 1991). Thus, group members confronted with divergent opinions have several reasons to strive for consensus, or uniformity of opinions: lack of consensus or lack of uniformity of opinions may introduce an obstacle to group locomotion, may lead the individual to doubt whether he or she harbours a valid representation of reality and may lead the individual to doubt whether he or she is an acceptable group member. Therefore, it is assumed that group members exert pressures towards uniformity.

Majority influence and conformity

How will a cognitive conflict for a minority member of a group be solved if that member sees him- or herself confronted with a disagreeing majority? The classic experimental paradigm for studying the influence of a majority on a minority was developed by Asch (1951, 1956). In a typical Asch study, four to nine people (usually students) meet. Their task is to estimate the length of lines. In total, there are eighteen trials. In each trial a card with a standard line is presented, which has to be compared with a card depicting three other lines. One after another the group members have to state aloud which of the three lines has the same length as the standard line. This task is simple enough: one of the three lines corresponds exactly with the standard line and it is extremely difficult to make an error. All group members are confederates of the experimenter except one, who has to respond next to last. On the first two and on four other trials, the confederates are instructed to give the correct answer. On twelve trials their answers are incorrect. What are the answers of the one group member who naively participates in the twelve trials in which that member finds him- or herself deviating in opinion from the majority of the group?

Of the 'naive' subjects, about 20 per cent completely ignored the wrong answers of the majority; they always gave the correct answer. Five per cent complied with the wrong answers of the majority on all twelve trials. About 75 per cent of the subjects gave at least one incorrect answer in agreement with the majority. In total, about 37 per cent of all answers were erroneous. In contrast, in a control condition in which subjects were confronted with no majority influence, 0.7 per cent errors were made.

The Asch situation has a number of striking features. First, in trials in which the majority gives the incorrect answer, the (only) naive subject – the minority in this group situation – is led to doubt the validity of his or her own internal representation, since other group members give an opinion that is discrepant with what the naive subject has learned in the past. Second, this discrepancy creates another conflict: if the naive subject complies with the majority, that subject apparently rejects his or her a priori representation, but the subject may consider him- or herself an acceptable group member; on the other hand, the subject may maintain his or her a priori representation, but in that case may fear that he or she will not be considered a member of the group. Third, Moscovici (1985) has pointed out another conflict. He argues that a subject knows that his a priori representation of the judgement will be shared by all people outside the specific group situation. If the naive subject nevertheless complies with the judgement of the majority, his behaviour is not only inconsistent with his own a priori representation of the reality; it is also inconsistent with that of all people outside the laboratory. Thus, compliance with the majority of the group may be considered in conflict with the naive subject's a priori representation, which is presumably shared by all people outside the laboratory. So the problem a naive subject faces is whether to stay close to his own internal representation and to associate with all people outside the laboratory, or to comply with the present majority in order to associate with the present group.

Of all responses, 37 per cent showed compliance with the laboratory majority, i.e. were incorrect. Conformity is often considered to be the adaptation of judgements, opinions, evaluations, feelings and behaviours to a majority in a group. It has been demonstrated to occur with different subject populations and on a wide variety of perceptual tasks and opinion and information items. To give examples of the latter types: college students at Berkeley conformed with statements like: 'The United States is largely populated by old people, 60 to 70 percent being over 65 years of age'; 'These oldsters are almost all women, since male babies have a life expectancy of only 25 years'; 'Besides, most people would be better off if they never went to school at all'; 'Not surprisingly, I cannot do anything well' (Krech, Crutchfield and Ballachey, 1962, p. 513).

In later research Asch and others studied the effects of several circumstances that stimulate or diminish conformity (Allen, 1965, 1975; Kiesler and Kiesler, 1969). Five principal circumstances were found to enhance conformity.

(1) The more ambiguous the stimulus and the more difficult the task appears to be, the more conformity occurs. For example, Asch (1952) found more conformity as the differences between the lines became smaller.
(2) There is greater conformity if a subject estimates his own ability to be low and/or the competence of the majority to be greater. For example, subjects showed more conformity if they were informed that their earlier individual performance on the task had been poor.
(3) Conformity increases with the size of the unanimous majority. This tendency, however, diminishes gradually. For example, Gerard, Wilhelmy and Conolley (1968) found 20 per cent conformity with a majority of two persons, 25 per cent with a majority of three persons, with a gradual increase to about 30 per cent with a majority of seven.
(4) There is more conformity if membership in the present group is more attractive, if group cohesion is strong, if the personal relations in the group are good and if the group has more prestige.
(5) There is more conformity if the response of the naive subject is given in public, so that it becomes known by the majority, than when the answer remains private.
(6) In contrast to these circumstances, which increase conformity, there is one important factor that decreases it. Conformity is diminished if the majority is not unanimous. It makes little difference whether a second person disagrees with the majority in accordance with the naive subject or shows disagreement in another direction, i.e. the break down of the unanimity among the majority is crucial.

In view of what we explained before, the relevance of these circumstances is understandable. For example, a non-unanimous majority is less likely to evoke conflict with the naive subject's internal representation. Moreover, non-conformity in this case may not arouse the feeling that one is not part of the laboratory group.

So far we have defined conformity as adapting thoughts, feelings or behaviour to a majority in a group. Naive subjects may change their response, or more generally, their behaviour, in the direction of the majority because they really become convinced that their original standpoint, judgement or opinion was wrong. They change not only the answer or behaviour that is visible to others in the group, but also their internal response. In terms of Figure 3.2., SO is accepted as evidence about reality and, in the integration of Rc.1 and Rc.2, the latter receives a greater weight. This change is called *private conformity, conversion* or *private acceptance.* If subjects conform in this way, according to Deutsch and Gerard (1955), they have undergone *informational influence.* Another form of conformity occurs when naive people do not really change their internal representation (Rc.1 in Figure 3.2.), but only adapt their behaviour to the majority (Ro in Figure 3.2.). This change is called *public conformity* or *compliance.* Why should a person conform in this way? According to the analyses of Deutsch and Gerard and others, people not only strive for correct opinions (see Festinger's social comparison theory), they also want to be liked and accepted by others in general and by important others in particular. To avoid dislike or rejection, they may adapt their overt behaviour to the behaviour of others. If people conform in this way, they have undergone *normative influence,* that is, 'an influence to conform to the positive expectations of others, expectations whose fulfillment by another leads to or reinforces positive rather than negative feelings and whose nonfulfillment leads to the opposite' (Deutsch and Gerard, 1955, p. 629). Although, in principle, these two forms of conformity seem quite different, they are, in fact, not mutually exclusive. They may co-occur, since public compliance may induce conversion. The latter process is predicted by Bem's (1972) self-perception theory, which states that persons infer their internal mental states partially by observation of their own overt behaviour.

So it may very well be that private acceptance of the judgements of the majority takes place because one wants to be an acceptable member of the group. However, since conforming would imply that one is not true to one's own internal representation of reality, one may change one's internal representation. It should be noted that Turner has recently argued that the distinction between informational and normative social influence is rather senseless, and that social influencing is always involved (Turner, 1991; see also Turner and Oakes, 1989). He seems to suggest that non-conforming means sticking to previously learned representations that have been validated in interaction with relevant others outside the laboratory. Public conforming is a consequence of wanting to be a part of the ingroup, i.e. it is affected by the influencing laboratory majority. Private acceptance takes place if naive subjects attach so much more importance to the present laboratory group than to the society in which they have validated their internal representations that they change their representation of reality.

In line with the general ideas about the hierarchical organization of self that were explained in chapter 1, Turner stresses that persons may categorize, i.e. may consider themselves, at an interpersonal level, at a group level and at a still higher hierarchical level of organization (e.g. being a human being and not an animal). He sketches the cognitive conflict for naive Asch subjects as one in which subjects have to choose at what level they want to consider themselves. Self as distinct from other should stick to the learned internal representation of reality (Rc.1). Self as a member of the laboratory group and not a member of another group should side with the majority, possibly even by rejecting the original personal representation in favour of the representation evoked by the majority (SO). Self as part of society at large should stick to the original representation, since that representation is presumably consistent with the representation of all people outside the laboratory.

Minority influence and innovation

Although Asch was not only interested in the influence of the majority, it was Moscovici (1976, 1985) who explicitly addressed the question of what the influence of minorities on the majority might be. Moscovici, Lage and Naffrechoux (1969) reversed the Asch situation, and formed groups with four naive subjects and two confederates. The groups were shown a series of clearly blue slides, which varied in brightness. The task was to judge the colour of the slides and to announce that judgement in the presence of the group. In one condition the two confederates consistently stated that the slides were green. It was found that 32 per cent of all naive subjects in this condition judged at least one slide as green and that the slide was described as green in about 8.5 per cent of all answers. In a control condition the groups consisted of six subjects without any confederate. In this condition 0.25 per cent of the judgements were 'green'. In another condition the answers of two confederates were inconsistent, i.e. sometimes green, sometimes blue; this resulted in only 1.25 per cent green responses by the subjects. So it appears that a consistent minority evokes more conformity than an inconsistent minority. Further evidence suggests that the consistent minority influenced the answers given not only in the group, but also in a later task. In a second part of the study, subjects were individually presented with coloured cards. Three cards were gradations of pure blue, three were pure green, and ten were ambiguous blue-green. The task was to label the cards as blue or green, and compromise answers such as 'bluish-green' were not allowed. Subjects who had been exposed to a consistent minority earlier judged more cards to be green than did subjects in the control condition. An interesting result was that the after-effect of the consistent minority showed up not only for subjects who had shown conformity before, but also for some of the subjects who had rejected minority influence during that first session. Moscovici (e.g. 1976, 1985) calls this private acceptance of a minority position *innovation*, so as to distinguish it from the private acceptance of a majority position.

Innovation has been demonstrated in other tasks involving attitudes and opinions in a wide variety of areas, for example foreign workers, feminism, air pollution and jury decision making (Maass and Clark, 1984). Innovation appears to be particularly strong if the minority consists of two persons and the group as a whole has five to seven members.

According to Moscovici (1976, 1985) minority influence rests upon the behavioural style of the minority, which in turn has two main components: consistency and confidence. A consistent minority receives the attention of the majority. Their conspicuously deviant position, together with consistency and confidence, creates a cognitive conflict in the group. The majority will exert pressures towards uniformity, but by resisting these pressures with consistency and with confidence, the minority perpetuates the cognitive conflict in the majority. The conflict cannot be resolved by compromising, as in the Sherif situation. The majority can resolve the conflict in only two ways: by rejecting and expelling the minority from the group, or by privately adopting the minority position.

Further experimental studies (Mugny and Perez, 1991) have shown that additional conditions have to be fulfilled if the influence of the minority is to be successful. The majority must consider the minority as part of the ingroup: the minority must basically share the norms and values of the majority; otherwise the minority can be regarded as belonging to another group, an outgroup, which can be ignored or rejected. Also, it must be impossible for the majority to attribute the minority responses to personal idiosyncrasies.

To summarize, the research by Moscovici and colleagues has convincingly demonstrated that a minority in a group may create a cognitive conflict in the members of the majority, and may influence them, mainly by demonstrating a consistent and confident behavioural style. Although it is difficult to make a fair comparison between the results of Asch's majority studies and those of Moscovici's minority studies, it should be noted that public compliance in majority studies (37 per cent) seems to be greater than minority influence (8.5 per cent).

Asch never investigated the after-effects of majority influence on a related task, whereas Moscovici found that on a second, related task, so-called innovation did occur. Moscovici (1980, 1985) argues that majority influence, as investigated by Asch, is evoked primarily by the naive subject's desire to belong to the group, whereas minority influence is elicited by the challenge from the side of the minority to re-evaluate one's internal cognitive representation. Therefore, Moscovici reasons, majority influence is more likely to change public behaviour, i.e. to lead to public compliance, whereas minority influence is more likely to trigger cognitive processes, leading to internal representations through innovations (see also: Maass and Clark, 1984; Maass, West and Cialdini, 1987). However, other researchers (Latané and Wolf, 1981; Tanford and Penrod, 1984) oppose the view of a dual process. Several recent studies (e.g. Chaiken and Stangor, 1987; Kruglanski and Mackie, 1990; Turner, 1991) acknowledge that, depending on situational circumstances, personal motives and issue relevance, both majority and minority influence may lead to a re-evaluation of initial representations (private acceptance) as well as to public compliance, although Kruglanski and Mackie (1990) still see some grounds for a weaker version of the dual process explanation of Moscovici.

Minority influence and divergent thinking

The research discussed thus far was focused on the question of whether people in groups will adopt the judgement or opinion of a disagreeing majority or minority. The results can all be described in terms of response integration, which is depicted in Figure 3.2, and in terms of J.R.P. French's (1956) formal theory of social power. In an interesting line of research Nemeth (1986, 1992) extended our knowledge of the influence of majorities and minorities by focusing on creative divergent thought processes and more elaborate information processing. Nemeth (1986) argues that a unanimous majority induces a fixation in thought and attention on the majority position. This is so because people have a general tendency to assume that a majority is correct, which is termed a consensus or social validation bias (Chaiken, 1986; Cialdini, 1986). Moreover, the majority has not only informational influence, but also normative influence, which can generate stress, which in turn impedes attention and thought. So, a cognitive conflict evoked by a majority induces convergent thinking and leads to focusing on the discrepancy between the subject and the opposing majority.

A consistent minority, on the other hand, implies a challenge to the consensus bias, but does not induce the same amount of stress, because the minority usually has no normative influence, i.e. does not elicit a desire among majority members to belong to the minority. Therefore, the cognitive conflict evoked by a minority is likely to stimulate attention and careful consideration of the disagreement and its possible causes, i.e. divergent thinking. In a study by Nemeth and Kwan (1985) subjects were confronted with either a majority or a minority who stated that blue slides were green. Afterwards they were asked to give associations with the words green and blue. Subjects exposed to the minority judgements gave not only more, but also more original, associations than subjects exposed to majority judgements. In another study, Nemeth and Kwan (1987) presented their subjects with letter strings (for example, tNOWap) and asked them to name the first three-letter word they saw. All subjects were requested to name a word formed by capital letters from left to right, that is, forward sequencing was emphasized (e.g. NOW). Subjects acted in groups containing a majority of confederates in the majority condition and a minority of confederates in the minority condition. These confederates were instructed to form names by backward sequencing (for example, to construct words like WON). It appeared that subjects indeed adopted the backward strategy of the majority (of confederates) at the expense of forward sequencing. Their rated performance was about equal to that of subjects in a control condition, in which there were no confederates.

The performance of naive group members in the minority conditions (with a minority of backward sequencing confederates) was best. They employed forward and backward strategies, and a novel combination of forward and back-ward sequences (e.g. NOT, WANT) as well. So being exposed to a diverging minority stimulates creativity and leads to better performance than does being exposed to a divergent majority, which merely leads to fixation of thought and adaptation. Further support was found in a study by Mucchi-Faina, Maass and Volpato (1991). They asked their students how the international image of the city of Perugia could be improved. Students were exposed to either original or conventional proposals that originated either from a majority or a minority. It appeared that original proposals made by the minority evoked more new pro-posals than did original proposals made by both the majority and the minority or original proposals made by the majority, suggesting that an original minority stimulated divergent thinking, as Nemeth (1986) had predicted.

In sum, a minority is not only able to resist the majority's pressures to uniformity (Moscovici, 1985); an original minority is also able to discount the pressure towards uniformity exerted by majority members.

Group polarization

In the research discussed so far in this chapter, the influence of a majority or a minority was manipulated by the experimenter; for example, in the studies of Asch and of Moscovici and others the majority and the minority consisted of confederates, or role players. Also, in these studies interaction and discussion were restricted. One wonders what would happen if these limitations were absent. A new line of research on groups without these restrictions has been initiated by Stoner (1961), who presented groups of students with risky choice dilemmas. Each dilemma describes a person who has to choose between two alternatives. One alternative has a certain but moderate attractiveness. The other alternative is risky: in the case of success it is very attractive, but in the case of failure it is extremely unattractive. An example is the dilemma of the electrical engineer. He finished his degree five years ago and works at an intermediate level in a firm in a secure position, but with a modest salary and without much prospect for promotion. He is offered a job at a new firm, with the possibility of big pro-motions in the near future, but also with the possibility that the new firm will have to be liquidated. The subjects were asked to imagine that they had to advise the engineer. Which minimal chance of success is considered a pre-condition for adopting the risky alternative? What must be the chance that the new firm will survive if the subject is to advise the engineer to accept the new job? Low odds (for example, 1 in 10) are generally considered more risky than high odds (for example, 9 in 10). Stoner first asked his subjects to respond to the choice dilemmas individually. Next he had groups of four or five members discuss the dilemmas and reach unanimous group decisions. As may be recalled, Sherif (1936) in his autokinetic effect experiments found that, in groups, individual judgements converged to the mean of a priori individual judgements. Stoner, however, found something puzzling: group decisions appeared to be more risky than the means of individual answers before the discussions. After the group decision, subjects were individually asked to choose again. The means of these individual answers were not as risky as the group decisions, but riskier than the responses before the group discussions. So, group discussions induced more risk taking. Subsequent research showed that if group members as individuals were initially inclined to take risks, group discussion enhanced that tendency. This phenomenon has been named 'risky shift'. However, the reverse phenomenon was also observed: if group members as individuals were inclined to be cautious, for example, if they had to respond to a choice dilemma in which health was at stake, group discussion enhanced mean cautiousness. This movement towards more caution has been coined 'cautious shift'.

In 1969 some French researchers wondered whether the shifts were due to the risk- or caution-inducing content of the task. Moscovici and Zavalloni (1969) and Doise (1969) reported a risky-shift-like phenomenon on non-risk-involving tasks. For example, their subjects were requested to evaluate opinion items about General de Gaulle, 'the Americans' and their school. If the mean answers before the group discussion were positive, the group decisions showed a mean movement towards the positive pole of the answer scale. However, the group decisions showed a mean movement in the negative direction when the mean individual answer before the discussion was negative. These movements were called 'choice shifts' (Pruitt, 1971) or 'group polarization' (Moscovici and Zavalloni, 1969). These results met with astonishment, which is amazing in itself because an experiment on group polarization (under another name) had been carried out by Bechterew and de Lange (1924) forty-five years earlier. In one of their studies, 'auf dem Gebiet der kollektiven Reflexologie', they gave teachers a picture showing how a boy, having stolen apples, was beaten by a farmer with a stick. Group discussion led to an increment in ethical statements and to stronger condemnation of the farmer. The picture was shown to medical students as well. Here the reverse was observed: medical students considered the punishment more justifiable after the group discussion than before. In the following, we will deal with group polarization in greater detail; and next we will discuss several possible explanations for the phenomenon.

By and large, the concept of group polarization as introduced by Moscovici and Zavalloni (1969) has been adopted by several authors. Myers and Lamm define group polarization as the process by which 'the average postgroup response will tend to be more extreme in the same direction as the average of the pregroup responses' (Myers and Lamm, 1976, p. 603). Before we start to elucidate the specific details of group polarization, it is necessary to describe the procedures of the experiments in somewhat greater detail. The standard procedure can be sketched as follows:

1 Subjects are presented with a number of statements and they have to respond to them individually, for example, on a 7-point Likert scale with response alternatives ranging from strongly agree (3), agree (2), neutral (0), to strongly disagree (–3).

2 Groups are composed at random, and usually have three to five persons; group members have to discuss the items one by one (group discussion); the discussion time is about five minutes for each item.
3 Often, but not always, the groups are requested to reach consensus or to make a group decision.
4 After the group discussion (and eventually after the group decision) the subjects have to respond to the items again individually (post-test).

The 'initial direction' is defined for each item as the mean of the individual answers on the pre-test of the whole sample (1). Group polarization is assessed by a comparison of the mean of (1) with the mean scores of all subjects on the post-test (4). If the mean score on the post-test (for example, $M = 2.5$) is located on the same side of the scale as that on the pre-test (for example, $M = 1.5$), but is further away from the neutral point, then group polarization is assumed to have taken place, e.g. $2.5 - 1.5 = 1.0$. Related to, but distinguished from, group polarization is the phenomenon of choice shift. This is the difference between the mean of the pre-test answers in a group (1) and the group decision (3) (Hinsz and Davis, 1984; Kaplan, 1987). Group polarization has to be distinguished from group extremization (Moscovici and Doise, 1974). Group extremization occurs when the mean score on the post-test (4) is more extreme than the mean of the pre-test (1), irrespective of direction. A mean shift from -1.5 at (1) to $+2.5$ at (4) is an example. Group polarization can be considered a special case of group extremization. It should be noted that, even if group polarization seems to occur in a study, there may be groups which show no shift at all, and that there may also be groups which contribute to this mean shift, not by polarization but by extremization. And even if a separate group shows polarization, this does not necessarily imply that each member has shown polarization or extremization (cf. McCauley, 1972).

A review of the literature leads to the conclusion that group polarization occurs when three conditions are fulfilled (Moscovici and Doise, 1974): (1) the initial individual responses (or the response-predispositions if a pre-test was not performed) in the sample should show a dominant tendency, e.g. positive; (2) the responses (or response-predispositions) in the discussion groups should vary, i.e. show some dispersion; and (3) discussion should have taken place in the group. Under these conditions, group polarization is observed in risk taking, in the risky or cautious direction on the choice dilemmas used by Stoner (1961), as well as in gambling tasks, blackjack and investment decisions. Group polarization is furthermore observed in non-risk-involving choice dilemmas and attitude statements concerning a wide variety of topics, ranging from pacifism to women's liberation, and in the choice of aspiration level, jury decisions, impression formation tasks, and so on. These shifts have been established not only in a great variety of tasks, but also with widely divergent samples, including American undergraduates, students, teachers, drug-users, foremen and toddlers; not only in the industrialized western countries, but also in Japan, Mexico, Colombia and Uganda (Lamm and Myers, 1978; Myers and Lamm, 1976). In general the polarization is rather weak: on average the shift amounts to 1 to 1.5 points on a 7- to 10-point scale. At least two studies (Johnston, 1968; Wallach, Kogan and Bem, 1962) demonstrated that group polarization may be an enduring effect that can continue for several weeks. More than 90 per cent of the research on group polarization has been conducted with *ad hoc* groups in a psychological laboratory. In real, pre-existing groups it appears to be far more difficult to study the phenomenon, mainly because the necessary measurements are not easily obtained. In addition to this, the phenomenon is often influenced by factors such as the history of the group, strong existing norms and hierarchical relationships. Therefore, group polarization outside of the laboratory has been studied with varying, but mostly weak, success by experimental researchers (Fraser and Foster, 1984; Lamm and Myers, 1978). On the other hand, at least fifteen field studies have been conducted by researchers who were not looking for group polarization, but nevertheless found comparable results (Lamm and Myers, 1978). Examples are the radicalization of opinions held by religious sects, residents of student houses, and therapy groups.

Group polarization: explanations

Since the research of Stoner (1961) quite a number of explanations have been presented for the occurrence of risky shift, cautious shift and group polarization. In the following we will focus on three explanations: one based on normative influence, one based on informational influence and one based on referent informational influence. For simplicity's sake we will discuss these explanations as they apply to the risky choice dilemma involving the electrical engineer, because similar explanations apply in other risky or cautious choice dilemmas and other decision tasks.

Social comparison and normative influence

Among the possible explanations of the risky shift phenomenon which were formulated after the study of Stoner (1961), the risk-as-a-value hypothesis (Brown, 1965, 1974) has been especially popular among researchers. This explanation consists of three propositions:

1 In general one strives to think and to behave according to (the subjective content of) existing norms and cultural values. In the western world and especially in the USA, taking risks is a general value which is also relevant in the situations described in the risky choice dilemmas: one wants to be at least as willing to take risks as similar other people. Therefore, the overt or covert response on an item may be not only right or wrong as in the Sherif, Asch or Moscovici situation, but also value-bound. Two research findings are in agreement with this proposition. First, when subjects were requested to indicate what their admired or 'ideal' point of view was with regard to risky choice items, it appeared (without any group discussion) to be more risky than their

own response. Second, when requested to indicate (also before the discussion) what they thought the responses of the other group members would be, subjects surmised that others would be more cautious than themselves.

2 If group members see that their responses are less risky than the mean response of their group, they will shift towards more risk in order to maintain the idea of making decisions in agreement with the general cultural value with respect to risk. Brown (1965, 1974, 1986) terms this the image-maintenance mechanism.

So, because subjects want to maintain the idea that they are at least as willing to take risks as others, when they find out during and after the group discussion that they are more cautious than other group members, they become more risk-taking. It should be noted that this explanation merely capitalizes on what has been called 'normative social influence': group members want to belong to their group. Without explicit (external) pressure from other group members (as in Asch's situation) they show a shift in the culturally desired direction. Furthermore, it should be noted that Brown's explanation is rather silent about whether group discussion affects only the overt responses or also the internal representations of shifting group members.

3 The risky shift is caused primarily by the exchange of information on the individual responses at the pre-test. Seemingly in agreement with this proposition is the fact that group members show small shifts in the valued risky direction when they are confronted with the responses of others without any group discussion (Isenberg, 1986).

Brown (1965) first proposed the risk-as-a-value hypothesis, but upon learning that cautious shifts were also observed, he introduced the caution-as-a-value hypothesis. Since then, shifts have been observed on all kinds of attitudinal topics, as mentioned before. In view of these findings, the question is whether there is a more general theory that can explain all these findings, so that new values do not have to be introduced for every kind of shift observed.

Festinger's social comparison theory (Festinger, 1954), which makes a distinction between comparison of opinions and comparison of abilities, has served as a way out. For opinions, a tendency to compare with similars, i.e. comparison with similar others, is proposed. Assuming now that in risky shift situations group members were exchanging opinions, it should follow that something like converging in groups would have occurred. So comparison of opinions with similars cannot explain the risky shift phenomenon. However, Festinger (1954) also referred to comparison of abilities. In this case, one would also compare with similars, but in an upward direction, i.e. more able persons would be selected as objects of comparison. Jellison and Arkin (1977) and Jellison and Riskind (1970) have indeed shown that subjects consider taking more risk as indicative of greater competence, from which it follows that one should compare with group members who take greater risks.

However, in view of other contexts in which group polarization has occurred, the risk-as-an-ability hypothesis does not seem tenable as a more general explanation.

A more promising social-comparison explanation is that proposed by Codol (1975), an explanation that agrees with what we discussed in chapter 1 on the self-reflective view. Codol launched the so-called 'Primus-Inter-Pares' or PIP-effect, which implies that one wants to see oneself as more conforming than others to all kinds of norms; that is, with regard to conformity to cherished norms, one wants to be superior in comparison to one's similars. In twenty studies, Codol found support for a 'superior conformity of self'. Myers and Lamm (1976) reported that businessmen considered themselves more ethical than the average businessman and people regarded themselves as less prejudiced than the rest of the group. According to Codol (1975), the PIP-effect is the result of two tendencies. On the one hand, people are inclined to conform to the norms of comparison others, their reference group, in order to present a favourable image of the self to other group members and to themselves. On the other hand, people want to distinguish themselves in order to maintain an identifiable independent identity, this again in the eyes of self and others. These tendencies agree with what we proposed in chapter 1 with regard to integration and differentiation, which have both descriptive and prescriptive implications. More specifically, in order to describe who we are, we have to establish to what representation (e.g. group) we belong. However, this should lead simultaneously to adherence to the norms and behaviours of that group, i.e. to prescription. On the other hand, self may see self as part of a specific category or representation (e.g. group), but self is a nobody if its identity coincides entirely with that of the group. Therefore, within a group, self should distinguish itself in describing itself as part of the group, and in the prescription of its own behaviours. In a similar vein, Codol maintains that 'there is only one way to present oneself as different from others without infringing on one's conformity to social norms and that is by asserting that one is more in conformity with these norms than the others' (Codol, 1975, p. 484). This suggests a liberal view of social comparison theory. The comparison of abilities and the drive upwards are merely a special case of a more general tendency towards differentiation in a socially desirable direction. The PIP-effect may explain risky shift, cautious shift and group polarization in general. In fact, a twofold shift may be assumed. First, the subjective estimate of the socially desirable response should shift (see also Ono and Davis, 1988). Next, a second shift should occur through the operation of the image-maintenance mechanism, as described by Brown (1965, 1974). It should be noted, however, that social comparison processes are not sufficient to explain polarization or choice shifts after group discussion, because shifts induced by discussions are usually greater than shifts induced by the mere exposure to others' responses without discussion.

Argumentation and informational influence

According to the persuasive arguments theory (Burnstein, 1982; Burnstein and Vinokur, 1975, 1977; Burnstein, Vinokur and Trope, 1973; Vinokur and Burnstein, 1974, 1978), the ultimate cause of risky shift, cautious shift and group polarization in general is not social comparison but exchange of relevant information. According to this theory, the initial individual response is the result of a weighing of the advantages and disadvantages (facts, presumptions, evaluations, deliberations) of the risky and cautious alternatives against each other. Arguments are considered risky if they contain the advantages of the risky alternative and the disadvantages of the cautious alternative. Conversely, cautious arguments are pro-caution and anti-risk. The more, or the more important, one's risky arguments, the more attractive the risky alternative is. Conversely, the more, or the more important, one's cautious arguments are, the more cautious the individual response will be. The content of these arguments depends on the issue; in the case of the choice dilemmas it can be described reasonably in terms of the Subjective Expected Utility Model (Vinokur, Trope and Burnstein, 1975). Generally, social reality (Festinger, 1950) and cultural norms and values determine the weight and social desirability of the arguments.

If, before group discussion, the mean initial risk taking of a group is high, and if the group members exchange the arguments which led them to their individual responses, then the group discussion will contain predominantly risky arguments. After the discussion most group members will have more, and more risky, arguments than before, and therefore they will take a greater risk. The result is a risky shift or a choice shift in the risky direction. These shifts will be stronger, according to the theory, as the exchanged arguments are more convincing and novel to the group members. Conversely, if before the group discussion group members tended to show caution, the group discussion will feature predominantly cautious arguments, and shifts towards more caution will result. In accordance with this theory, a number of studies have shown that the risk taking of individuals and groups can indeed be influenced by presentation of arguments: presentation of risky arguments leads to higher risk taking and presentation of cautious arguments leads to more cautious decisions. Also, risky and cautious shifts can be predicted from the proportion of risky arguments during the discussions. These predictions, based on informational influence, are fairly accurate if they concern mean differences between items (ignoring differences between groups). However, these predictions are much less accurate if they concern differences between groups (on one single item). So, for a full understanding of group polarization, additional processes during the group discussion have to be explored.

Referent informational influence

In recent years the general point of view has been that the two explanations of group polarization, social comparison processes and informational influence processes, may be reconciled (Isenberg, 1986; Kaplan, 1987; Kok, 1983;

Meertens, 1980). A meta-analysis (Isenberg, 1986) of twenty-one publications with thirty-three independent effects showed a much stronger effect under standard laboratory conditions of relevant arguments (mean effect size r = .75) than of comparison of positions (r = .44). If the two explanations are complementary, then further research should establish possible interaction effects with other variables and the external validity of obtained results. Both tasks are rather awkward and unrewarding, and partly as a result of this, the amount of research on group polarization has declined over the last decade.

Recently, Turner and his associates (see Turner, Hogg, Oakes, Reicher and Wetherell, 1987; Turner, 1991) have re-animated attention to the paradigm while launching an interesting reconciliation of what had been separately labelled social comparison of positions and processing of arguments. Moreover, an interesting reconciliation of minority and majority influence was pursued. Turner's self-categorization theory (e.g. Turner *et al.*, 1987; Turner and Oakes, 1989) places social identification with the group and ingroup-outgroup categorization at the forefront. Social influence is mainly seen in terms of intra-group and inter-group processes.

Generally the theory supposes that one expects other group members to agree if these others are categorized as similar to oneself with respect to the topic at hand. One expects agreement with members of one's own category and one expects disagreement with people of the other category ('we' against 'them', ingroup versus outgroup). Following self-categorization theory, people within a group tend to converge to a position on a response continuum which is perceived as representing the shared views of the group members. This position best represents the group as a whole, is the most 'prototypical' (cf. Rosch, 1978) for that group. In the theory, the prototypicality of a position is usually defined by the Meta Contrast Ration (MCR). The MCR of a particular position on a response continuum (or of a group member occupying that position) is the mean absolute distance of the position from all outgroup positions, divided by the mean absolute distance of the position from the positions of the other ingroup members. In other words, a position is more prototypical, or representative for a group, as it differs less from the other positions within the group, and as it differs more from all possible positions outside the group.

The self-categorization theory has two important implications. First, convergence of positions to a mean, as in the Sherif and Asch situations, and convergence towards a scale pole (group polarization) can be explained by the same psychological process: movement towards the most prototypical position. Second, the contrast between exchange of positions and exchange of arguments becomes irrelevant, and the distinction between normative and informational influence becomes useless. Therefore, Turner does not speak of social comparison of positions or of argumentation, but of referent informational influence:

> the basic influence process is one where the normative position of people categorized as similar to self tends to be subjectively accepted as valid. The validity of

information is (psychologically) established by ingroup norms. People shift towards persuasive material, but what is persuasive is not a matter of information that can be abstracted from the social context but of the degree to which the material has been validated through its participation in an ingroup consensus.

(Turner, 1991, pp. 171-172)

The self-categorization theory leads to predictions which have recently been tested (see Turner *et al.*, 1987; Turner, Wetherell and Hogg, 1989). There is growing empirical support for the prediction that group polarization is stronger when the identification with the own group and the differentiation from another group are greater. Also, in line with referent informational influence, it appears that arguments arising from persons of the same group or category have more influence than those from persons of another group or category.

In a modification of the Stoner situation by Turner, Wetherell and Hogg (1989) four-person groups had to discuss and to reach consensus on a risky and a cautious choice dilemma. Subjects were informed beforehand either that they were risky or cautious individuals, or that risky or cautious groups had been formed. The results showed that risky groups shifted towards risk and cautious groups shifted towards caution, but for groups that were not labelled as risky or cautious, no shift was observed. These differences in shifts were predicted by referent informational influence theory.

To conclude our discussion of referent informational influence theory, we want to make two comments. First, it may be noted that, theoretically, referent informational influence can be integrated into J.R.P. French's (1956) formal theory of social power: the MCR of each group member's position can be considered to refer to the concept of weight or force, as implied by French. Second, the theory accounts for minority influence by assuming that a minority can influence the majority in a group as long as the minority is perceived as belonging to the same social representation or category and not belonging to another category. As soon as the majority categorizes the minority as an out-group, for example mentally disturbed people or people that represent views that are incongruent with the higher-order values of the ingroup, the minority will lose its influence (Turner, 1991).

CONCLUSIONS AND SUMMARY

In the present chapter we have tried to sketch some general findings and theoretical points of view about why cognitive conflicts may be experienced in groups and how they are resolved.

It may be concluded that a rather important ingredient of cognitive conflict is whether group members experience a conflict between their previously learned internal representations (i.e. judgement policies, positions and arguments) and the ones communicated by other group members. This was clearly the case in Asch's experiments in which subjects were exposed to judgements of other group members (confederates) that strongly contrasted with previously built-up representations. This is less the case in other experimental situations. For example, the minority group members in the rather ambiguous choice situation designed by Moscovici did not have strong prior evidence in favour of one of the two possible responses (blue or green).

The assumption that one experiences a cognitive conflict between one's own cognitive representation and the ones communicated by some other group members has another consequence. It may create another cognitive conflict, namely the question of how self as a representation of self is related to higher representations in which self may be included. For example, in the Asch experiments it may very well be, and this has been accentuated by Moscovici (1985), that a group member has to make a choice in self-definition in that self may relate itself to all people outside the lab, or to the society at large, or may feel tempted to see self as a part of the present group. Such a conflict is less likely in Sherif's autokinetic situation, since there the subjects presumably had no knowledge about how others outside the laboratory would make judgements. However, Sherif also had sessions in which subjects first had to make individual judgements (which led to an individual reference point (anchor)) and thereafter were exposed to the representations of other group members. As may be recalled, conforming in the latter condition was less pronounced than in groups in which subjects had not made individual judgements before the group session. This means that it is rather likely that in the Sherif situation the subjects who had made individual judgements before the group session were confronted with another kind of conflict than Asch's subjects. Not only did they see some discrepancy between their own learned representations, but they also had to decide whether they would consider self as an individual or define self as a subpart of the group, a conflict that is due to the fact that self as a representation may define itself on several hierarchical levels of organization, as we explained in chapter 1. An even more complicated problem may have arisen in the choice dilemmas introduced by Stoner (1961). Confrontation with divergent representations (choices) of other group members is assumed to pose the question of self-definition. Brown's (1965) explanation of risk and caution as values emphasizes that self may define itself as part of its culture, and, in that case, the conflict may imply that self may define itself as a representation of its culture or as a part of the present group. Turner (1991) starts from the idea that group members want to be part of the present group, that is, membership (identification) in the present group is desired. One is a part of the ingroup, that is, self may define itself in terms of group membership, if one is a prototypical group member. In order to become an ideal group member, a subject should shift in the direction of the prototypical group member. The result that minorities have no effect if they are not considered a part of the group at large seems to be in agreement with this notion.

On the other hand, Turner (1991) also argues that self may define itself at an interpersonal, at an inter-group and an inter-societal level. So one may wonder why this freedom of self-categorization is not a part of Turner's theorizing about group polarization. We are inclined to attribute this partly to the specific experimental situations investigated by Turner. As one might remember, in Stoner's paradigm all subjects are naive. As a consequence, a strong conflict involving a subject's own view, representation of the choice dilemma, is not induced. Thus, the conflict between self-categorization in terms of self in itself and self-categorization in terms of membership in the present group is presumably rather weak.

So, we argue that a cognitive conflict elicited by the communication of divergent representations of the task may simultaneously evoke a conflict over the hierarchical level at which self should define itself. Put differently, self is not only concerned about building up representations of cognitive contents (e.g. opinions about topics), but is simultaneously concerned about how self relates to others in a hierarchical sense, and these two cognitive processes are interrelated. For example, subjects resisting majority influence in Asch's experiment might have been aware that they did not adapt their previously established representations concerning the task's content, and they might also have been aware of the fact that they did not identify with the majority and preferred to categorize themselves as an outgroup member, as an independent individual or as part of the society at large outside the lab. Conversely, some of Asch's subjects, who afterwards showed private acceptance of the 'false' judgements of the majority, might have been aware of the fact that they had changed their previously established internal representations with respect to the content of the task, and they might also have been aware that they identified themselves as members of the group, while looking away from membership of society at large.

In view of the dual relation between representations about task content (*en soi*) and social representations (*pour soi*), it is not surprising that responses to cognitive conflicts are difficult to predict. Take, for instance, a Stoner situation in which no group discussion occurs (see, for instance, Isenberg, 1986), in which positions are merely exchanged and in which subjects find themselves in a prototypical position. Assuming that subjects are highly self-confident about their initial positions, that they have built up strong representations in the past, their initial judgement is strongly connected with self in itself and self as member of society at large.

There may be several reasons for rejection of previous judgement in favour of public acceptance of the judgement of the prototypical group member, and these reasons run parallel with those pointed out by Asch (1951, 1956).

1 Subjects may publicly adapt, but privately reject, their new judgement. This allows them to keep their previously learned representation intact and also allows them to categorize themselves as part of their culture, while simultaneously pretending that they are faithful members of the ingroup.
2 Subjects may also be converted. This is more likely if defining themselves as members of the present group is more important than keeping their previously learned representations. In that case they readjust their previously learned representation. Does that mean they are unfaithful to their culture and their

previously defined self? Not necessarily; they may also look away from other levels of categorization. In any case, this example demonstrates how divergent judgements communicated by a prototypical group member may give rise to a revision of previous representations. Does this imply that if a group member is converted, that member always starts by taking notice of positions that activate new representations, which in turn are responsible for the conversion? Not necessarily; if divergent and new arguments are exchanged, then new connections between cognitions may be established in a direct way, that is, by focusing mainly on the arguments, as the persuasive-arguments theory maintains. However, in this case the process of the revision of one's internal representation may also be facilitated by the circumstance that the arguments came from members of a group to which one wants to belong, i.e. a group that is important for one's self-definition.

Chapter 4

Reflective tuning

In chapter 1 it was argued that one is not automatically inclined to meet task requirements and to elaborate on a task in a cognitive way, but that reflection plays a role. Reflection refers to the process of weighing the consequences of one's activities, and it is assumed that group members strive for a reasonable probability of satisfaction.

Reflection in groups concerns two major aspects of group task performance. First, there is reflection on task engagement, task continuation and task abandonment. Second, there is reflection on the relationship between (potential) group members, i.e. their efforts and the potential or actual outcomes of group performance. In the following we will start with an illustration of how group members reflect on goals to be set.

REFLECTION ON EXPECTED REWARDS

In the section on social loafing (see chapter 2) we pointed out that individual group members in some circumstances (for example, when they are allowed to 'hide in the crowd') pay less attention to the ultimate group success than is desirable from the perspective of the group as a whole. Analytically, such a choice to pursue individual satisfaction may be described in terms of the reflection process proposed by Thibaut and Kelley (1959), which suggests in essence that group members imagine a number of possible behavioural alternatives, like contributing versus withholding efforts, that may affect group performance. The consequences of these behavioural alternatives are assessed in terms of satisfaction, and the behavioural alternative that provides the highest probability of satisfaction is chosen.

Suppose, for example, that a specific group member is involved in a group rope-pulling task, that her own group is very large and that her own contribution to the group remains invisible (see chapter 2). Assume further that she expects her own group to win the contest regardless of how much she exerts herself. In this case she faces two behavioural alternatives. She can exert herself, which is costly ('exert'), or she can decide not to exert herself ('no-exert' option). Because in the case of the 'no-exert' option she obtains the same rewards (such as sharing in the glory of her group) without incurring any costs, according to Thibaut and Kelley she will prefer the 'no-exert' option.

Thibaut and Kelley (1959) make the assumption that the value of a behavioural alternative depends on the actor's expectations. In the foregoing example, the performer expected that her group would win with or without her exertion. What would she decide if she were convinced that her group could only win with her exertion? In this case the behavioural alternative or option of 'no exertion' may be less preferred than the 'exertion' option, because exertion leads to group success, and although she has to endure the costs of exertion, the outcome – the reward – is better than in the case of no exertion, because the latter option is associated with group failure. So, in contrast with her decision in the first example, she may now decide to exert herself, and this is so because she departs from different a priori expectations.

Thibaut and Kelley's analytical concepts are closely related to what Mitchell and Beach (1990) later called the 'profitability' test, a comparison of the consequences of behavioural alternatives in terms of profits, i.e. forthcoming rewards minus costs (see chapter 1); however, the ideas of Thibaut and Kelley also share the weakness of the profitability test in that what is considered rewarding or costly is rather difficult to assess, because the assessment of rewards and costs, as well as the weighing of their respective values, depends on psychological interpretations made by the task performer him- or herself. To illustrate, one can only guess at what the rewards or costs implied in group success and group failure, respectively, may be. Moreover, effort expenditure may be considered a cost to a tired task performer, but a reward to an overactive task performer who has not had the opportunity to expend his or her energy. And even when group success is seen as rewarding and effort expenditure as costly, there remains the measurement problem of how to assign value to the different kinds of rewards and costs and how to compare them so that a net profit can be determined.

Nevertheless, we argue that the ideas of Thibaut and Kelley (1959) are analytically very useful for describing several reflective moments before and during task performance when potential social relationships are considered. In the following we will explain this.

The choice between acting with a partner and remaining solo

Quite often – think of writing a book – one may consider engaging in a task alone or with one or more others. In such cases Thibaut and Kelley's analysis suggests a distinction among behavioural alternatives: acting solo, or acting with person A or with persons A and B. For each of these behavioural alternatives a profit analysis (rewards minus costs) is made and the behavioural alternative that promises most profits is chosen. This reflective analysis shows that (if one has the freedom of choice) one remains solo if that behavioural alternative is considered to be more profitable, and one will form a group (with one or more others) when that alternative is considered to be more profitable.

Continuation or change of group

When an actor performs in the context of a social relationship (a group), he or she may experience the profits (rewards minus costs) associated with that current relationship. The consequences of the behavioural alternative that is selected are referred to as the actor's actual outcomes. The profits resulting from such a relationship may be higher than, equal to or lower than those the actor had reason to expect before engaging in the group activity, and it is these expectations that form an actor's so-called comparison level, a standard against which other behavioural alternatives are measured. The comparison level is formed in the past and is based on an accumulation of experiences in other relationships and knowledge concerning still other relationships that the actor has observed, heard of or read about. Depending on the results of the comparison between an actor's actual profits from his or her current relationship and the comparison level, the actor may be disappointed (comparison level [or standard] is higher than actual outcomes), content (comparison level and actual outcomes are equal) or very satisfied (a priori expectations [comparison level] are lower than actual outcomes). An implication of this is that the relationship between comparison level and actual outcomes determines whether a group member is attracted to the group, i.e. the social relationship in which the actual outcomes are produced. For example, group members who experience actual outcomes that are higher than those expected beforehand are likely to be more attracted to their group than group members who experience actual outcomes that are lower than the comparison level. However, there is another circumstance that may affect group members' attraction to their group, namely, the outcomes that group members might experience in an alternative group. These expected outcomes form the comparison level of alternatives.

Sometimes it is possible for group members to enter an alternative relationship, i.e. another group. When this is feasible, group members are assumed to take three things into account: the comparison level (a priori expected outcomes), the actual outcomes of group performance and the outcomes or profits expected from the alternative group(s). To describe this reflection process we will give an example. Assume that a group member is dissatisfied with the actual outcomes of his or her own group when these outcomes are compared with a priori expectations, the comparison level. Assume further that a group member anticipates that he or she may or may not become a member of another group which promises to provide higher profits than his or her present group, that is, the comparison level for alternatives is higher than the actual outcomes, and the actual outcomes are lower than a priori expectations, i.e. the comparison level. When group members think it possible to become members of an alternative group, they will be less attracted to their present group and more attracted to the alternative group, that is, they will be tempted to disrupt or leave the present relationship. However, when alternative relations are not available – for example, when there is no other group, or group members are not allowed to change groups – the expected outcomes of the alternative relationship will be low and although group members may be somewhat discontent with present actual outcomes, this discontent will not be aggravated because the expected comparison level of alternatives is rather low. Because in this case group members have no viable alternative, their attraction to the group will be rather strong, in spite of the low actual outcomes. Another consequence of having no viable alternative group is strong dependence on the present group: in spite of possible discontent with the present group, there is no viable alternative group that promises higher profit than the present relationship.

Some of these ideas are nicely illustrated in a number of recent experiments performed by Ellemers (1991). In one of her experiments half of the subjects were told that their group was quite successful, whereas the other half of the subjects received the information that their group was failing. An additional variable was the promise that group members either could (permeable group boundaries) or could not (impermeable group boundaries) be promoted to the other group. The results indicated that members of a successful group were more attracted to their group than group members who were told that their group was failing, which is understandable because the actual outcomes experienced as a result of group membership were higher for members of successful groups. More interesting was the following result. Members of failing groups who had no viable alternative group (impermeable group boundaries) felt more attracted to their group than did members of failing groups who had the option to become a member of the superior group, that is, who had a high alternative comparison level of expected outcomes.

GOAL SETTING BY GROUPS

The way in which group members reflect upon task engagement as a consequence of previous task behaviour was investigated by Zander (1971) in his group aspiration studies. The procedures used in these experimental studies are fairly standard. Group members have to perform a task consisting of a series of trials. After a trial the group receives feedback in the form of a score. Thereafter group members are requested to indicate the score they believe their group will be able to attain in the next trial. A frequently used task is the 'group ball-propelling task', in which all group members are asked to stand in a single file, to grasp a long pole, and to manoeuvre it in unison so that the end of the shaft strikes a wooden ball, causing it to roll down an extended tunnel. The ball stops next to one of several numbers painted on the side of the tunnel, and this number indicates the score for that shot. Five shots make a trial, and the group may earn up to fifty points in each trial. When a group performs several trials of this task, it is observed (Zander, 1968, 1971) that the level of aspiration agreed upon by the members tends to be close to the immediately preceding one. Zander suggests that a future preferred group score is generally close to the previously established one. However, there is one qualification: aspiration levels are raised following improved performance more often than they are lowered following diminished performance, i.e. groups (like individuals) are more sensitive to success than to failure feedback. Why? To explain this result Zander makes the assumption (derived from achievement-motivation theory: see McClelland, 1961, and chapter 1 on 'engagement') that group members try to optimize their expected satisfaction. Because success leads to greater satisfaction when it is difficult as opposed to easy tasks that have been successfully performed, group members are inclined to prefer more difficult future tasks to easy tasks. However, group members also weigh the feasibility of success, and expectations of future success derive from previous task performance. Thus, the group aspirations that are chosen are those that strike 'a balance between what would be a most satisfying outcome (success at a very difficult goal) and what would be an achievable outcome (success at a recently achieved level)' (Zander, 1968, p. 419).

Do groups faced with success set goals that are different from those set by groups faced with impending failure? This question was addressed in another experimental study described by Zander (1968). In the 'lose' condition group members received chips they could lose, whereas in the 'win' condition group members received no chips beforehand but could earn chips as a result of successful performance. Moreover, in the 'lose' condition it was stressed that greater losses would be involved when the group failed at more difficult tasks, whereas in the 'win' condition subjects learned that more chips could be obtained when more difficult tasks were successfully performed. In both conditions the groups performed a number of trials of a task. No verbal communication was possible, but unanimity about the goals to be set had to be reached by balloting (sometimes repeatedly). In this and other experiments it was shown that group members in 'win' conditions selected new tasks of intermediate difficulty, whereas in the 'lose' condition either very easy or very difficult goals were set.

Individual and group aspirations

With respect to individual task performance as well, it is well known that individuals are more sensitive to success feedback than to failure feedback in the sense that the increase in the aspiration level after success feedback is greater than the decrease in the aspiration level after failure feedback. So the afore-mentioned regularity 'success-raise and failure-lower', which is qualified by a greater sensitivity to success than to failure, might be fully ascribed to individual and not to group motivation.

Zander (1983) found another resemblance between individual and group performance. As may be recalled from chapter 1, individuals with a strong desire to avoid failure – as measured by the TAT – select either very difficult or very easy tasks, whereas achievement-oriented individuals select tasks of intermediate difficulty. Similarly, it was found that groups composed of failure-oriented group members chose either very easy or very difficult tasks and worked less hard than groups consisting of success-oriented group members, who not only had more moderate aspirations but also worked harder and were more successful, i.e. performed better.

Another parallel between individuals and groups is that when no feedback about task performance is provided, both individuals and groups overestimate their performance and consequently set unattainable goals. In the domain of actual performance, there is still another similarity between individuals and groups. Zander (1968) found that groups, like individuals, that set goals of intermediate difficulty perform at a higher level compared with groups that set very easy or very difficult goals. This was shown in a study conducted in an industrial environment. The foremen of a number of crews were informed of particular goals that their groups were to attain within six months. One third of the crews were given very easy assignments, one third received very difficult assignments, and the remaining third were given goals of moderate difficulty. At the end of six months the crews with the moderately difficult tasks had improved their perform- ance more than those with the easier and those with the more difficult goals.

What is different about group aspirations?

Zander (1983) argues that the main difference between group achievement motivation and individual achievement motivation is that the desire for group success is not a permanent trait of individuals, but rather a motive that develops in particular situations. One of these circumstances is whether groups see themselves as cohesive. In one of Zander's experiments cohesive groups consisted of members who were told that they matched quite well, who were addressed as a team and who chose a group name, whereas the members of less cohesive groups were informed that they did not match very well in terms of abilities and temperaments and were addressed as individuals. It turned out that highly cohesive groups developed moderate aspiration levels more often than less cohesive groups.

Zander asked himself whether group-oriented motives act independently of motives for individual achievement and failure. To settle this issue, an experiment was designed in which subjects (high school boys) had to perform a number of domino tasks. Before they started they were shown domino patterns which ranged from very easy to very difficult (depending on the number of pieces required). The group task was arranged so that the first member to place a domino was more responsible for the chosen pattern. In each three-person group there was one achievement-oriented member, one failure-oriented member and one intermediate member as measured by the TAT (see chapter 1). Two conditions were realized. In the achievement-oriented group the first member to place a domino was achievement-oriented, and in the failure-oriented group the first member was failure-oriented. It turned out that achievement-oriented group members selected tasks of intermediate difficulty regardless of the position they occupied. When failure-oriented group members were in the less important (later) positions they indeed selected either very difficult or very easy tasks. However, when they acted in the first and more important position they acted like achievement-oriented group members: when placed in the first position they selected goals of intermediate difficulty. From this and a number of other experimental studies, Zander concludes that, 'in appropriate circumstances group responsibility and spirit can overtake the effects of trait-like individual differences' (Zander, 1983, p. 468).

Consequences of group aspirations

Group performance has two notable consequences: it has implications for the way a group member assesses his or her own abilities, and it affects the way group members appreciate the group and its task. In the following we will deal with these consequences.

Self-appraisal

When group members have no reliable knowledge about how they have contributed individually (as in the case of the group ball-propelling task), self-ascribed competence is strongly affected by the performance of the group. Experimental evidence (see Zander, 1983) shows that a group member's self-evaluation is more strongly affected by group success than by group failure. When the group succeeds a member is fully prepared to see him- or herself as highly competent. However, when the group fails the member is inclined to blame the group and not him- or herself, that is, group members protect their individual self-esteem by denying that they performed as ineptly as the group's score suggests.

Appreciation of the group and its task

The above-mentioned tendency to associate oneself with success and to ascribe group failure to a circumstance outside one's own control is, of course, an example of a self-serving bias (see chapter 1). This tendency to take credit for group success and to dissociate oneself from group failure has been documented in other research as well. Fiske and Taylor (1991) report evidence that when groups succeed, group members are inclined to attribute that success more to their own contributions than to those of their fellow group members, whereas the reverse occurs when group failure is at issue. In the latter case one's own contribution to group failure appears to be discounted.

Zander (1968) suggests three consequences derived from the tendency to associate oneself more strongly with group success than with group failure: (1) after success one has more positive feelings about one's group than after failure, for example, one feels more attracted to one's group after group success; (2) when the group succeeds, the group score is considered to be more reliable than when the group failed; and (3) after group success one has more positive feelings about the task, which one also has a greater desire to repeat, than after group failure.

The foregoing suggests that group goal setting is a reflective activity indeed: one weighs the behavioural outcomes before, during and after group performance. Zander summarizes this reflective process as follows:

> The tendency of group members to select a given level of aspiration for their unit is a multiplicative function of the strength of the members' desire to attain group success or to avoid group failure, the perceived probability that engaging in the task will provide desired outcomes, and the value placed upon these outcomes. The resultant tendency to engage in any task is determined by the strength of the members' tendency to approach that task minus their tendency to avoid it.

> (Zander, 1968, p. 424)

We have shown that there are several similarities between individual and group aspirations: (a) there is adherence to the 'success-raise and failure-lower' rule, but greater sensitivity to success; (b) achievement-oriented group members and individuals select tasks of intermediate difficulty and perform better than failure-oriented groups and individuals, who select either very easy or very difficult goals; and (c) with no feedback about task performance, individuals and groups overestimate their performance. We have also indicated that a group situation is not always a summation of individual reflections. This was shown in the domino study. Moreover, we have tried to show that performing as a group member has consequences for one's self-appraisal and one's appreciation of the group and the task.

As an introduction to the section on 'task interdependency' it should be noted that in Zander's experiments (1968, 1971) a tacit assumption is that the personal interests of members coincide with the interests of the group as a whole, that is, work takes place under cooperative conditions, and indeed the experiments were designed to evoke cooperation in group members. The same research also suggests that this assumption is not entirely justified. For example, Zander (1968) reports that members of failing groups are less attracted to their group and the group task than are members of successful groups, which might suggest that the motivation to be cooperative, i.e. to exert oneself for the benefit of the group as a whole, co-varies with group success.

ATTAINING HIERARCHICALLY LOWER GROUP GOALS

Goals in Zander's groups were set by the group itself, that is, these groups were fairly autonomous in setting their own goals. In daily life, for example, in industrial settings, goals are usually set by agencies such as supervisors and boards of directors. In a car factory, for instance, the goal of number of cars to be produced will usually be set by the directors of the company, who prescribe the number of cars to be produced by groups of workers on the shop floor. These directors are responsible for the hierarchically higher levels of goal setting, whereas groups of workers themselves have to execute these plans. The workers are then responsible for the effecting of hierarchically lower goals.

In the present section we will deal with the task performance of groups that have to execute goals which are set by authorities that may be part of the larger organization, or by the circumstances involved. An example of prescription by circumstances is provided in a study by Torrance (1954). Torrance studied a group of 200 Air Force personnel brought down over enemy territory during World War II or the Korean War, focusing on the efficiency of the crews' attempts to survive. His main measures were costs and efficiency of performance, changes over time, indices of interpersonal relations among group members and member relationships with the surroundings. He found that two conditions were rather detrimental to survival: (a) unstable social relations among group members; and (b) insufficient insight into how to survive, i.e. lack of competency to develop lower hierarchical levels of task organization. Torrance found that these conditions were likely to lead either to random, trial-and-error behaviour, or to the development of a feeling of hopelessness which usually led to surrender to the enemy.

One of the early, now classic, studies of productivity in an industrial setting in which groups of workers have to meet the goals set by their supervisors was carried out in the Hawthorne plant of the Western Electric Company during the Depression (see Roethlisberger and Dickson, 1939). The researchers intended to investigate the effect of physical conditions such as lighting. To their surprise they found that production rose regardless of whether lighting conditions were improved, degraded or left constant. Further investigation showed that in experimental conditions in which groups worked together in the presence of a researcher who kept track of the flow of materials, units of products produced, etc., production usually improved as compared with that of control groups that did not receive the researcher's attention. Thus, it turned out that groups reacted favourably to being studied rather than to the lighting circumstances themselves. This sensitivity to receiving attention, which may affect task performance, has since then been called the Hawthorne effect. Its implication is that human relations – increased social interaction, increased personal attention – may affect productivity in tasks. That is not to say that increased intra-group interaction within experimental groups always leads to higher productivity. This is shown by the results for some of the experimental groups. It appeared that some groups developed high internal cohesion but agreed upon rather low performance goals. These groups applied negative sanctions to productive members, who were addressed as 'rate busters', and effectively kept members from producing either too little or too much. This study shows that reflective activities take place in groups. When groups set production goals, group members' behaviours (production rates) are carefully observed in order to keep track of whether members conform. Conformity leads to satisfaction among group members (but not necessarily to satisfaction of their supervisors when goals are set too low). When individual group members perform under or above the common goal, these group members are punished to stimulate compliance with the consensual production level. In this way, the rewards of potential deviation are counteracted by applied sanctions, or costs. By applying sanctions, the group tries to guarantee that the agreed-upon group goal provides the highest profits (or satisfaction) as compared with personal goals (e.g. lower performance), which may involve higher rewards but in this case also the higher costs that are imposed by other group members. In this way it is ensured that conformity to the common goal is likely to remain the most attractive behavioural alternative. This study also demonstrates that agreed-upon goals have a descriptive aspect (e.g. a high, moderate or low production level) and a prescriptive aspect (members should comply with the goals set) for group members (see the introduction to chapter 3).

Subsequent studies have indicated that (a) group members reflect upon group goals; (b) group members are influenced in such a way that they conform to the goals set; (c) cohesive groups influence their group members more than less cohesive groups; and (d) such influences can serve to raise or lower members' productivity, depending on what goals groups have set. An illustration will be presented in the following.

Schachter, Ellertson, McBride and Gregory (1951) investigated whether group members' production performance is affected by the influence attempts of their fellow group members and whether conformity to influence attempts is more complete when one is acting in a cohesive as compared with a non-cohesive group, where cohesion was defined as the attractiveness of the group for its members. In their experimental procedure subjects are requested to work – ostensibly as a part of a three-person group – on a three-part checkerboard problem. The three parts consist of cutting out squares, pasting them onto a board and painting them. All subjects – who are placed in separate rooms – are assigned to the same part of the task (cutting cardboard squares). Their alleged group mates are presumed to be performing the other two parts (painting and pasting) in adjacent rooms. Communication takes place only by means of written messages delivered by the experimenter. During task performance, the experimenter delivers a series of pre-planned notes to the subject. Two kinds of production messages are delivered. Half of the subjects receive downward messages that urge the subject to keep his or her production rate down, so that the subject's output does not stack up too much work for the group mates. The other half of the subjects receive upward messages, which urge the subject to achieve a high production rate so that the group can produce many checkerboards. Besides the factor 'direction of production message' cohesion of the group is also varied. In the high-cohesive condition subjects are led to believe that, 'there is every reason to expect that the other members of the group will like you and you will like them', whereas in the low-cohesive condition it was announced that, 'there is no particular reason to think that you will like them or that they will care for you'. The main dependent variable is change in the subject's production rate from before to after receipt of the production messages.

The results indicated that upward production messages led to an increase in the subject's production rates, whereas downward production messages led to a decrease. The results for cohesive versus non-cohesive groups were somewhat unexpected. Following downward ('slow-down') messages the decrease in production was indeed stronger for high-cohesive than for low-cohesive group members; however, following upward ('speed-up') messages no effect for cohesion was observed, i.e. irrespective of the cohesion of the group, subjects in the speed-up conditions increased their production. How can these results be explained?

Closer inspection of the reported results indicates that the magnitude of change after speed-up induction (upward messages) was more pronounced than the magnitude of change after slow-down messages. This may suggest that one of the rewards for group members is an increase in group productivity, a tendency which is consistent with what we described in the section about group aspirations, and which Schachter *et al.* (1951) call 'a force to do a good job'. The second reward or 'force' (Schachter *et al.*, 1951) is acceptance as a group member, which may be assumed to be greater under high- than under low-cohesive conditions.

Schachter *et al.* point out that in the speed-up (upward messages) conditions the reward associated with 'doing a good job' is apparently so strong that it does not matter whether the extra reward to be received is larger (high cohesion) or smaller (low cohesion). However, under slow-down conditions (downward production messages) the two rewards (or forces) apparently oppose each other: to do a good job demands that one should speed up; however, to be accepted as a good group member demands that one should slow down. The results indicated that in the low-cohesive slow-down condition the inducement to slow down had no effect: no shift in production occurred. Apparently, the two opposing rewards balanced each other out. However, in the high-cohesive slow-down condition the reward for being a good group member was stronger, and therefore, slow-down high-cohesive group members were more compliant with the slow-down inducements than were slow-down low-cohesive group members.

This experimental study demonstrates that reflective processes are involved. Whereas Schachter *et al.* are inclined to describe this process as a weighing of forces, we prefer to refer to this process as a weighing of costs and benefits. For example, a slow-down high-cohesive group member faces the decision to slow down his production. The behavioural alternative of slowing down is costly from the point of view of doing a good job, but rewarding from that of being an accepted group member. Conversely, for such a member in a slow-down high-cohesive group the decision to speed up is costly (a negative reward) in view of the desire to be an accepted group member, but rewarding in view of the desire to do a good job. The choice between these behavioural alternatives depends on the net rewards or profits that are associated with them. Admittedly, the weighing of costs and benefits and the expression of each behavioural alternative in terms of a single profit function is a troublesome problem. However, it may be argued that Thibaut and Kelley's (1959) analysis is the best analytical framework available for examining the decisions people make in concrete circumstances like those in the study just described.

TASK INTERDEPENDENCY

Quite often the success or failure of some group members can have positive or negative consequences for other group members. This was probably the case from the perspective of the subjects who participated in the above-reported experiment by Schachter *et al.* (1951). For example, if the person cutting the squares cannot perform his or her subtask, the other two members cannot fulfil their subtask and the group as a whole cannot complete the three-part checkerboard problem. This type of task provides an instance of *positive* interdependency: one group member's success directly facilitates the success of other group members. We call this a cooperative task. Another example is a team sport, like soccer: one team player's good (or bad) performance during a match has beneficial (or detrimental) consequences for the other members of the team.

At the other extreme, group members may be confronted with a task involving a negative interdependency. In that case the success of one group member inhibits the success of other group members, and the failure of one group member has positive consequences for other group members. For example, Brown (1988) refers to the practice in some companies of providing financial incentives based on individual performance relative to other group members. Such a task is called a competitive task, because a loss for one group member means a gain for the other group member(s), and the reverse.

The distinction between cooperative and competitive may be described more precisely in terms of goal-directed behaviour or goal achievement. A cooperative task is a task in which the goal achievement of one group member has positive consequences for the goal achievement of other group members. In a competitive task the goal achievement of one member has negative consequences for the goal achievement of other group members. Thus, in cooperative tasks the achievement of one group member and the achievement of the other group members are positively related, or positively interdependent, whereas in competitive tasks the goal achievement of one member and the goal achievement of other group members are negatively interdependent.

Another way to describe cooperative and competitive tasks is in terms of the absence and presence of a conflict of interest (see the introduction to chapter 3). In cooperative tasks the interests of group members coincide because the task achievement of one member also serves the interests of the other group members. In competitive tasks the task achievement of one member has negative implications for the interests of other members.

As Deutsch (1949a, 1949b) has rightfully pointed out, there are very few purely cooperative and competitive tasks in real life. Most tasks involve a mixture of positive (cooperation) and negative (competition) interdependency, because individuals may be cooperatively or positively interdependent with respect to one goal and competitively or negatively interdependent with respect to another goal. For example, members of a soccer team may be cooperatively interdependent when it comes to winning the match, but competitively interdependent with respect to being the star of the day.

Moreover, the distinction between these pure types of tasks does not imply that group members always act in the way that is demanded by the task characteristics. Kelley and Thibaut (1978) suggest that, by psychological redefinition or transformation, purely cooperative and competitive tasks may be transformed into their counterpart. For example, soccer players who as a team have a cooperative task may be encouraged to compete with one another when they are aware that headhunters for other clubs are watching their individual performance. Or the reverse can occur: on a lazy day two chess players, who are basically involved in a competitive game, may before the match agree not to try to beat each other but to end with an easy draw, and by doing so transform a competitive task into a cooperative task.

Task type and performance

How will type of task affect group performance? Deutsch (1949b) set up an experiment to answer this question. Deutsch argued that in situations in which a group member's locomotion towards a goal (success in a task) has positive consequences for other group members (cooperative tasks; positive inter-dependency), group members will be motivated to help one another, they will like one another, and the group as a whole will be strongly propelled towards the group goal. In groups faced with a competitive task, group members will hinder one another, they will learn to dislike one another, and the group as a whole will be less likely to produce a good group product than it would be if it had to perform a cooperative task.

The groups in Deutsch's experiment worked at a series of human-relations and logical problems over a period of five weeks, and their discussions were monitored by observers. In addition, self-report measures of attitudes towards the task and fellow group members and objective measures of performance were taken. Half of the subjects received cooperative, the other half competitive task instructions. In the cooperative instructions condition it was stressed that the subject's own group was in competition with other groups, but that all members of the same group would receive the same grade, which would depend on how well the group performed in comparison with other groups in the psychology course. So *within* these groups, group members were positively interdependent. In the competitive instructions condition the students were informed that they would receive individual grades according to how well they performed in the group, the best students receiving the highest grades. So within these groups, group members were negatively interdependent: assignment of the highest rank to one group member meant that this rank was not available for other group members. The results were as anticipated. Cooperative groups achieved a higher level of objective group performance, and group members liked one another more, communicated more, were more friendly to one another, were less aggressive and less competitive. Moreover, they liked the task itself and the group more than competitive groups. Deutsch suggests that cooperative or positive interdependency evokes greater group or organizational productivity. Moreover, the communication of ideas, coordination of efforts, friendliness and pride in one's group appear to be disrupted when members see themselves to be competing for mutually exclusive goals. Competitiveness produces greater personal insecurity due to anticipation of hostility from others than does cooperation. Pointing to the practical implications, Deutsch (1949a, 1949b) suggests that a competitive grading system should be re-examined as an educational tool, because it leads to a decrease of personal security, less communication and worse interpersonal relations, effects which hamper personal development.

As has been pointed out by several investigators (see Brown, 1988), Deutsch's experiment has several shortcomings: (1) the (only) ten groups were not formed randomly, which may have affected the reported results; (2) in the cooperative condition there was a mixture of intra-group cooperation and inter-group competition, so the results for the cooperative condition may be ascribed to inter-group competition instead of to intra-group cooperation; (3) the measures taken were not very reliable; and (4) the observers were not entirely independent. However, in spite of these deficiencies later research that does not share these shortcomings has corroborated Deutsch's findings.

An example is the work of Rosenbaum *et al.* (1980), who studied group performance in three-person groups. These groups had to construct towers, and the degree of positive and negative interdependency was carefully controlled. The task of each of the groups (which were run independently so that the possibility of inter-group competition was excluded) was to build towers as high as possible. Interdependency – from positive to negative interdependency – was induced by financial incentives. Maximum positive interdependency (co-operation) was created by means of the rule that the group prize would be higher as more blocks were added, whereas maximum negative interdependency (competition) was induced when it was suggested that all the money would go to the member (the winner) who had contributed most blocks. By means of a clever variation of financial compensations, intermediate levels of positive and negative interdependency were also induced. The results confirmed Deutsch's findings in that the greater the positive interdependency (a) the greater the productivity (the number of blocks used); (b) the more coordination of efforts; and (c) the higher the interpersonal attraction among group members. This conclusion was also confirmed in an extensive comparison of the results of 109 studies by Johnson *et al.* (1981), who compared groups that had performed cooperative and competitive tasks. They found that 56 studies supported, whereas only 8 disconfirmed Deutsch's findings. After a review of these studies, Brown (1988) remarks that, 'This apparently unassailable superiority of cooperation should cause us to question seriously the overwhelming emphasis on *competitive* arrangements in our educational institutions and workplaces. The evidence is that such arrangements are quite literally counterproductive' (Brown, 1988, p. 32).

PROFIT INTERDEPENDENCY

In the foregoing section on task interdependency it was shown that group members reflect upon their individual profits. When personal profits are more served by contributing to the group product, as in cooperative task settings, one tends to contribute more effort to the group task than under conditions in which personal profits are higher when one performs better than other group members, as in competitive conditions, as was shown in the experimental studies of Deutsch (1949b) and in those more than thirty years later by Rosenbaum *et al.* (1980).

In these experiments group members in the cooperative and competitive task conditions could influence their definite profits (or net rewards) by working for the group or for themselves, respectively. It should be noted that in these studies on task interdependency group members could indirectly influence their profits by means of task effort, i.e. via task performance. In the present section we will deal with situations in which group members may affect their profits in a more direct way, that is, group situations in which group members have to decide (before or after task performance) how the group's profits should be assigned to individual group members.

Allocation of profits

Before and/or after task performance group members are quite often faced with two problems associated with the division of profits available as a result of group performance. It may be necessary to determine a reasonable criterion on which to base the allocation of profits in a situation in which profits for some members are not available to other members, i.e. a situation which involves a potential for competition. Should the allocation of profits be based on effort, ability or some other criterion? In the following we will illustrate two complementary kinds of approaches that are available, approaches that make identical predictions.

To illustrate, suppose that group members are entirely equal on any imaginable criterion (ability, effort, seniority, gender, etc.). How should the group profits be allocated? If each group member claimed all group profits for her- or himself, then an endless competition for the group's scarce profits would be the result: if one group member claimed all profits for her- or himself, all other group members would be excluded from having a share of the group profits. As a consequence – for this is maximal competition – groups would fall apart (as many philosophers, e.g. Spinoza and Hobbes, have argued), and in the future no group performance would be possible. To escape from this undesirable consequence, two important ways out are proposed, namely normative and rational co-ordination, which we will explain in the following.

Normative coordination

Adams (1965) and Homans (1974) propose that in the past people learned to adhere to norms and that these norms coordinate behaviours so that discrepancies from what is fair or equitable are redressed.

Adams proposes a distinction between inputs and outcomes. Inputs are resources (like effort, ability, gender, etc.) that an actor, such as a task performer, invests in an exchange relationship, for example in the group's production.

Outcomes are the profits that the actor receives from these relationships, for example rewards that become available as a result of the group's achievements.

The formula for a fair or equitable relationship is quite simple, namely that there should be equality between actor A's outcomes or profits divided by A's inputs and actor B's outcomes divided by B's inputs, and so on.

In formula:

$$\frac{\text{A's outcomes}}{\text{A's inputs}} = \frac{\text{B's outcomes}}{\text{B's inputs}} = \frac{\text{C's outcomes}}{\text{C's inputs}}$$

The above illustration makes it clear that when group members are entirely equal as to their investments, or inputs, they should receive equal outcomes.

Rational coordination

Another explanation is that it is rational to divide outcomes equally when group members have contributed equally. The underlying reasoning is that group members reflect upon the behavioural alternatives, and the behavioural alternative that provides the highest profits is selected. From this perspective each of the group members in principle would prefer to have all group profits for her- or himself. However, at the same time each group member realizes that the other group members also reflect upon the outcomes they derive from the group's performance. So if one group member were to profit more than any other group member, then she or he is likely to be aware that the other group members may be faced with outcomes that do not provide their best behavioural alternative. In such a case, one or more other group members might reduce their efforts or even leave the group. Conversely, leaving the group and reducing one's efforts are also ways open to a group member who expects to receive less than the other group members.

So, in order to establish and to maintain group relations, it is rational or reasonable to propose that each member should receive equal outcomes when group members are equal with respect to all possible sources of investment. As compared with the normative approach, the rational approach can explain why certain outcome allocation situations do arise. However, a weakness of the rational approach is that it suggests that group members always make complex calculations about the outcomes attached to all behavioural alternatives for self and others. The strength of the normative approach is that it assumes that people more or less automatically conform to rules of fairness, and its weakness is that it cannot explain why particular norms come into being or are maintained during group interaction.

In the following we will not continue the debate between the proponents of the normative approach (e.g. Lerner, Miller and Holmes, 1976) and the rational approach (for example, Walster, Walster and Berscheid, 1978) but suggest that the two approaches are complementary: quite often the content of a rule of fairness is rational or functional; however, a rule or norm of fairness may be applied without people being aware of its invested rationality. This is also true for more complicated relationships in groups.

Thus, on the one hand there are researchers who endeavour to show that allocation decisions are based on rather complex reflections about the expected utility of the behavioural alternatives available (see, for example, Campbell and Snowden, 1985), while on the other hand there are experts who start from the idea that people automatically conform to rules of fairness and that people only start to reflect upon their behavioural alternatives when rules or norms are violated. Most noteworthy in this respect is Adams's (1965) work on equity theory, which we will deal with in the following.

Equity in work groups

The formula presented in the previous section may also be employed when group members are not equal with respect to all possible investments or inputs. For example, members of a three-person work group may be convinced that person A has invested three times more effort in a group task than B, while B has invested three times more effort than C. How will they allocate the group's profits? According to equity theory, A's outcome/input ratio should be equal to B's ratio and to C's ratio. Since the inputs of A are three times as great as those of B and nine times as great as those of C, it is equitable that A should receive three times more of the outcomes than B and nine times more than C, i.e. in this way their ratios are equal. Furthermore, equity theory assumes that when these ratios are equal, satisfaction is experienced (Adams, 1965). What will happen when these ratios are not equal?

For simplicity's sake, two kinds of initial inequality or inequity may be distinguished. In the case of a two-person work group consisting of A and B, suppose that A has worked three times as long as B. Equality or equity is realized when A's outcomes are also three times greater. Employing the previous formula we find that the ratios are equal, as presented below in (a). In (b) A has again invested three times more than B.

(a)

$$\frac{\text{outcomes A} = 3}{\text{inputs A} = 3} = \frac{\text{outcomes B} = 1}{\text{inputs B} = 1}$$

(b)

$$\frac{\text{outcomes A} = 1}{\text{inputs A} = 3} < \frac{\text{outcomes B} = 1}{\text{inputs B} = 1}$$

However, A's outcomes are equivalent to B's profits, i.e. the ratios of A and B, who presumably are involved in social comparison (see chapter 3), are unequal. In their relationship, A will feel undercompensated and B overcompensated: A's and B's investments are non-equivalent, whereas their profits or outcomes are the same. Of course the inequality may vary, for example if A's inputs are equal to 3, and B's inputs equal to 1, but A's outcomes are 1 and B's outcomes are 3. A and B have more reason to feel undercompensated and overcompensated, respectively, in (b).

What are the predicted reactions to feeling inequitably treated? Adams (1965) proposes that inequity will be experienced as unpleasant and that inequity creates a state of dissonance, which tends to be reduced. Several ways of reducing dissonance are open in the case of inequity. To sum up for the case of (b) above:

1 A may reduce his or her inputs so that they are equal to 1.
2 B may increase his or her investments so that they are equal to 3.
3 A and B may cognitively distort their inputs so that it looks as if A and B have invested the same amount. For example, by discounting A's inputs (to 1) equity can be established.
4 A and B may cognitively distort their profits. For example A and B may believe that B's outcomes have a value of 1/3 of what they are worth to A.
5 A person (e.g. person A) may leave the work group and associate him- or herself with another group in which an equitable exchange may take place.
6 Person A may communicate to person B that the ratios are not equal and that if B does not increase his or her inputs (e.g. effort), A will slow down, or conversely that the outcomes or profits of a group should be redistributed in a more equitable way. For example (in b): A's outcomes should become three times larger than B's outcomes.

In the following we will present some evidence, and we will briefly note a number of problems with a straightforward application of equity theory. We will discuss the following issues: (a) equality concerning outcomes and investments: equality to what? (b) situational constraints with respect to the rule of fairness that applies in a given situation; (c) the importance not only of outcomes, but also of procedures: outcomes or distributive justice versus procedural justice.

Bystander allocation

The allocation of outcomes in groups has been investigated primarily in two kinds of experimental situations, namely in situations in which group members themselves have to divide the outcomes and situations in which an employer, or a bystander, has to act as an allocator. We will give some examples of these investigations, which show that reflective weighing influences the allocation of outcomes by a bystander.

In a review of equity studies, von Grumbkow and Wilke (1974) hypothesized that subjects applied theoretical notions of equity more strictly in questionnaire studies than in 'real life' settings. To examine the plausibility of the hypothesis that the research method has consequences, von Grumbkow, Steensma and Wilke (1980) performed a study in which subjects had to allocate money to workers. Half of the subjects did this by allocating money after having read a description of the performance of two workers (hypothetical condition), while the other half allocated the money after having seen these two workers actually perform (real life condition). Besides the 'questionnaire' versus 'real life' variation, the performances of A and B were varied (e.g. performance of A equal to performance of B; A fulfilling 18 more tasks than B, and the reverse). It appeared that the differences in allocated outcomes matched the differences in investments or performance more closely in the hypothetical situations than in real life situations.

In another study (von Grumbkow, Steensma and Wilke, 1977) subjects allocated rewards to eight hypothetical subordinates, in a procedure that is similar to the one used by Leventhal and Whiteside (1969). Half of the subjects received instructions from the experimenter, who remained in the presence of the subject during the task. The other half of the subjects received identical instructions but did not see the experimenter. It was expected and found that subjects who allocated in the presence of the experimenter made allocations that were less strictly equitable than those made in the absence of the experimenter. The interpretation of these results was that the subjects were more concerned about the experimenter's evaluation of them when he was present than when he was not. These results agree with data reported by Leventhal, Michaels and Sanford (1972) indicating that allocators behave less equitably if the application of strict equity gives rise to tension.

In an earlier study (von Grumbkow, Deen, Steensma and Wilke, 1976), subjects allocated rewards to two actors whose performance they observed. Half of the subjects expected to interact with the actors, whereas the other half did not. In both conditions, worker A decoded seventy questionnaires in the same time that worker B decoded thirty questionnaires. The results indicated that subjects consider the costs of a strict application of equity rules when they anticipate future interaction. Since it might be costly to have to justify large differences in rewards, the subjects expecting future interaction with the workers decided to compensate more equally (but less equitably) than subjects who did not expect future contact.

The above-presented findings suggest that when outside allocators feel more dependent on the group members who receive outcomes from them, they are less likely to compensate according to the equity principle, a finding that has been replicated in several experimental studies (e.g. Leventhal *et al.*, 1972; Pruitt, 1972) and in field studies in organizational settings as well (see von Grumbkow, 1980).

Allocators profiting from the allocation of outcomes

In groups it is quite often group members themselves who have to allocate outcomes. When the total number of outcomes is constant, outcomes allocated to another group member cannot be allocated to oneself. It is not surprising that in such a situation one is inclined to apply the equity principle in one's own favour (see Turner, 1980). Such a conflict of interests seems rather absent in situations in which a group member may allocate outcomes to self and the other as two independent acts. Nevertheless, in such a situation a so-called 'egocentric bias' also occurs. This was demonstrated by Messick and Sentis (1979), who explicitly asked their subjects to allocate money in a fair way and found that subjects selected higher outcomes for themselves than for their fellow group members. For example, subjects who worked ten hours when another group member worked seven hours judged on average that their own pay should have been $35.24 when the other person had been paid $25. However, when they themselves had worked seven hours and had been paid $25, subjects judged the fair pay to the other for ten hours of work to be $30.29. This difference of nearly $5 reflects what is called an egocentric bias, a tendency for subjects to consider more money to be fair for themselves than for someone else in the same situation.

While explaining their data in another study, Messick and Sentis (1983) reported evidence that the egocentric bias involves at least two components. First, subjects prefer an outcome allocation scheme that best serves their interests. When subjects worked seven hours and the other ten hours in an identical situation, subjects were more inclined to prefer an equal split allocation, whereas subjects who worked ten hours whilst the other worked seven hours preferred unequal allocations. So the most advantageous allocation scheme was selected. The second component was demonstrated in the data for subjects who showed a preference for unequal allocations, that is, a preference for equal outcomes per hour. It appeared that these subjects thought it fair to be paid more than someone else in an identical situation. Messick and Sentis (1983) relate the second component of egocentric bias to the egocentric bias in attribution of responsibility documented by Ross and Sicoly (1979): if successful, people take more credit for the group product than others would accord them; people think it fair for them to get more than others in a similar situation because they think they have contributed more to the group product.

It should be noted that in the above-reported studies positively evaluated group outcomes had to be allocated. What is to be expected when negative outcomes (e.g. losses after failure) are involved? The egocentric or self-serving bias literature suggests that (1) one will prefer that allocation which best serves one's interests, i.e. one will allocate the least (negative) outcomes to oneself; and (2) one will discount one's investment or contribution to the group failure, i.e. there will be underestimation of one's own part and overestimation of the others' share in the negatively evaluated group product (see, for example, Weary and Arkin, 1981).

To sum up, the above-reported studies show that one is inclined to match investment and outcomes. However, departures from equity show up if this is in one's interest: (1) an outside allocator is less inclined to apply the equity principle when the allocation of outcomes might imply negative outcomes (costs) to the allocator; and (2) when one directly profits from the allocation of outcomes one adheres to the equity principle, but in an egocentric way.

Multiple criteria for equity

In the above-presented studies the allocation task was rather simple since group members only differed in one respect. For example, in the study by von Grumbkow *et al.* (1977) group members only differed in terms of the number of questionnaires decoded, whereas in the study of Messick and Sentis (1979) investment differences pertained to the number of hours group members had supposedly worked. Moreover, outcomes were expressed by one measure: money allocated. An example of a more complicated study, in which managers had to allocate money to 10 types of employees in their firms, is that of Hoekstra and Wilke (1972), who analysed the wage recommendations of 432 managers participating in one of Bass's exercises (Bass, 1965). These employees were said to differ with respect to performance and certain other criteria as well; for example, advancement potential, working in a low-prestige subsidiary, working in an uncongenial environment, dullness of job, and having an offer to join a competitive firm. It appeared that wage increase recommendations were based mainly on past performance. However, other criteria were also taken into account. For example, the employee Ed who had no opportunity for further advancement in the same firm was given a lower wage increase than Jim, who had received a competitive offer from another firm. These data indicate that when multiple investment criteria and one outcome criterion (wage increase in terms of money) are involved, performance differences count heavily, but that other investment criteria also play a role.

Some researchers (e.g. Farkas and Anderson, 1979; Jasso and Rossi, 1977) have investigated the relation between multiple investment criteria and a single outcome criterion more thoroughly. Their research question was how various criteria (e.g. age, gender, marital status, performance, effort, ability) are combined to arrive at evaluations of deservingness for a particular outcome, such as payment. One of the models proposed was the 'equity integration model' (Farkas and Anderson, 1979), which pertains to situations in which investments are rather dissimilar, for example seniority and past performance. According to the model, separate outcome estimates are derived from each single investment criterion and then arranged or combined in some way to arrive at a final equity judgement. The results of studies in which outsiders or bystanders had to make judgements about the deserved payment appear to support this model, which fits in rather closely with other models designed to predict outcome differentials when multidimensional investment criteria are involved (see Cook and Yamagishi, 1983). These studies pertain to performance situations in which many investment criteria and one outcome criterion (pay) are the topic of investigation. The results indicate that performance and ability are important determinants of payment. However, it should be noted that in daily life an even more complicated question evolves: namely, how are multiple outcomes (such as pay, promotion, social esteem) allocated given multiple investments (such as performance, seniority, ability)? This research question has not yet been addressed as far as we know.

Types of interdependency

It may be concluded that in work groups outcomes are equitably allocated and based on task-related investment criteria like performance and ability. However, this does not imply that the allocation of outcomes will always be based on performance differentials. Quite often in friendship groups outcomes are allocated equally, that is, performance differentials are neglected in favour of group membership, on the basis of which group members are equal and consequently group outcomes are allocated equally. And to complicate matters, in other types of groups, for example close relationships like families, outcomes are allocated according to need. In close relationships outcome allocation is usually not based on performance differentials but on who has greatest need. For example, in family relationships it is not the wage earner who obtains the most outcomes, but that family member who has the greater need (see further Mikula, 1984).

Procedural justice

Multiple investment criteria, multiple outcome criteria and type of inter-dependency (task-related, friendship and close relationships) are not the only things that can complicate the application of the equity rule; the procedures by which outcomes are allocated also appear to be of importance, and some researchers even argue that the fairness of the allocation procedure ('procedural fairness') quite often has a greater impact than the resulting outcomes them-selves, i.e. so-called 'distributive or outcomes justice' (cf., for example, Tyler and McGraw, 1986). Distributive fairness refers then to the perceived fairness of the outcomes, whereas procedural justice refers to the fairness of the procedures used to determine those distributions.

Focusing on legal procedures in court or dispute-resolution procedures, Thibaut and Walker (1975) found that litigants' reactions to their experiences in court were affected not only by the outcomes of their cases but also by their judgements about the fairness of the process through which such outcomes were produced. Satisfaction was higher for cases won than for cases lost. Satisfaction and acceptance of verdicts (independent of outcomes) was higher after fair than after unfair procedures. In a laboratory study by Greenberg (1987) subjects had to perform a task on which they subsequently received a positive, a neutral or a negative evaluation, i.e. outcomes were varied by means of the suggestion that one particular subject performed better than average, average or below average. Moreover, the procedures through which the evaluations were communicated were varied. In the diary condition the experimenter accurately kept a diary, in the observation condition the experimenter observed the subject's performance without recording, and in the negligence condition the experi-menter did not pay much attention to the performance, but merely evaluated the subject. At the end of the experiment the experimenter posed separate questions about the perceived fairness of the outcomes and the procedures. Regarding the rated fairness of the procedure it turned out that the ratings for the diary condition were higher than those for the observation condition, which in turn were higher than those for the negligence condition. Ratings of procedural fairness were also different in the outcome conditions, namely ratings in the positive and neutral evaluation conditions were higher than those in the negative evaluation condition; however, this effect (the variance explained by the evaluation factor) was much smaller than that for the procedure conditions.

The ratings of the fairness of the outcomes were higher after positive evalua-tion than after neutral evaluation, which in turn were higher than those following negative evaluation. However, it was also observed that the perceived fairness of outcomes was considered to be higher in the diary condition than in the obser-vation condition, while the fairness of outcomes in the latter condition was judged to be higher than it was in the negligence condition.

What do these results mean? One implication is that, more than negative evaluations, positive evaluations of workers lead to a higher ascribed fairness of outcomes and of procedures. A second implication is that, more than unaccepted procedures (like in the negligence condition), well-accepted procedures of recording performance lead to higher ratings of perceived procedural justice, as well as to higher ratings of distributive (outcomes) justice. Together these results suggest that judgements of procedural and distributive justice are fairly closely related.

The above-presented insights suggest that group members strive for equality, and that equality is at the heart of justice. The most prominent issue is then on what dimensions or aspect of the situation equality should be established. Should equality be based on equal outcomes of permitted investment (e.g. number of hours worked), on need or on group membership? Or should equality be based on procedural equality, i.e. equality in the application of rules? Messick and Sentis suggest that the problem of finding fair arrangements for groups is 'not one of equality versus inequality but one of equality with regard to what' (1983, p. 68).

CONCLUSIONS AND SUMMARY

The major proposition of this chapter is that rewards and costs are taken into account. This concerns both individual group members and groups as a whole. For individual group members it was shown that the choice between remaining solo and performing with a partner and the choice between continuing as a member of a group and changing groups are made after reflection, implying that one prefers the behavioural alternative that is most rewarding or least costly. For individuals and for groups, success is more rewarding than failure. It was shown that individual and group aspirations are subjected to the 'success-raise and failure-lower' rule of adjustment of goals after receiving feedback on past performance.

Group goals are not always autonomously set by group members. Quite often they are set by others outside the group. It was shown that these goals have to be accepted by the group, because (a) group members reflect upon group goals; (b) group members are influenced in such a way that they conform to the goal set; (c) cohesive groups influence their members more than less cohesive groups; and (d) such influencing can serve to raise the performance of a less productive group member.

The nature of the task may affect the relations between group members: regarding task outcomes, group members may be positively or negatively interdependent, i.e. tasks may be either cooperative or competitive. The research presented in this chapter indicates that cooperative task interdependency leads to higher productivity than does competitive task interdependency.

Reflection on costs and rewards is also an important determinant of the way in which explicit outcomes of group performance are distributed among group members. It was argued that since each group member strives for maximal rewards at the least cost, normative coordination is necessary. The way in which rules of distributive and procedural justice operate was also described.

Chapter 5

Communicative tuning

Individual group members may have individual cognitions about themselves, the group and the task environment (chapter 3). They may reflect upon the goal to be set and the outcomes involved (chapter 4). And finally, it is by communication that these cognitions and reflections are put forward and integrated so that the group may act as one task-performing unit.

In the following we will discuss the findings of researchers who have investigated communication within groups. We will start with Bales's (1950, 1958) analysis of interacting groups. One of Bales's conclusions is that in groups influence differentials always arise, that is, some members always have more influence than others. Expectation States Theory, which explains the emergence of influence differentials in groups, will be presented thereafter. The theory predicts that members with a (status) advantage with respect to a cue or status characteristic, such as competence related to the group task, exert more influence and are themselves less influenced by others than group members who have a (status) disadvantage. Subsequently, it is shown that status characteristics or discriminating cues may also emerge during the interaction process, and that such cues may have a stronger effect than cues available before interaction. In the final sections we systematically elucidate six reasons for communication in groups and elaborate some of the relevant research findings.

INTERACTION ANALYSIS

The study of communication within task groups goes back to the 1950s and started with the seminal work of Bales. Bales's work was mainly descriptive in nature; he observed how task groups actually communicate in time and how specific group members communicate during group interaction. Bales's groups (see Bales, 1950, 1958) held discussions in a well-lighted room. In an adjoining room observers listened and watched these discussions from behind one-way mirrors. This set-up was explained to the members of the group. One of the problems group members were asked to discuss concerned a human relations case. First a 5-page presentation of facts relevant to a problem faced by an administrator in an organization was read. After the case had been read, group members were given about 40 minutes to assemble the information, to discuss why people were behaving as they were, and to decide on a recommended course of action. During the discussion the observers in the adjoining room observed and recorded every step of the interaction. Each observer had a small machine with a moving paper tape on which he wrote in code a description of every act. Acts ordinarily occurred at a rate of 15 to 20 per minute. The recorded information on each act included identification of the person speaking and the person spoken to and classification of the act according to 12 predetermined categories. The 12 predetermined categories form what is referred to as the 'interaction-process analysis'. Bales made a distinction between four main areas. The area of Positive Reactions comprises the following interaction categories: (1) shows solidarity; (2) shows tension release; and (3) shows agreement. The area of Problem Solving Attempts includes the categories: (4) gives suggestion; (5) gives opinion; and (6) gives orientation. The area of Questions comprises the interaction categories: (7) asks for orientation; (8) asks for opinions; and (9) asks for suggestions. The area of Negative Reaction comprises: (10) shows disagreement; (11) shows tension release; and (12) shows antagonism. Besides observation scores, Bales also collected ratings from group members concerning liking, best ideas, etc. The results of this research programme revealed that there was differentiation in groups as to the kind of activities and as to the amount of emphasis on particular activities at different points in time and by different persons, results we will describe in somewhat greater detail below.

Overall differentiation in activities

Bales (1958) reported on how 24 groups (ranging in size from 2 to 7 persons) scored on the 12 categories. Since the groups had to solve a problem, it is not surprising that Problem Solving Attempts were observed most frequently (±56 per cent), followed by the area of Positive Reactions (±26 per cent). Questions and Negative Reactions, on the other hand, were less frequently observed (±18 per cent). So problem-solving activities received most attention. However, the relatively high frequency of observations in the Positive Reactions area suggests that positively evaluated social-emotional relations are also of importance in task groups.

Task differentiation in time

Bales and Strodtbeck (1951) hypothesized that during group interaction the emphasis would shift from orientation activities, via evaluation activities, to control activities, and that positive and negative social-emotional reactions would increase over time. The total discussion time was divided into three stages. It was found that during the first stage groups scored higher on orientation (categories 6: gives orientation and 7: asks for orientation) than in stage 3. The frequency of evaluation (categories 5: gives opinion and 8: asks for opinions) increased from stage 1 to stage 3, as did control activities (categories 4: gives suggestions and 9: asks for suggestions). Moreover, positive reactions (categories 1: shows solidarity and 3: shows agreement) and negative reactions (categories 10: shows disagreement and 12: shows antagonism) increased from stage 1 to stage 3. Although Bales and Strodtbeck's terminology is somewhat different from the concepts sensing, testing and effecting that we introduced (see chapter 1), their results suggest that during the first stage, sensing (or orientation in the terms of Bales and Strodtbeck) does occur and that sensing decreases over time. Testing whether the chosen criterion is being realized (or 'evaluation' in the terms of Bales and Strodtbeck) and effecting (or 'controlling' in the terms of Bales and Strodtbeck) appear to increase over time.

Status differentiation

Early in the research programme Bales (1958) started to collect judgements from group members about how much they liked other group members and to what extent they thought each group member had contributed ideas to the problem-solving task. Bales's first guess was that the group member who was considered to have contributed most (the 'Idea man') would also be the group member who was liked most (the 'Best-liked man'), i.e. Bales started from the idea of a single status order. He analysed the results of discussion groups that had to discuss problem-solving tasks during four successive sessions. His results indicated that after the first session the Idea man was only in 50 per cent of the cases considered to be the most liked person, and this percentage dropped after sessions 2, 3 and 4 to 12 per cent, 20 per cent and 8.5 per cent, respectively. This result led to a second hypothesis, namely: could it be that there was something about arriving at the top-status position that tended to make the Idea man lose friends and alienate people? Further analysis of results for other problem-solving groups suggests that in discussion groups quite often two kinds of specialists may be distinguished: socio-emotional and task leaders. On the initiation side of interaction, the Idea man initiates more heavily in the area of problem-solving attempts and the Best-liked man in the area of positive reactions. On the reception side of inter-action, the Idea man receives more agreement, questions and negative reactions, while the Best-liked man receives more problem-solving attempts, more solidarity and tension release. Bales summarizes these findings by suggesting that, 'the general picture is thus one of specialization and complementarity, with the Idea man concentrating on the task and playing a more aggressive role, while the Best-liked man concentrates more on socio-emotional problems, giving rewards and playing a more passive role' (Bales, 1958, pp. 441–2).

Bales's work on communication in groups is noteworthy for several reasons. (1) For the first time ingroup communication was observed by means of an observation scheme. (2) In interpreting these observational data Bales suggested that in discussion groups status differentials pertaining to task and socio-emotional leadership do arise, and he suggested that the Idea man and the

Best-liked man fulfil complementary functions. Moreover, he analysed the sequence of group activities, that is, influence processes in discussion groups. In the following we first describe an experimental project launched by Berger and his co-workers (e.g. Berger, Rosenholtz and Zelditch, 1980) that was highly inspired by Bales's ideas about influence differentials. Thereafter we will describe communication processes and a research programme on influence processes in task groups (by Festinger, 1950) that was also launched during the 1950s, but was quite independent of Bales's achievements.

THE EMERGENCE OF INFLUENCE DIFFERENTIALS

Whereas Bales and his co-workers observed that influence differentials in groups do arise, in an extensive and impressive programme Berger and his co-workers posed the question of why this is the case (see, for a recent review: Berger, Webster, Ridgeway and Rosenholtz, 1986).

Their theory – the Expectation States Theory (EST) – builds further on the findings of Bales and his co-workers that some group members consistently participated more than other group members and that these highly active group members were perceived more often as task and socio-emotional leaders than less active members. In the following we will first explain the theory and thereafter we will present some empirical findings that are relevant to it.

Expectation States Theory

According to Expectation States Theory, the interaction of members in a task-oriented group always leads to influence differentials. How do these influence differentials emerge? The theory assumes that, during group interaction, group members form expectations about possible competencies and that they behave in accordance with these expectations. A performance expectation is a belief about one's own and others' capacity to make successful contributions to the group task. The higher the performance expectations held of one group member relative to other group members, the more that group member will receive opportunities to contribute to the group's task, the more these contributions will be positively evaluated and the more that group member will be able to influence the behaviour of other group members. Thus, the theory maintains that group members always try to assess or evaluate each other's potential contributions to group success. The question is then how these performance expectations are formed. The theory assumes that, during interaction, group members always search for cues (or status characteristics) that may be of relevance as predictors of future group performance.

To form expectations, all kinds of cues or status characteristics may be employed. A distinction is made between diffuse and specific status characteristics. A specific status characteristic is quite relevant to the group task, since such a cue directly relates to the group task. For example, when a group has to solve a judicial problem and it is known or it appears during interaction that one of the group members is a lawyer or for some other reason has greater competence in judicial matters, then the other group members use this cue or status characteristic in forming performance expectations. Since that group member is likely to be considered as most able to promote the group's success, that specific group member receives most behavioural opportunities (e.g. others are likely to listen). Moreover, that group member is more able to influence the behaviour of other group members.

Diffuse status characteristics are culturally related to high and low ability, and are not self-evidently related to particular tasks. To give an example, in some cultures there exists a stereotype that males are more able than females. Suppose now that a two-person group consisting of a man and a woman has to solve a judicial problem. EST predicts that the gender cue will be employed to form expectations about potential contributions to group success. The man will be ascribed greater potential competence than the woman. As a consequence the man receives more behavioural opportunities and is likely to influence the woman more than the reverse. EST assumes that diffuse status characteristics are employed as a starting point in the forming of expectations, unless such a cue (e.g. sex or race) is explicitly made irrelevant. This means that, in our example, sex as a status characteristic will be used as a basis for expectations unless group members contest this cue as being irrelevant to the given situation, and demand proof that the cue is of importance to the task. Of course, specific status characteristics like competence differentials will be considered better predictors of future success than diffuse status characteristics. EST accounts for this by postulating that status characteristics may vary in path of relevance. Because knowledge in judicial matters is more relevant than race or gender in a group task involving a judicial problem, the path of relevance (the predictive value) of the cues will differ.

In sum, EST explains the emergence of influence differentials in groups by assuming that group members always search for one or more cues or status characteristics. Having selected or being presented with a status characteristic, group members form performance expectations. That group member who is ascribed the highest performance potential receives the most opportunities during the interaction process and will have the most influence.

Compliance: influence acceptance

To measure compliance in dyadic task situations, Berger employed a standard procedure in many experiments (see Berger *et al.*, 1980, 1986), which we will explain in somewhat greater detail. In this procedure two subjects are invited to the laboratory at the same time. Usually subjects are assigned to two separate cubicles so that they cannot establish personal or otherwise meaningful contacts with one another. Each cubicle is equipped with a panel featuring a number of buttons and light bulbs. First, subjects receive instructions about how to use the equipment. Thereafter, the subjects are told that they will be working with another subject, who is referred to as their 'partner', on a cooperative task.

In the first phase of experiments investigating the effect of a diffuse status characteristic, group members are told that they differ in sex, race, age, etc., and some practice trials are run. In the experiments investigating the effects of a specific status characteristic, that is, competence, the first phase is dedicated to the communication of competence differentials. The subjects then have to perform an individual task, such as one involving 'contrast sensitivity', 'rational ability' or 'spatial arrangement'. When the task involves contrast sensitivity, subjects are presented with a series of slides, each having a number of black and white squares. Subjects then have to indicate whether there are more white than black squares on each slide. Since the exposure time for each slide is rather short, the correct answer is very difficult for subjects to ascertain. After a number of trials, bogus feedback about the subjects' relative performance is provided. It is communicated that one subject performed better or worse than the partner or that the two performed equally.

In the second, or group, phase of the experiment, partners have to perform a collective task, that is, they are to receive a reward each time both partners give a correct answer on a trial, and the more trials in which both provide the correct answer, the higher the group rewards. In each trial subjects give a preliminary answer, then receive information about the preliminary answer of the partner, and lastly give a final judgement, about whether there are more black than white squares on the slide. In actuality, the information about the preliminary answer of the partner is faked by the experimenter. On some (neutral) trials it is suggested that the subject's preliminary response agrees with the response of the partner, whereas on critical trials the bogus feedback indicates that the partner has made the opposite preliminary judgement. The dependent measure is the number of critical trials in which the subject complies with the preliminary judgement of the partner, i.e. changes his or her judgement.

EST research has focused mainly on two issues, namely whether one status characteristic or status cue leads to influence differentials and what happens when more than one status characteristic is involved. We will deal with these research questions in the following.

One status characteristic

As already explained, EST makes a distinction between specific and diffuse status characteristics. In the case of specific status characteristics, subjects are usually informed that they have greater, equal or lower competence than their partner. Results indicate that subjects comply more often with the preliminary judgements of the other when they believe themselves to be less competent than the other. In the case of diffuse status characteristics it appears that females comply more often with the recommendations of males than the reverse. Also, males more often initiate behaviours and are more often elected as leaders (see, for example, Lockheed, 1985). A similar pattern of results is observed for the interaction between whites and blacks (Riches and Foddy, 1989). Blacks more often comply with proposals from whites than the reverse. The study of other status characteristics suggests that a higher occupational and military rank, a higher educational background (e.g. college students versus high school students) and greater age give rise to less acceptance of influence or compliance.

Two status characteristics

Numerous studies have been devoted to the question of whether information on two cues or status characteristics affects compliance. An example is a study by Wagner, Ford and Ford (1986). They gave males and females information about whether they were more or less competent than their partner of the other or same sex. It appeared that these cues or status characteristics had a combined effect: competent women accepted more influence than competent men but less than incompetent men, suggesting that the two types of status information were combined. Similar results were found when researchers investigated other pairs of sources of status information, namely race and competence (Riordan and Ruggiero, 1980), two competence dimensions (Kervin, 1977) and age and competence (Knottnerus and Greenstein, 1981).

Do the above-reported studies provide conclusive evidence that multiple status cues are combined? In a number of other studies it has been shown that attention is paid to only one of the status cues at the expense of the other one. Some researchers found that the effect of a diffuse status characteristic disappears as soon as information about specific competence differentials becomes available (Wood and Karten, 1986). Others (e.g. Martin and Sell, 1980) suggest that the weight of the status cue on which one scores higher than the partner will be enhanced, i.e. one seems to attach greater importance to information proving that one is more competent than the other, while discounting a status cue that provides information that one is inferior as compared with the partner. Lastly, Lee and Ofshe's (1981) experimental results suggest that the status cue that has been induced more saliently has a higher probability of affecting compliance. In that study subjects' reactions to videotaped discussions were registered. By way of the videotapes two variables were manipulated: occupational status of the discussant (high, moderate and low) and demeanour (the discussant behaving in a deference-demanding, a deferential or a neutral way). It appeared that the subjects' reactions (evaluation of the interaction and estimated influence differentials) were more affected by demeanour than by the occupational status of the discussant (see further Sherman, 1983).

Initiation or influence exertion

EST predicts that group members with higher competence (1) show less compliance, i.e. accept less influence; and (2) show a stronger tendency to exert influence than group members with lower competence. The above-reported results indicate that hypothesis 1 is supported by abundant experimental evidence. What about the prediction concerning initiation or exertion of influence?

In Bales's studies (see Bales and Slater, 1955) it was found that group members who initiated more communication also received more communication and were perceived as having more influence. The question is then why do some group members exert more influence than others? EST proposes that status cues may be responsible for influence differentials.

In a study by Ridgeway, Berger and Smith (1985) it was made known prior to a group task that some subjects were men and others were women, that is, a diffuse status characteristic was involved. In the group task a number of items were presented simultaneously to both subjects, and they were instructed to respond as soon as they thought they knew the correct answer. It was found that males were more ready to give their answer than females. In another study Connor (1977) found that subjects who had higher competence provided the group answer more often than subjects who had lower competence. Finally, de Gilder (1991) investigated exertion and compliance in one study. First competence differentials were communicated. Thereafter half of the subjects first worked at a group task in which compliance was investigated. This task was similar to the well-known group task employed by Berger. Subsequently they had to work in circumstances that were similar to the one established by Connor (1977), i.e. exertion of influence was established. The other half of the subjects worked at the two group tasks in the reverse sequence. It appeared that more competent subjects complied less with the preliminary responses of their partner, but they initiated more influence than less competent subjects. Moreover, in all experimental conditions compliance and initiation of influence were negatively correlated.

To summarize, where Bales and his co-workers established that influence differentials always arise in discussion groups, EST makes it plausible that influence differentials arise in task groups because group members form performance expectations. The formation of performance expectations may be based on task cues about specific abilities, so-called specific status characteristics. Performance expectations may also be based on rather general cues like gender, seniority, and occupational status. These diffuse status characteristics are culturally associated with high and low ability, and are not self-evidently related to particular tasks. EST predicts that unless such a characteristic is (made) explicitly irrelevant, it is employed by group members as a basis for forming expectations.

Contrary to Bales's studies, within the EST tradition it was possible to investigate the causal relation between group members' relative positions on status characteristics (higher or lower) and influence differentials. Two kinds of influence differentials were distinguished: compliance, or acceptance, of influence, and exertion, or initiation, of influence. It was found that group members having a higher position on a status characteristic accepted less influence and initiated more influence than group members having a lower position. As for the strength of the influence differentials, as it appeared from differences in influence rates between group members having a higher and group members having a lower position on a status characteristic, it was shown that expectations based on more relevant cues, that is, cues that are perceived as more strongly associated with the group task, have a stronger effect in establishing influence differentials than cues that are perceived to have a weaker association with the group task.

BEHAVIOURAL EVENTS

A contrast between the above-reported studies originating from EST and Bales's studies is that in Bales's studies, group members could influence one another during group interaction, whereas in the EST experiments, one-sided compliance and exertion or initiation were investigated. Moreover, whereas EST is concerned with the emergence of influence differentials as a consequence of performance differentials derived from status cues, there is less emphasis on consequences of group interaction itself, and a relevant question is whether a priori performance differentials are so strong that they have a greater effect on the influence differentials than do behavioural events during group interaction.

A study by Levinger (1959) suggests that behavioural events during group interaction are at least as important in establishing power or influence rankings in small groups as are a priori available status cues. In dyadic groups, where there was always one stooge (an accomplice of the experimenter) and one real subject, in the course of a number of trials dyads had to make decisions about the best building site for a number of buildings, such as a school, a fire station, and a supermarket. Before the group task, subjects were informed that the other stooge had more or less experience, i.e. performance expectations were established. During the group decision task, the real subject and the stooge initially disagreed upon the site to be chosen in a number of the trials. In the acceptance condition, the stooge complied with the proposals of the subject on most of these trials, whereas in the rejection condition the stooge maintained his or her initial choice. The results indicated that, at the end of the group task, subjects estimated their influence to be greater when it had been suggested that they had more experience than when it had initially been suggested that they had less experience. Influence ascribed to self was greater in the acceptance than in the rejection condition. The results suggest that the effect of experience on ascribed influence was much smaller than the effect of the behavioural events, i.e. acceptance and rejection of influence during the task.

As such, the results of the Levinger experiment fit quite well with the prediction of EST in that it was shown that experience and behavioural events served as status characteristics or cues that together led to performance expectations and to influence differentials. However, the larger effect of the behavioural events suggests that, during group interactions, behavioural events may be more important in establishing influence differentials than a priori competence differentials like experience. This seems to be more true for task groups that have a longer history of interaction than the groups employed in EST research.

Further, it should be noted that although Levinger's study may be considered a demonstration of the plausibility of EST before EST had been proposed,

Levinger's theoretical concepts are slightly different. He argues that group members have certain resources (such as experience) at their disposal and that these resources are used to pursue personal and group goals. As group members start to interact with other members they receive initial information about one another, which leads to the formation of first perceptions. These first perceptions determine their first actions towards the others, and their actions are likely to modify their perceptions of one another. Their behaviour, in turn, will be shaped according to their modified perception and will probably induce a readjustment of the group members' initial perceptions, that is, it is conceived that inter-personal perception and behaviour develop as the products of a circular process of interaction, and that the individual continually generates and receives information concerning the individual's own and others' social resources. Admittedly, this supposed process does not differ greatly from the process proposed by EST; however, it does pay more attention to the dynamic properties of the interaction process of groups that have to solve problems.

COMMUNICATION PROCESSES

Reasons to communicate

In Bales's groups, members communicated. A relevant question is why group members in task groups communicate at all. There are several important and related reasons to communicate: (1) to test reality; (2) to organize the task; (3) to organize the group itself; (4) to solve conflicts of interests; (5) to solve cognitive conflicts; and (6) to make group decisions. In the following we will explain these reasons and some of the relevant research findings in somewhat greater detail.

1 *Reality testing.* When one is confronted with a task environment one may not be very confident about what the task entails, what a proper solution of the task is, etc. Social comparison theory (Festinger, 1954) proposes that one turns to similar others to reduce one's uncertainty about the task environment (see further chapter 3), that is, one turns to fellow group members.

2 *The organization of the collective task.* Another reason to turn to fellow group members is to arrive at a common interpretation of the task, i.e. one has to build up sensing, testing and effecting schemes so that the collective task can be solved. As we argued in the introduction to chapter 3, this has descrip- tive and prescriptive implications. Descriptive implications refer to charac-teristics of the task itself, whereas prescriptive implications refer to how the task should be performed. Communication in groups about the task serves both goals simultaneously: if one has reached agreement about what the ingredients of a task are, a consensual interpretation regarding how the task should be performed has also been achieved.

3 *The organization of the group itself.* Group tasks usually cannot be per-formed without a division of labour, and communication is required if the

group is to arrive at an agreement about who has to do what. In this context, too, communication has both descriptive and prescriptive implications: consensus about which roles can be distinguished and assignment of these roles or task positions to specific group members (description) has implications for how these group members should function, i.e. for their prescribed behaviours. It seems self-evident that in the early stages of interaction within a new group a larger proportion of the communication will be devoted to the organization of the group itself than during later stages, when the structure of the group is more established.

4 *Solving conflicts of interests.* As explained in chapter 4 on reflective tuning, group members may differ as to their expected rewards or profits. In groups, several kinds of rewards may be distinguished: there are not only rewards for group performance (see chapter 4) but also rewards implied by the division of labour, since some positions (e.g. leader) may be evaluated more positively than other ones (e.g. followers). And even when there are no problems with the division of labour (for example, because the task does not require a subdivision of roles), a problem may arise about who will exert more influence during group interaction, that is, a struggle for dominance may emerge.

5 *Solving cognitive conflicts.* A cognitive conflict may concern the organization of the task or the organization of group members, or a combination of task and group. Because chapter 6 on managerial tuning will deal with cognitive conflicts as far as the organization of the group is concerned, we will restrict ourselves here to cognitive conflicts concerning tasks.

When a group member finds other group members interpreting the collective task differently, he or she is faced with a cognitive conflict: should that member believe his or her own perceptions and interpretations, or should the views of others be trusted? Although individual group members may respond differently to features of the task, the demand for uniformity of opinions generated by such a situation seems inevitable. Asch (see also chapter 3) describes this cognitive conflict by suggesting that,

> the individual comes to experience a world that he shares with others. He perceives that the surroundings include him, as well as the others, and that he is in the same relation to the surroundings as the others. He notes that he, as well as the others, is converging upon the same object and responding to its identical properties. Joint action and mutual understanding require the relations of intelligibility and structural simplicity. In these terms the 'pull' towards the group becomes understandable.
>
> (Asch, 1952, p. 484)

A consequence of this is that when group members do *not* have the idea that they share a common surrounding, they are not inclined to experience a cognitive conflict, and consequently no converging or conforming will take place. An illustration of this is the study of Crutchfield (1955) in which subjects were asked to express their preferences in aesthetic matters. It appeared that in a group session, which was comparable to the one employed by Asch involving visual judgements (see chapter 3), virtually no subject changed preference.

6 *Making group decisions*. Often the group's ultimate task is to solve a problem and to make a decision. Examples of decision-making groups come easily to mind: committees deciding on investments, teams of physicians choosing one of several therapies available to a patient, juries bringing in verdicts, appointment committees choosing one of several candidates, cabinet members adopting a political course of action. Making group decisions can be conceived of as a process of problem solving with four phases (e.g. Zander, 1982). First, the problem has to be identified and defined; second, possible solutions have to be generated; next, one of these alternatives has to be chosen; and finally, action has to be taken to implement the chosen solution. Each phase may, in turn, require sub-decisions, involving the five foregoing communication processes.

Communication rules

The communication of group members necessary to reach consensus is a complex process, because there are a number of prerequisites for successful communication. We restrict our discussion to intentional verbal transmission of information.

According to Rommetveit (1974), subjects must have established a 'shared social reality', i.e. must have a common definition of the here and now of the situation; otherwise the communication is doomed to failure. Another precondition is that subjects share their perceptions of the ways in which the communication process is regulated. People have to agree on the premises underlying the communication process, for example, on interpersonal relations and appropriate language use given these relations and the social situation; otherwise a misunderstanding will result. A third precondition for successful communication is the ability and willingness to take the perspective of the other persons involved; otherwise the communicator cannot formulate what he or she wants to transmit in such a way that the listeners understand it. In order to fulfil these preconditions, subjects have to follow a number of prescriptions, which have been coined by Higgins 'general rules of the communication game'. Higgins formulated seven rules for communicators and six rules for message recipients.

For communicators:
1 Communicators should take the audience's or recipient's characteristics into account.
2 Communicators should convey the truth as they see it.
3 Communicators should try to be understood (i.e. be coherent and comprehensible).
4 Communicators should give neither too much nor too little information.
5 Communicators should be relevant (i.e. stick to the point).

6 Communicators should produce a message that is appropriate to the context and circumstances.
7 Communicators should produce a message that is appropriate to their communicative intent or purpose.

For message recipients:
1 Recipients should take the communicator's or source's characteristics into account.
2 Recipients should determine the communicator's commmunicative intent or purpose.
3 Recipients should take the context and circumstances into account.
4 Recipients should pay attention to the message and be prepared to receive it.
5 Recipients should try to understand the message.
6 Recipients, when possible, should provide feedback to the communicator concerning their interpretation or understanding of the message.

(Higgins, 1981, p. 348)

In the ideal situation all these rules are to be followed during the communication process; ignoring these rules will hamper the communication process, which may lead to mutual irritation, and defective decision-making may result. However, following these rules may have unintended negative implications. For example, if communicators follow rules 1, 3, 6 and 7, they have a mental set to transmit information, while message recipients following rules 3, 4 and 5 have a mental set to receive information. The influence of these two different mental sets on the processing of information was investigated for the first time by Zajonc (1960) in his research on cognitive tuning. Experimental studies by Zajonc and others (see Guerin and Innes, 1989) indicate that people who are tuned to produce messages have a tendency to unify and to sharpen cognitively the information they want to transmit to others. They are also reluctant to consider additional complicating information, and they reject additional inconsistent information. The simplifying and biasing of information in order to transmit the message to the recipient may, in turn, affect the communicator her- or himself. For example, Higgins (1981) has demonstrated that subjects who had to describe a stimulus person to another person simplified the available information and took the attitude of the recipient towards the stimulus person into account in formulating their message. Afterwards, the cognitions of the communicators became increasingly consistent with the description they had given in the message.

On the other hand, subjects who are tuned to receive communication have a tendency to keep their cognitive organization somewhat more flexible and general. However, recipients of communication may misjudge the characteristics or intentions of the communicator and accordingly may form an inadequate mental representation of the information in the message. Recipients may also underestimate the amount of sharpening in the message by the communicator. For example, Higgins (1981) has shown that labels used by communicators to describe a somewhat ambiguous stimulus person strongly influenced recipients' memory of that person. In some cases such an influence may be even stronger than the communicators intended.

In summary, successful communication is a delicate and fragile process. It requires at least some 'implicit insight' into the 'rules of the game' and skills to follow these rules. However, it also requires 'intuitive insight' into unintended consequences of following these rules.

CONFLICTS OF INTEREST AND COMMUNICATION

Groups may develop a struggle for influence among the members during inter-action, that is, a struggle for dominance. Mazur (1985) argues that usually influence differentials emerge in a cooperative way, because in most groups there exists consensus about group members' positions, a theoretical argument that has also been put forward by EST (Berger *et al.*, 1980). However, when there is no consensus, a competition for influence may arise. In investigating dominance contests, Mazur has mainly focused on non-verbal communication. For example, facial expressions, such as the position of the eyebrows, appeared to be related to perceived dominance, and group members who, at the initiation of an interaction, stare down at their fellow group members appeared to receive more behaviour opportunities during subsequent interaction, for example, they were allowed to speak more often than others.

Whereas Mazur (1985) suggests that a contest for power or dominance might only occur in competitive situations, Mulder's power theory argues that power or dominance contests always occur in groups (Mulder, 1977). He posits that people always strive to have more influence, and the more so the more influence they already have. Mulder, making a distinction between 'upward behaviour' directed by less powerful group members towards more powerful members of the group and the 'downward behaviour' of more powerful towards less powerful members of the group, makes predictions concerning the strength of upward and down-ward behaviours depending on the magnitude of difference in power in a group with a well-established hierarchical order. He predicts that a more powerful member will show a negative attitude towards less powerful members and that this tendency will be stronger when the power difference between the two group members is greater. Conversely, a less powerful member will have a positive attitude towards the more powerful member, again the more so as the difference in power between the more and less powerful members is greater. In a number of experiments Mulder (1977) established that the attitudes of more powerful members were more negative the more remote (the more 'steps' away) the less powerful group members were, i.e. more powerful members protected their higher power positions less when a less powerful person was in power. More interesting with respect to the potential for conflicts of interest among less powerful members was the finding that less powerful members showed a more positive attitude towards the more powerful member as there were fewer steps between themselves and the more powerful member. Moreover, less powerful members showed a stronger aspiration to take over the position of the most powerful member as the number of steps they were from the most powerful member decreased. The fact that it was a cooperative task that had to be performed in these experimental studies suggests that even in cooperative groups some conflict of interest in terms of what Mazur (1985) coined a 'dominance contest' may arise: even in cooperative task settings some competition for higher positions in a power hierarchy may emerge (see also Bruins and Wilke, 1992). Although Mulder did not investigate actual communication, it seems self-evident that some of the communication in groups will be about status protection and status pursuit by more and less powerful members, respectively. It seems plausible to propose that a larger proportion of the communication will be devoted to power contests when there is more competition for scarce resources within groups, for example, for the prestige attached to a higher power position.

COGNITIVE CONFLICTS AND COMMUNICATION

If groups experience cognitive conflicts between members concerning tasks, they try to reduce task uncertainty by achieving common standards or norms. In chapter 3 we discussed laboratory experiments on cognitive conflicts. We now turn to two studies which illustrate the influence of group cohesion (Cartwright, 1968) on the process of achieving common norms.

A field study on the operation of standards in informal groups was performed by Festinger, Schachter and Back (1950). By means of interviews, they determined the cohesiveness of various residential courts in two housing projects and the attitudes of the residents towards a tenants' organization. They showed that cohesive courts in which there were a large number of mutual connections were likely to have more uniformity in attitudes towards the organization and more uniformity of behaviour in the degree to which members participated in the organization, that is, highly cohesive courts had fewer members who were not actively involved in the organization. It was also shown that persons who were deviant with respect to the standards within a court were less likely to be accepted as friends by the other people living there, and the more so the higher the interconnectedness or cohesion within a court.

So there is some evidence that in more cohesive groups there is a greater pressure towards uniformity and less tolerance for deviance than in less cohesive groups. Why do deviant group members succumb to pressures towards uniformity? Cartwright (1968) argues that this is so partly because group members who side with the majority expect to receive rewards like social approval and esteem from their fellow group members, whereas deviants are likely to receive punishments like social disapproval and even expulsion from the group. And because the likelihood that punishments will be administered is greater if others know that a member is deviant than if he is successful in concealing his non-conformity, Cartwright argues, behaviour in public is likely to be more conforming than private behaviour and overt acts are more likely to conform to group expectations than covert beliefs, an insight that agrees with what we have labelled 'reflective tuning': group members make assessments of forthcoming rewards and punishments.

As Cartwright (1968) has explained, in experimental studies cohesion is measured in various ways. In the study of Festinger *et al.* (1950) the investigators asked the residents to name their friends in the entire community and then examined the number of in-court friends as a proportion of the total number of friends. Other methods of measuring the cohesiveness of groups are to ask group members for an evaluation of their group, to request them to express to what extent they identify with the group and whether they desire to remain in their group. Another question then is why tolerance towards deviant group members is lower in highly cohesive groups than in less cohesive groups. Here Cartwright refers to what we have labelled 'reflective tuning': group members in highly cohesive groups derive their satisfaction or rewards more from their ingroup, they are more concerned with the reality testing and goal locomotion of their group than members of less cohesive groups, who presumably have more rewarding alternatives outside their group. Since deviance in a group is threatening to the goals of the group as a whole, deviance by group members might mean that group goals will not be reached and that no group rewards will be forthcoming. Since members of highly cohesive groups are more dependent on their rewards from the functioning of their present ingroup than members of less cohesive groups, any blocking of the group goals by deviant group members will be experienced as more negative in highly cohesive groups. Since this is so, members of highly cohesive groups are more inclined to pursue uniformity and act against deviance than are members of less cohesive groups.

Experimental evidence for this line of reasoning is provided by an experimental study of Schachter (1951) with four kinds of clubs. In highly cohesive clubs, members had indicated beforehand that they were 'moderately' to 'extremely' interested in the club's activities, whereas less cohesive clubs consisted of individuals who had indicated that they were not interested in their club's activities. High- and low-cohesive clubs had either to discuss a topic that was highly relevant or that had no relevance for their specific club. Accordingly, each of the four clubs represented one of the conditions in the cohesion (high versus low) × relevance (high versus low) factorial experimental design. Each club consisted of five to seven members. In each of the clubs there were three accomplices of the experimenter, each of whom played a role. The 'conformist' always agreed with the naive subjects; the 'deviant' always disagreed; and the 'slider' disagreed during the first part of the discussion but conformed to the judgements of the majority during the second half of the discussion. Before the discussion each group member read the case of 'Johnny Rocco', which consisted of the short life history of a young juvenile delinquent; the story ended as Johnny was awaiting his sentence for a minor crime. The question was, 'What should be done with this kid?' Several answers were provided, ranging from 'providing Johnny with warmth and love' to 'Johnny should be harshly punished'. After reading the case, group members were invited to state their initial position on this love versus punishment scale. Subsequently the discussion took place for forty-five minutes. Trained observers recorded who spoke to whom at what time during the discussion. After the discussion several measures, such as sociometric rankings and assignments to more or less important committees, were taken.

The results indicated a number of important regularities. First, it was demonstrated that the deviant was rejected more than the conformist and the slider. This appeared both from the sociometric measures (the deviant was less frequently chosen as a desirable member of the club) and the assignment to committees, that is, deviants were assigned to the least desirable committee. Second, with 'cohesiveness' held constant, more than in discussing an irrelevant topic, rejection of the deviant was stronger in clubs that considered the Johnny Rocco case highly relevant to their club's primary mission. Third, with 'relevance' held constant, the deviant was rejected more often in the high-cohesive than in the low-cohesive clubs. Also interesting were the results on the communication process. It appeared that, throughout the discussion, the conforming role player received less communication than the deviant and the slider. Communication addressed to the deviant increased over time, but at a later point in the discussion the communication decreased, demonstrating that pressures towards uniformity were operating but that at a certain moment the naive group members gave up trying to persuade the deviant. When the slider took a deviant position he or she was treated like the deviant. However, after 'conversion' the slider was treated more like the conforming role player. The above-reported results indicate that some of the communication within a group is aimed at solving cognitive conflicts. The antecedents and consequences of this type of communication have been described by Festinger (1950), and Wheeler has provided a recent summary, which we will cite in the following:

Pressures to communicate:
1 increase with perceived opinion discrepancy in the group,
2 increase with the relevance of the opinion to group functions, and
3 increase with the cohesiveness of the group (resultant of all the forces acting upon the members to remain in the group).

Pressures to communicate to a particular person in the group:
1 increase with the opinion discrepancy between the communicator and that person,
2 decrease with the perception that the person is not a member of the group or is not wanted as a member of that group, and
3 increase with the perception that communication is likely to change the person in the desired direction.

The amount of change in opinion resulting from having received communication:
1 increases with pressures toward uniformity in the group,
2 increases with the resultant force for the recipient to remain in the group, and

3 decreases to the degree that the opinion is anchored in other groups or serves important need satisfying functions for the person.

The tendency to change the composition of the psychological group (pushing members out of the group):
1 increases as the perceived discrepancy in opinion increases, and
2 increases as the cohesiveness of the group and the relevance of the issue to the group increases.

(Wheeler, 1991, p. 4)

As explained in chapter 3 (on minorities and innovation), Moscovici (1985) has questioned the tacit assumption in the study of Schachter (1951) that it is always the majority of the group that exerts pressure towards uniformity and that it is always the minority that shifts in opinion.

In sum, the above-reported insights and empirical evidence suggest that part of the communication within groups stems from pressures towards uniformity. Pressures towards uniformity or consensus apparently serve two aims, namely achieving a collective representation of the task environment and group loco-motion towards task completion.

DECISION MAKING AND COMMUNICATION

Groupthink

An interesting line of research on group decision making, with which most of the intra-group conflict and influence processes we have discussed so far are related, was initiated by Janis (1972). He was shocked by the decision of the Kennedy administration in 1961 to invade the Bay of Pigs in Cuba in order to combat Cuba's communist president Castro. The invasion was a complete failure. Janis tried to find social psychological explanations for the occurrence of this dis-astrous decision, as well as for a number of comparable political and military fiascos in recent history. Well-documented cases are those of the Chamberlain cabinet, negotiating with Hitler (1938), Pearl Harbor (1941), the Truman cabinet, becoming involved in the Korean War (1950), the decisions of the Johnson cabinet concerning the escalation of the Vietnam War (1964–1965), and the Nixon group on the Watergate affair (1972–1973) (Tetlock, Peterson, McGuire, Chang and Feld, 1992).

These poor decisions are usually contrasted with two historical cases which were handled extremely well, the Marshall Plan (1947), which consisted of economic support for Europe from the USA, and the Kennedy cabinet's handling of the Cuban missile crisis (1962) (Tetlock *et al.*, 1992). In his theoretical analyses of the bad and the good decisions, Janis (1972; 1982; Janis and Mann, 1977) developed a theory or model of 'groupthink', which he defined as 'a mode of thinking that people engage in when they are deeply involved in a cohesive in-group, when the members' strivings for unanimity override their motivation to realistically appraise alternative courses of action' (Janis, 1982, p. 9). The model of groupthink as depicted in Figure 5.1 describes the antecedent conditions and the consequences of groupthink. Janis (1982) discusses three groups of factors that may contribute to the occurrence of groupthink. The first factor (A in Figure 5.1) is the strong attractiveness of the group to its members, the high value of group membership; in short, the cohesiveness of the group. Older experimental evidence for the relation between group cohesion and pressures towards uniformity has been presented by Schachter (1951) in an experiment that is described in the preceding section of this chapter.

A second group of factors (B–1 in Figure 5.1) concerns the environment and the internal organization of the group. In most cases studied by Janis, the group had isolated itself from the environment in such a way that possible relevant information from outside was simply ignored. Moreover, in most cases, the group leader (e.g. Kennedy, Johnson, Nixon) had a disproportionate amount of influence during the discussion on the courses of action they proposed. In the section on Expectation States Theory we have explained why it is that leaders have a disproportionate amount of influence, i.e. reject more influence and accept less influence than regular group members.

For the most part, the influence of the leader(s) on the discussions was not counteracted by extensive procedural rules which could have resulted in a more balanced information search and appraisal. These procedures would have been all the more useful because the group members shared a common background and ideology from the start. The third set of factors that Janis distinguished (B–2 in Figure 5.1) includes the specific situational circumstances of the group: the situation was experienced as stressful because of the pressures to reach an immediate decision. Also, some group members probably did not have enough self-confidence or self-esteem to oppose the proposals of the principal decision maker.

Together these factors lead to groupthink, which has, in turn, three sorts of consequences. Groupthink is considered by Janis as a 'disease' with eight 'symptoms' that are listed in box C of Figure 5.1. Symptoms 1 to 4 are ways to restore the balance between the sources of stress and emotional stability. If the power of the group is overestimated, if rationalizations for the course of action are available and if extreme negative stereotypes of outgroups are formed, difficult and costly decisions seem to be more justified. However, the group can only make these stressful decisions if every group member agrees or at least appears to agree publicly. The group exerts strong pressure towards uniformity. If there are minority members, their disagreeing views are censored by themselves or by other group members, with an illusion of unanimity as a result. During concurrence seeking, a minority in the meaning of Moscovici (1985) has no reason to be confident, and is not in a position to be consistent because of the antecedent conditions. So, according to Janis, groupthink leads to defective decision making (box D in Figure 5.1), which in turn raises the probability of an unsuccessful outcome of the decision process. The two political decisions described by Janis (1982) that were successful (the Marshall Plan, 1947, and the Cuban missile

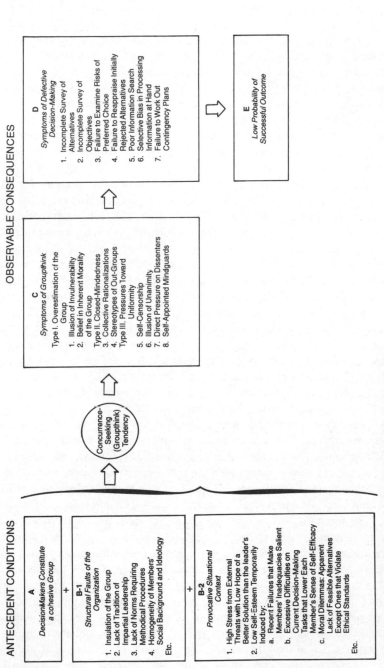

Figure 5.1 Theoretical analysis of groupthink (Janis, 1982)

Copyright © 1982 by Houghton Mifflin Company. Used with permission.

OBSERVABLE CONSEQUENCES

ANTECEDENT CONDITIONS

A
DecisionMakers Constitute a cohesive Group

+

B-1
Structural Faults of the Organization

1. Insulation of the Group
2. Lack of Tradition of Impartial Leadership
3. Lack of Norms Requiring Methodical Procedures
4. Homogeneity of Members' Social Background and Ideology

Etc.

+

B-2
Provocative Situational Context

1. High Stress from External Threats with Low Hope of a Better Solution than the leader's
2. Low Self-Esteem Temporarily Induced by:
   a. Recent Failures that Make Members' Inadequacies Salient
   b. Excessive Difficulties on Current Decision-Making Tasks that Lower Each Member's Sense of Self-Efficacy
   c. Moral Dilemmas: Apparent Lack of Feasible Alternatives Except Ones that Violate Ethical Standards

Etc.

Concurrence-Seeking (Groupthink) Tendency

C
Symptoms of Groupthink

Type I. Overestimation of the Group
1. Illusion of Invulnerability
2. Belief in Inherent Morality of the Group

Type II. Closed-Mindedness
3. Collective Rationalizations
4. Stereotypes of Out-Groups

Type III. Pressures Toward Uniformity
5. Self-Censorship
6. Illusion of Unanimity
7. Direct Pressure on Dissenters
8. Self-Appointed Mindguards

D
Symptoms of Defective Decision-Making

1. Incomplete Survey of Alternatives
2. Incomplete Survey of Objectives
3. Failure to Examine Risks of Preferred Choice
4. Failure to Reappraise Initially Rejected Alternatives
5. Poor Information Search
6. Selective Bias in Processing Information at Hand
7. Failure to Work Out Contingency Plans

E
Low Probability of Successful Outcome

crisis, 1962) had different antecedent conditions, especially the structural aspects of the organization and the situational context. To summarize, groupthink may be conceived of as a strong mixture of cognitive conflict, pressures towards uniformity, the absence of a consistent minority (cf. chapter 3), and one-sided influence potential, plus restricted communication processes in which the rules of the communication game (Higgins, 1981) were violated.

Various criticisms have been directed at Janis's analyses (see Tetlock *et al.*, 1992). The first criticism is methodological. It has been argued that the case study method used by Janis does not permit the strong tests of hypotheses needed to confirm or reject the theoretical model. On the other hand, simulation of these decisions and group conditions in a laboratory situation (see, for example, Flowers, 1977) is weak in comparison to the real world circumstances. The second criticism is theoretical, and it concerns the causal relations depicted in Figure 5.1. In particular, the relative influence of the cohesion factor has been a topic of debate (Longley and Pruitt, 1980; Steiner, 1982). In an elaborate recent study, Tetlock *et al.* (1992) used a new methodology, Group Dynamics Q Sort (GDQS) to analyse the cases described by Janis (1982) and two other decisions; that of the Ford cabinet to rescue the captured ship *Mayaguez* by launching an attack on Cambodia (1975), and the Carter cabinet on the Iran hostage rescue attempt in 1980. The GDQS consists of one hundred bipolar statements on cards that describe group processes; for example, 'The group leader is insulated from criticism / The group leader is exposed to a wide range of views and arguments'. Judges had to read historical accounts of the group processes and to place each card in one of three stacks. In the first stack had to be placed all those cards for which the first statement best characterized the group; in the second deck had to be placed all those cards for which the second statement was characteristic for the group. The remaining cards formed the third stack. Next, the judges had to reconsider each statement and make a finer division of the cards into nine stacks, ranging from, 'the first statement is extremely characteristic' (score 1), to 'neither upper nor lower statement is characteristic' (score 5), and finally to 'the second statement is extremely characteristic' (score 9). The number of cards in each stack was fixed for all judges, following a normal distribution (e.g. 5 cards had to be placed in the first and last stacks, 18 cards had to be placed in the middle stack). The reliability of the resulting Q-sort scores could be estimated in three ways: agreement between judges on the same historical text; agreement between different historical accounts; and agreement between conceptually related statements. The three reliabilities appeared to be sufficient. The GDQS data made it possible to test Janis's theoretical model (Figure 5.1) and a reduced Janis model, without links between box A, B–2 and the Concurrence Seeking Tendency. The reduced model could predict groupthink as well as the original Janis model. So, the single most important factor leading to groupthink consists of structural faults in the organization of the group (box B-1 in Figure 5.1). Tetlock *et al.* (1992) also found that groups with groupthink tendencies differed from groups without concurrence seeking in the following respects in particular: (1) the leader restricted the range of viewpoints consulted; and (2) he was insensitive to other points of view; in addition (3) the information flow between the leader and lower levels was restricted; and (4) the communication was highly formal, with few breaches of protocol or sharp disagreements. The results also showed a very strong relationship between symptoms of groupthink and symptoms of defective decision making.

These results were in agreement with a field study of panels evaluating medical developments (Vinokur, Burnstein, Sechrest and Wortman, 1985). The products of the discussions were reports that summarized the group consensus on a new technology, for example a total hip-joint replacement. Vinokur *et al.* constructed various measurements to evaluate the quality of the conference process and the reports. The quality of the reports appeared to be strongly related to the behaviour of the chairpersons, who facilitated or inhibited focused discussions, helped or hindered the identification of areas of agreement and disagreement, and generally encouraged or discouraged participation.

In sum, the studies on groupthink clearly demonstrate that leaders may influence communicative tuning in groups. Their behaviour has implications for reality testing, for the organization of the task and the group, for the resolution of cognitive conflicts and conflicts of interest, and finally, for decision making.

Pooling of unshared information

In the case of groupthink, defective decision making can be explained primarily by the behavioural style of the chairperson and various motivational factors within the group. In an interesting line of research, Stasser (see, for a review: Stasser, 1992) focused attention on an additional, non-motivational factor, which may contribute to the one-sidedness of group discussions. He argues that an important aspect of decision making in groups is the presentation of items of information relevant to the discussion topic at hand; this information is made available to the group members beforehand and is to be recalled during the discussion. Shared information is information available to each of the group members before discussion. In that case all group members receive all arguments before discussion. Unshared information is the information that is known to some of the group members prior to group discussion, but not to others.

What is the effect of unshared information on decision making? The sampling advantage of shared information over unshared information (Stasser, Taylor and Hanna, 1989) may lead to what Stasser (1988) names 'hidden profiles' and ineffective decision making. A hidden profile 'occurs when the total profile of information available to the group favours one decision alternative, but the pattern of information received by individual members before discussion favours another alternative' (Stasser, 1992, p. 158). As a hypothetical example, imagine a three-person group which has a choice between two alternatives. The group members share three items of information supporting A, and one item supporting B. In addition, each group member has one unique item supporting B. In this case, each individual profile of information favours alternative A, with three items, while the hidden collective profile supports alternative B, with four items of information.

In a study by Stasser and Titus (1985) subjects had to choose one of three candidates for presidency. If all available information was presented individually, 67 per cent of the subjects favoured candidate A. If four-person groups were composed in which all information was shared before discussion, 83 per cent of the group decisions were in favour of candidate A. If the same information was divided between group members, only 18 per cent chose candidate A. In a later study (Stasser, Taylor and Hanna, 1989) it was found that three- and six-person groups discussed 45 per cent of the information items that were shared by all members, and 18 per cent of the unshared items. In addition, it was found that unshared items, even if they were introduced, were less often repeated and less often discussed than shared items.

Finally, it was found that procedural instructions to group members to discuss all the information available to them led to more discussion about unshared information, but increased the difference between shared and unshared information. For example, in six-person groups, 19 per cent of unshared items were discussed; due to the procedural instructions this number increased to 23 per cent. However, without instructions 58 per cent of shared items were discussed; due to the instructions this number increased to 67 per cent.

So, pooling of unshared information cannot easily be enhanced by procedural instructions. The results of a recent study (Stasser and Stewart, 1992), however, suggest that the sampling disadvantage of unshared information may depend upon the group members' perception of the nature of the task. Groups had to discuss a murder case under the (shared) impression that sufficient evidence was presented to determine the guilty suspect (problem-solving task set), or that insufficient evidence (judgemental task set) was available. If critical information was unshared before discussion, 35 per cent of groups with a judgemental task set identified the guilty suspect, while 65 per cent of the groups with a problem-solving task set succeeded in doing this. If all critical information was shared before discussion, the frequency of correct group responses was more than 90 per cent. Thus the sampling disadvantage of unshared information may be ameliorated by the belief that the task has a demonstrably correct answer.

So, hidden profiles that are evoked by unshared information may be less of a problem to a group when the group focuses on problem solving, which may be another way to reduce groupthink.

CONCLUSIONS AND SUMMARY

Besides engaging in cognitive and reflective tuning, group members also communicate. An important feature of communication in groups is that group members differ widely in the communication they send and receive, which is in turn related to influence initiation and acceptance of influence or conformity. Expectation States Theory is able to explain these influence differentials. Expectation States Theory postulates that group members search for cues to determine how much each of the group members may contribute to the group task. These cues are called status characteristics. In task groups competence differentials quite often serve as a status characteristic. It has been shown that more competent group members initiate more and accept less influence than less competent group members.

In addition to the organization of the collective task emphasized in Expectation States Theory, there are a number of other interrelated reasons for group members to communicate: reality testing, the organization of the group itself, the resolution of cognitive conflicts and conflicts of interest, and decision making. This chapter has presented some insights and research findings that demonstrate the implications of these interrelated reasons to communicate.

First it was shown that in order to build up a 'shared reality', communication rules are necessary, and the general rules of this communication game were explained. Second, communication may result from a conflict of interest, because some group members may strive for dominance in the pecking order of the group. Third, communication is necessary for solving cognitive conflicts, and the factors that affect the pressure towards uniformity in groups was described. Fourth, communication is necessary to make decisions. Antecedent and consequent conditions of 'groupthink' were discussed. It was shown how different behaviours of group leaders may induce or reduce the tendency towards 'groupthink' with dramatic consequences. Lastly, it was explained that it may be difficult for group members to pool unshared information, and that unshared information may have consequences for the kinds of decisions group members make.

Chapter 6

Structural tuning

In task groups there is a task and there are group members. In the previous chapters we argued that group members organize the task and the group by means of cognitive, reflective and communicative processes.

The central theme of the present chapter is that these processes lead to the emergence of structures. The concept 'structure' may be defined as a cognitive (descriptive) and normative (prescriptive) social representation of how parts (i.e. group members and tasks) are interrelated. It is a social representation because, at a certain moment during group interaction, group members may reach consensus about how they relate to the task and to other group members. It implies cognitions or descriptions because group members are more or less aware that specific relations among group members and regarding the task have emerged. The concept of structure also implies norms, prescriptions, or rules of conduct, since the agreement about how group members do relate to one another and to the group task also has implications for how group members should relate to one another and to the group task. Furthermore, structure may be considered a product of cognitive, reflective and communicative processes within a task group that restricts subsequent cognitive, reflective and communicative processes within the group. This does not mean that in permanent groups a specific structure exists forever: new information about the task environment and/or about the relations among group members may give rise to 'new' cognitive, reflective and communicative processes, that is, structure is a consensually achieved description and prescription of the ongoing task and the group members' interrelatedness at a given moment in time.

Lastly, in task groups there is not one structure or one representation of how task and group members are organized. Several aspects of task group functioning may be distinguished. For example, the pattern of liking relationships ('socio-emotional structure'), the pattern of who influences whom ('influence structure'), the structure of how outcomes are distributed among group members ('outcomes structure'), the structure of who usually communicates with whom ('the communication structure'), the consensual representation of the task ('the task structure') and the pattern of who is assigned to which subtask so that the total group task can be performed ('the role structure') may be distinguished in a group.

GROUP STRUCTURES

In the following we will elucidate our approach by reporting evidence of what is known about the formation and consequences of structure in task groups. However, before we do this, we first present four examples showing (a) interdependent structures in a task group; (b) interdependent structures in an organization; (c) the emergence and change of structures; and (d) the interrelatedness of influence, outcomes and task structure.

Interdependent structures in a task group

Oeser and Harary (1962, 1964) have developed a mathematical model starting from the idea that a task group can be decomposed into three classes of elements: tasks (or subtasks), positions and personnel. Tasks are the environmental demands imposed on the group. Usually tasks can be split up into subtasks. Division of labour among group members allows for specific task specializations or role positions, such as carpenter, electrician, plumber, bricklayer, architect. Personnel refers to 'sets of attributes' required of the real person assigned to a position. Personnel assigned to a position should have the attributes laid down in the 'worker specification'.

Group structure is depicted in terms of a set of dots, some representing personnel, some (sub)tasks and some positions. Connecting lines between dots are used to represent the various relations among the elements of the group structure. A distinction is made between formal and informal structure. Formal structure refers to relations among role positions, and to personnel assigned to positions and to (sub)tasks. People brought together in a formal relationship develop a number of informal relationships not specified in the formal structure of an organization; informal relationships may involve things such as liking, respecting and communication. The complete structure of a group is conceived of as the combination of all formal and informal relations among positions. To illustrate this, in Figure 6.1(a) a five-person factory is presented in terms of the relations among positions.

Similar structures (or mathematical graphs) could be drawn to represent the relations among tasks, the relationship between positions and tasks, and the relationship between persons and positions.

Figure 6.1(b) represents all possible relations of a particular person, P5, the second worker. The lines in the lower part of the figure indicate that position 5 is responsible for task elements t1, t2, t3 and t4. The dotted line above P5 indicates that this person has been assigned to the hierarchical position 5. We also see that P5 receives his instructions from the foreman, P3. The upper part of Figure 6.1(b) shows that P5 has established specific informal relations with persons at position 3 and position 4. We

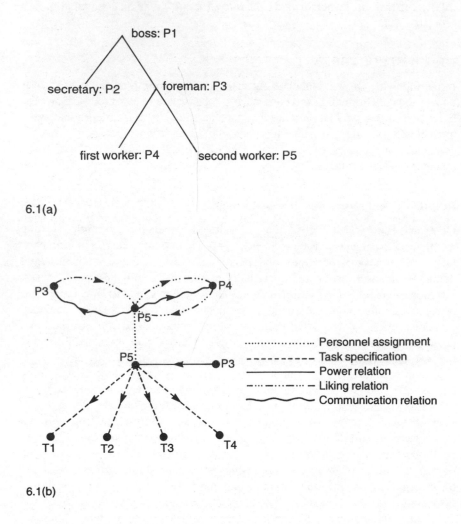

Figure 6.1 A five-person factory (adapted from Oeser and Harary, 1962)

see that P5 communicates with P3 and P4, but P3 and P4 do relatively little talking to him. Further on, we see that P5 does not like his foreman (P3), whereas P3 has positive feelings towards P5, and P5 and P4 show mutual liking.

Interdependent structures in large organizations

The above-presented example shows that in small groups several formal and informal structures may be distinguished and that a person's functioning in a work group is dependent on several formal and informal relations he might have. This is so not only for small task groups, like a five-person factory, but also for larger organizations. This was shown in a recent analysis (Wilke, 1987) that builds further on Mintzberg's approach to organizational structure (Mintzberg, 1979). In a large organization the complete task is divided so that the more general and abstract sensing, testing and effecting task levels are performed by the strategic top (board of directors), the intermediate level by middle management (e.g. plant managers) and the more specific task levels by the workers (e.g. assemblers). Mintzberg (1979) also makes a distinction between the formal and the informal organization. The formal organization may be described by a blueprint summarizing who is responsible (for information processing, testing and effecting) for which part of the total task. The informal organization pertains to all informal relations such as liking, informal communication, clique formation, etc. Mintzberg's main proposition is that the operation of organizations can only be understood if it is acknowledged that myriad interrelated (formal and informal) structures (and relations) are involved.

The emergence and change of structure

The above-presented examples suggest that in a group and in a large organization several structures may be distinguished: the formal structure, which is strongly related to the task structure, that is, the 'official' influence structure, and the informal structure that implies liking, informal communication and deference relations, which in turn also form structures or patterns of interrelatedness. Whyte (1948), in his field study of the restaurant industry, has shown what happens when small task groups increase in size, that is, turn into larger organizations. At stage 1 there is Tom Jones, a restaurant owner, who has two employees, but there is (almost) no division of labour – all three work as cooks, servers and dishwashers. So there are role positions (positions associated with subtasks), but there are no specific people assigned to these positions. At stage 2 the restaurant flourishes and additional workers are hired. There is now a staff of cooks, dishwashers and waitresses, that is, the beginning of a division of labour or task specification emerges, and Jones assigns himself the supervisor's role. At stage 3 the business grows in size, and because Jones has to hire extra personnel, it is impossible for him to supervise all the work. He hires a service supervisor and a food-production supervisor. One of his other employees is placed in charge of the dining-room as a working supervisor, and a head waiter is added to the staff to total bills for waitresses and to see that the food is served properly. At this stage Jones is a top management official and issues orders to his four second-line supervisors.

The Tom Jones study shows that as a task group increases in size, further task specifications (or differentiation in roles) are necessary to coordinate and to monitor the group's performance. Moreover, as the group grows, the number of formal relations (as described in this example) also increases. In the same vein, it may be assumed that informal relations also increase in number. Moreover, there is another aspect that deserves attention, namely the fact that during stage 1, Jones and his co-workers apparently acted on the basis of mutual adjustment, whereas at stage 3 more stringent norms or rules of conduct were introduced. In sum, as a task group increases in size, the number of formal and informal relations also increases, and it becomes necessary both to build in more monitoring by hiring medium-level managers and to introduce a stronger normative structure, that is, a pattern of rules applying to each of the role positions and the organizations at large.

The interrelatedness of influence, outcomes and task structure

As equity theory (see chapter 4) suggests, group members who have a higher (role) position in the formal structure of the group are likely to have more formal influence and should also be allowed higher outcomes in terms of salary, fringe benefits etc., suggesting that formal positions are strongly related to the outcomes structure. Whyte (1948) has shown that in work groups informal relations also have consequences for the outcomes structure derived from the task itself. He focuses on the prestige structure in a vegetable-preparation station of the Mammoth restaurant, consisting of eight women. He observed that the vegetables were ordered from very attractive (e.g. parsley and chives) to ordinary and undesirable (e.g. onions). It appeared that the women with more prestige tended to work on the more desirable vegetables, whereas the women with less prestige were assigned to work on the undesirable vegetables. And even when all women were working on the same vegetable, the high prestige workers handled later (i.e. cleaner) stages in the process of preparation. This real life example shows that informal relations, such as the prestige order in a task group, may be related to the outcomes structure, since high-prestige women were allowed to do the more attractive work. Moreover, the outcomes structure may be related to the pattern of task relations, i.e. to the task structure.

All in all, the above examples show that in task groups myriad formal and informal relations may be distinguished that together add up to 'the' group structure. These informal and formal structures are highly interdependent and may change over time in response to new information. The above-sketched analysis also demonstrates that it is rather impossible to theorize about and research all possible patterns or structures at the same time, and that is the reason why we will focus on the specific formal and informal structures that have been investigated to date. Before we start to present empirical research findings about formal and informal structures, we will demonstrate how cognitive, reflective and communicative processes lead to the emergence of structures and how structures – in turn – affect these processes.

TUNING PROCESSES

In the emergence and development of social structure three processes – namely, cognitive, reflective and communicative processes – play a role. Until now these processes have been approached separately. In the following we will argue that these processes are strongly interrelated.

Cognitive tuning: the learning of social structure

De Soto (1960) exposed his subjects to paired-association learning tasks. Subjects were told that they were participating in an investigation of learning about interpersonal relationships. Three types of relations were separately investigated, namely, liking relationships, influence relationships and confiding relationships. That is, in some tasks subjects had to learn the pattern of who likes whom, in other tasks they had to learn the pattern of who influences or controls whom and in other tasks they had to learn the pattern of who confides in whom. In the case of the liking pattern, subjects had to learn the specific liking pattern between Bill, Jim, Ray and Stan. The task proceeded as follows. Subjects received a specific card with the names of two persons printed on it; for example, Bill and Stan. The subjects then had to guess whether Bill liked Stan or not. After they had made their guess, they were to turn the card over, and from the back of the card they learned what was the case. Thereafter, a second card was presented. After subjects had seen all the cards and given their response, the experimenter reshuffled the cards and a new trial started. This procedure continued until the individual subjects had a perfect understanding of the liking relationships within the four-person group. In a similar way subjects had to learn influence and confiding relationships. The experiment had nineteen conditions, but for simplicity's sake we will focus on six of them: a 2 (structures: asymmetric, symmetric) × 3 (type of interrelationship: liking, influence, confiding) factorial design. Note that subjects again had to learn the specific patterns (i.e. the criteria) from the information on the back of the cards. Asymmetric relations were learned faster when subjects had to focus on who influences whom (mean number of trials to criterion = 8.9) than when subjects had to focus on liking (mean = 14.7) and trusting (mean = 16.2) relationships. Symmetric relationships were learned faster when subjects had to focus on 'likes' (mean = 10.9) and 'confides in' (mean = 10.9) than when they had to focus on 'influences' (mean = 12.9). De Soto's interpretation of these results is rather modern in that he suggests that it might very well be that the learning of a specific type of interrelationship (influence, liking or trust) evokes a scheme, a social representation that might be the residue of countless social orderings encountered in the past. So, the 'expectation of an ordering tends to produce an ordering'. Apparently, influence structuring in the past has been more asymmetric than symmetric and therefore a new asymmetric influence pattern is learned faster (mean = 8.9) than a new symmetric one (mean = 12.9).

This interpretation is rather modern because it assumes that subjects do not start a new task with a *tabula rasa*, but instead make use of cognitive representations built up on previous occasions. Thus, De Soto's experiment and reasoning suggest that social structure is a consequence of cognitive tuning: it was shown that recent associations between people are formed and it was suggested that these recent associations are learned against the background of learned schemata or cognitive representations from the past. On the other hand, it should be stressed that the new structure was learned because the backs of the cards showed that some responses were more rewarding than other ones. So the new social structure was learned through a mixture of cognitive and reflective accommodation. Lastly, it might be suggested that the specific interrelationships referred by implication to communication patterns. These communication patterns were provided in the format of the cards presented by the experimenter. For example, it was made clear that Bill influenced Jim, whereas Jim influenced or had control over Ray, whereas Ray had control over Stan. Moreover, Bill had control over Ray and Stan. So, although De Soto (1960) focused on cognitive tuning, it is evident that implicitly reflective tuning and communicative tuning were also involved.

Reflective tuning: social structure and exchange

The formation and development of social structure may also be approached from the perspective that social structure is a consequence of the exchange of rewards and costs, whereas the basic proposition is that group members strive for an optimalization of their rewards, i.e. reflective tuning is the central topic.

This approach is illustrated in a field study by Blau (1955). He investigated a group consisting of a supervisor, sixteen agents and one clerk who were part of a federal agency that was concerned with the enforcement of a certain set of federal (US) laws. An agent's task was to investigate whether a specific firm obeyed or violated federal laws. This task was assigned by the supervisor. In order to perform the task, an agent went to the office of a business firm where he obtained the necessary information. Having collected this information he wrote a report for his supervisor. Since his report might give rise to legal action against the firm, an agent had to be sure of his facts, his arguments and the clarity of his presentation. To illustrate some of the findings of this field study, in the following we make use of a description (by Homans, 1974, pp. 343–355) of some of its highlights.

(a) *Rewards and costs of consultation.* A consultation between agents can be considered an exchange of rewards and costs. As a result of consultation, the questioning agent can perform better than he otherwise would have. However, by asking for advice, he implicitly pays his respect to the superior ability of his colleague. This acknowledgement of inferiority is the cost of receiving assistance. The consultant receives prestige or status in return for the costs of the disruption of his own work. The consequence of this requesting and providing of advice is a social structure in which some agents served quite often as consultants in the top positions.

Of course, to obtain top positions agents had to be competent, but that was not the only requirement. It appeared that two of the more competent agents, who were not willing to exchange prestige for task disruption, received lower status positions. The top positions in the prestige order were occupied by agents who were more competent and willing to exchange as well.

(b) *Leadership*. The top informal leader (the supervisor was the formal leader) was the agent who was highly competent at his job and quite willing to act as a consultant (at the cost of task disruption). Moreover, he was ready to accept invitations to lunch with his social inferiors. After a while, his recognized authority had increased so much that when a committee was appointed to draft a change in the regulations, he dominated the discussion and others accepted his proposals. Moreover, he stood up for the other agents against the supervisor; he was highly successful in this, since the high regard in which he was held made his advice and opinion influential among fellow agents and even *vis-à-vis* the supervisor.

These field study examples show the rigor of reflective tuning. Less competent agents turned to more competent agents because in doing so they could prepare better reports. They did so although they had to incur the costs of acknowledged inferiority. Conversely, (some) agents were inclined to act as consultants, because they perceived that their costs in terms of task disruption were balanced by increased prestige. Referring to the principle of distributive justice (see chapter 4 on reflective tuning), Homans remarks that, in general, participants' costs and rewards in the federal agency were fairly balanced. Most noticeable was the behaviour of the informal leader of the agents. Because this competent agent quite often exchanged the cost of task disruption for the rewards of higher prestige, that agent was allowed to lead the informal group later on.

What has been demonstrated thus far? First, social exchange (or reflective tuning) leads to a cognitive or social representation of the informal group. Second, through communication the informal leader and the followers establish a social structure. Third, this social structure has consequences for communication patterns within the informal group.

Communicative tuning: attempts to lead under conditions of acceptance and rejection

In the following we will describe a study in which the central focus was the communication of group members. In an experiment by Pepinski, Hemphill and Shevitz (1958) group members had to work at a manufacturing problem. This task required the group members to organize a toy manufacturing concern and to operate their business for maximum profits. During the group interaction two trained observers, who observed the groups through a one-way mirror, tallied the frequency of attempts to lead by each group member. Two experimental conditions were introduced. In the 'rejection' condition two accomplices of the experimenter rejected a preselected 'real' group member whenever that group member made an attempt to lead. This role was reversed in the 'acceptance' condition: whenever a particular real group member attempted to lead, the accomplices indicated personal acceptance of the initiating group member. In both conditions, the accomplices were to comply with all direct requests or orders and were themselves to make no attempts to lead. The main dependent variable was the number of attempts to lead as observed by the two observers through the one-way mirror. The results indicated that in the rejection condition fewer influence attempts were made than in the acceptance condition.

This result is important in several respects. First, it demonstrates how group members' influence attempts can be increased and decreased by approving and disapproving communication, respectively. Second, since approval implies positive outcomes and disapproval negative outcomes for the group member attempting to lead, the results can also be understood from a reflective point of view: influence attempts can be facilitated by positive rewards and inhibited by negative rewards conferred upon group members who try to lead.

Another observation by Pepinski et al. (1958) allows us to generalize to one of the other antecedents of social structure as well. After the experiment, the experimenter requested group members to indicate how much they liked each of the other group members and how much they preferred them as leaders. It turned out that in the acceptance condition the stooges (or accomplices) were as liked as regular group members. However, in the rejection condition the stooges received a disproportionate share of the negative evaluations. These results might suggest that the behaviour of the stooges in the rejection condition was experienced as rather negative. Whenever a group member made an attempt to exert influence, the stooges disapproved of that influence attempt, and the mere fact that the stooges were providing negative outcomes for all real group members apparently led to a cognitive organization or social representation in which the stooges were disliked and less preferred as leaders than were regular group members. In sum, at first glance, the study of Pepinski et al. seems to reveal that social structure is a consequence of communication. However, further analysis shows that cognitive and reflective tuning are processes that also affect group structure.

As argued above, a myriad of interrelated structures can be distinguished in task groups. Since researchers have to restrict their topic of investigation, empirical evidence about task groups is limited to specific sub-areas like: (a) structure of the group task; (b) role structure; (c) communication structure; and (d) liking structures. We have decided to present these sub-areas separately. A very important sub-area is, of course, the influence structure. Because this topic has received more attention we will deal with leadership in our last chapter.

EMPHASIS ON TASKS

One of the most convincing classification systems for group tasks is that proposed by Steiner (1972, 1976), a system that is based on the requirements or rules that define when and how a task should be solved. We will describe that classification of tasks. Moreover, following Kelley and Thibaut (1969) and Keers

Question	Answer	Task type	Examples
Can the task be broken down into sub-components or is division of the task inappropriate?	Subtask can be identified	Divisible	Playing a football game, building a house, preparing a four course meal
	No subtasks exist	Unitary	Pulling on a rope, reading a book, solving a maths problem
Which is more important: quantity produced or quality of performance?	Quantity	Maximizing	Generating many ideas, lifting the greatest weight, scoring the most runs
	Quality	Optimizing	
How are individual inputs related to the group's product?	Individual inputs are added together	Additive	Pulling a rope, stuffing envelopes, shovelling snow
	Group product is average of individual judgements	Compensatory	Average individuals' estimates of the number of beans in a jar, weight of an object, room temperature
	Group selects product from pool of individual members' judgements	Disjunctive	Questions involving 'yes-no, either-or' answers such as maths problems, puzzles and options
	All group members must contribute to the product	Conjunctive	Climbing a mountain, eating a meal, relay races, soldiers marching in file
	Group can decide how individual inputs relate to group product	Discretionary	Deciding to shovel snow together, opting to vote on the best answer to a maths problem, letting leader answer question
How are group members interdependent as to their outcomes?	Commonality of interest	Cooperative	All examples above
	Conflict of interest	Competitive	Status struggle
	Cooperative and conflict of interest	Mixed motive	Commons dilemma

Figure 6.2 Task requirements: Steiner (1972) (adapted from Forsyth, 1983; Keers and Wilke, 1987)

and Wilke (1987), we will add another ingredient, namely whether according to the task instructions group members' interdependence is cooperative, competitive or a mixture of cooperative and competitive.

In Figure 6.2 we have presented a combination of Steiner's system of classification and Keers and Wilke's analysis. Four questions are posed.

Steiner's classification of tasks

The first question – *Can the task be broken down into subcomponents or is a division of the task inappropriate?* – compares divisible and unitary tasks. Reading a page of a book is essentially a one-person job; having two persons read alternate lines would serve no purpose, i.e. reading a page or solving a mathematical problem is a unitary task. Splitting up a unitary task makes little sense. Divisible tasks, however, can be broken into subtasks and assigned to different people. Playing a football game, building a house and planting a garden are tasks that can be broken down into subtasks. Thus, in unitary tasks mutual assistance is impractical, whereas in divisible tasks a certain division of labour is feasible. In this view, pulling a rope is a unitary task. To be sure, as Steiner remarks, this task can be conceived of as involving a number of subtasks, such as grasping the rope, bracing one's feet, contracting one's biceps, etc., but all phases have to be performed by a single individual. Several people may pull the same rope, but when this occurs, Steiner maintains, we have an instance of parallel performance rather than a division of labour.

The second question – *Which is more important: quantity produced or quality of performance?* – compares maximizing and optimizing tasks. When a task entails doing as much as possible of something, or doing it as rapidly as possible, we call this a maximizing task. For example, if an individual or group is requested to exert maximum force on a rope or if a group of mountaineers is asked to ascend a cliff as rapidly as possible, we call this a maximizing task, since the criterion of success is to complete the task in a maximum way. In contrast, optimizing tasks have as their criterion to produce some specific preferred outcome. When individuals or groups are asked to exert a force of exactly 100 lb, we speak of an optimizing task, since success is understood as the extent to which the specific criterion of 100 lb is achieved.

The third question – *How are individual inputs related to the group's product?* – gives rise to five possible answers. In additive tasks the contributions of various members are summed. For example, when several people shovel snow from a pathway, each performs that same act while taking care to stay clear of nearby co-workers. In this case group task performance can be expressed as the total surface cleared of snow. Compensatory tasks require a group decision from the average of individual members' solutions. Group members' estimates of, for example, the temperature of the room, the number of beans in a jar, or the number of cars in a parking lot may be averaged so that overestimates are pitted against underestimates; the two types of estimates balance each other out, and in the end the right answer may be achieved. Disjunctive tasks require that the group select one specific judgement from the pool of individual members' judgements. The horse-trading problem we dealt with in chapter 2 is a disjunctive task, since a group faced with such a problem might generate several judgements, from which one answer has to be selected. Conjunctive tasks require that all group members act in unison. The speed at which a group of mountain climbers can ascend a cliff is determined by the slowest member. Discretionary tasks are tasks which leave it to the group to decide how the task will be performed. For example, the group's decision about the temperature of the room can be arrived at in several ways. One person, the leader, may decide, with the other group members being bound by this decision. Another possible option is that some, but not all members may come to an agreement. The final group judgement may also be the average of all individual members' judgements. Thus discretionary tasks are those in which the group has freedom to select its own decisional procedures.

A fourth question – *How are group members interdependent as regards their outcomes?* – gives rise to a variety of interdependence situations that vary from pure cooperation, via combinations of competition and cooperation, to pure competition. Take, for example, a two-person group and a problem-solving task with only two response alternatives: a correct and an incorrect answer. In co-operative situations, members' outcomes resulting from group success are in perfect correspondence. In additive tasks the separate contributions of the members are simply added. Suppose A and B both give a correct answer. Under cooperative conditions both would receive, for example, 4 outcome units. If both give an incorrect answer, then both receive 0 outcomes. If one problem solver gives an incorrect response while the other gives a correct response, both receive 2 outcome units. Likewise, in purely cooperative disjunctive and conjunctive task conditions group members' outcomes always correspond. In a disjunctive task, both group members might receive the same outcome units when one of the group members provides the correct answer, whereas in a conjunctive task situation both group members have to give a correct answer and in that case also receive identical outcomes.

To complicate matters somewhat further, additive, disjunctive and con-junctive tasks may also be performed in competitive circumstances, implying that one group member receives all and the other one nothing. Especially when both group members have given a correct answer under a purely competitive distri-bution rule, the conflict of interests is not easily resolved, since a gain for one group member means a loss for the other one. If one member gives a correct solution and the other one does not, the group outcomes may be allocated by means of the equity principle (see chapter 4 on reflective tuning), with the correct member receiving all outcomes and the other group member receiving nothing. No conflict of interests is involved when both group members give an incorrect answer. Likewise, for disjunctive and conjunctive tasks under a competitive distribution rule, the conflict of interests is most severe when both members have provided a correct answer but outcomes have to be allocated to only one of the two group members.

Figure 6.2 provides another example of competitive interdependence, namely status struggle, which is said to exist when two group members strive for favourable outcomes in terms of a higher status position. Since higher status is only obtainable for one of the two group members (in a two-person group), this means that the winner gains all and the loser receives nothing or even negative outcomes in terms of lower self-esteem.

Group outcomes may be distributed in a cooperative or in a competitive way, but the distribution may also involve a mixture of competition and cooperation. An example of a mixed-motive situation is the 'commons dilemma'. Hardin (1968) referred to this dilemma when he described the adverse consequences individual actions may have for a group as a whole. The tragedy of the commons refers to the choice situation in which every herdsman on the common pasture is confronted with the choice between adding an extra animal to his herd and refraining from doing so. As long as the carrying capacity of the commons is sufficient, adding an extra animal has no consequences for the group at large. However, as soon as the upper limit of the carrying capacity of the common pasture has been reached, a mixture of competitive and cooperation interdependency emerges: every herdsman will be inclined to reason that the gains from adding an extra animal accrue to him personally, whereas the negative consequences of overgrazing are shared by all. Since the net outcomes are higher for adding an extra animal, an individual herdsman will be inclined to add an extra animal. Since that calculation counts for every herdsman, all will contribute to overgrazing, until finally the commons are exhausted. The commons dilemma has two properties: (1) every participant wants to add an extra animal to his herd, since the consequences for him personally are more positive than are the consequences of not doing so; and (2) if all participants add an extra animal, a tragedy results: all are better off when the herdsmen show some restraint by not adding extra animals to their herds than when each pursues his self-interest. Such a commons or social dilemma may arise in many task situations. In chapter 2 we described the social loafing or Ringelmann effect: being part of a group quite often leads to a decrease in motivation to contribute to the group's performance. This has been shown in groups having to perform additive tasks in which individual group members are not identifiable. This is a mixed-motive situation having two properties: (1) individual group members perceive that they are better off if they withhold their task efforts; and yet, (2) if all do so, the group is worse off than if all group members had contributed as much as possible to the group task.

Steiner's ingenious classification system has two attractive properties. First, it can be used to classify many tasks. Three examples will serve to demonstrate this. A tug-of-war contest involves a task that is unitary, maximizing and additive. Assembling a car is divisible, optimizing and conjunctive. Solving the afore-mentioned horse-trading problem is a unitary, optimizing, disjunctive task.

Second, Steiner's classification system allows us to make predictions about group performance. In the following we will show how group performance on a specific task is dependent on the group members' resources for dealing with the task. This approach is in agreement with our contention in chapter 2 that group productivity is equal to potential productivity plus or minus process gains and losses. The different classes of tasks demand different sorts of resources: skills, abilities and tools. If group members possess these human resources, the task demands are met and the task may be fulfilled successfully. If, in contrast, the group does not possess these necessary resources, group failure may result. In the following we will demonstrate the predictive value of Steiner's classification system in the case of additive, compensatory, disjunctive and conjunctive tasks. Thereafter we will briefly discuss the consequences of the distribution of outcomes for group performance.

Additive tasks

In additive tasks the individual contributions are added together, and therefore it is not surprising that it has been established that the more people in a group, the better the group performance. Especially in the case of unitary tasks, such as pulling a rope and clapping after a concert, the old saying 'many hands make light the work' applies. Since additive tasks have been extensively dealt with in chapter 2 and above, we will summarize the major conclusion: in additive tasks group performance is equal to the potential performance of group members minus process losses. Two kinds of process losses may arise, namely losses due to faulty coordination and losses due to decreased motivation. The Ringelmann effect, for example the failure of rope-pulling group members to live up to their performance potential, is due to these two types of losses, which also play a role in other additive tasks, like brainstorming, clapping and cheering. In Figure 6.3 our main conclusion regarding additive tasks is summarized.

Compensatory tasks

In compensatory tasks the group's product is the average of individual judgements. In a series of early studies (Knight, 1921; Gordon, 1924), individuals were asked to make private estimates of the temperature of a room, the number of beans in a jar and the number of pieces of buckshot in a bottle. It appeared that the statistical average of the many judgements came closer to the correct judgement than did the judgements rendered by most of the individuals. Shaw (1981) also comes to the conclusion that the bulk of evidence indicates that – in compensatory tasks – the average of judgements is more accurate than individual judgements. Steiner (1972, 1976), however, is more critical with regard to this conclusion. He points out that 'statisticized' groups occur rather rarely in daily life and may not be recognized as such when they do occur. Moreover, the average of all judgements only leads to superior group performance when no information about the competence of members is available and when individual prejudices may be presumed to generate errors that cancel each other out. When some individual judgements have more influence than others, or when some members abstain from expressing their judgement, then the average judgement is likely to be less correct. In addition it should be mentioned that even 'statisticized' groups that are not hampered by these drawbacks may fail. For example,

Task/motivation	Group productivity	Description
Additive	Better than best	Group out-performs the best individual member
Compensatory	Better than most	Group out-performs a substantial number of group members
Disjunctive (Eureka)	Equal to the best	Group performance matches the performance of the best member
Disjunctive (non-Eureka)	Less than the best	Group performance can match that of the best member, but often falls short
Conjunctive (unitary)	Equal to the worst	Group performance matches the performance of the worst member
Conjunctive (divisible with matching)	Better than the worst	If subtasks are properly matched to ability of members, group performance can reach high levels
Cooperative	Facilitates group performance	Depends on the cognitive rules of the task (see above)
Competitive	Deteriorates group performance	Group performance hampered by competing individual group members
Mixed motive	Group performance less than optimal	Better than under more competition, but worse than with pure cooperation

Figure 6.3 Group performance (adapted from Steiner, 1972; Forsyth, 1983; Keers and Wilke, 1987)

Klugman (1947) reported that groups of World War II soldiers overestimated how long the war would continue because they could not foresee how the atom bomb would shorten the war in the Pacific region.

Disjunctive tasks and Social Decision Schemes

Groups are very often confronted with disjunctive tasks requiring the acceptance of only one of the available individual contributions.

Interest in disjunctive tasks arose in the early 1930s (Shaw, 1932). In addition to the horse-trading problem, the so-called missionary/cannibal problem was quite often employed. This disjunctive task has the following content: 'Three missionaries and three cannibals are on one side of the river, and want to cross to the other side by means of a boat that can only hold two persons at a time. All the missionaries but only one cannibal can row. For safety reasons, the missionaries must never be outnumbered by the cannibals, under any circumstances or at any time, except when no missionaries are present at all. The question is, how many crossings will be necessary to transport the six people across the river?' The answer is thirteen crossings. Shaw (1932) observed that overall groups out-performed individuals on this task. These results were explained in terms of the enhanced opportunity of groups to correct errors and to reject incorrect suggestions.

Later on, successful and failing groups were compared more closely. Another explanation, the *Truth-Wins* explanation, was proposed. According to this explanation, if one group member proposes the correct answer, then it is likely that the group will succeed. This explanation does not always hold, though. For some problems the truth-wins explanation does apply, e.g. for the missionary/cannibal problem. However, for others, such as the horse-trading problem, it appeared quite often that having one successful member was no guarantee of group success.

This result was explained by pointing out that the missionary/cannibal problem has a very appealing solution, a *Eureka* appeal, while other tasks have a less obvious solution. The consequence of this is that if in a Eureka task group one member has the correct solution, the other group members more or less automatically adhere to this solution, which is not the case for problems that do not have such an obvious and insightful solution. For non-Eureka tasks, it can easily occur that the correct solution suggested by one member is not supported by the other group members or that a group member with an incorrect solution dominates the solution process. For non-Eureka problems, it is not Truth-Wins, but *Truth-Supported Wins* that explains group success.

Thomas and Fink (1961) described a three-step model which appears to encompass the critical aspects of group success on disjunctive tasks:

1 *Potential performance:* do group members possess the necessary resources for solving the problem?
2 *Motivation:* do group members who arrive at the correct solution actually propose this solution?
3 *Coordination:* do correct solutions elicit support more often than incorrect solutions?

In the same vein, Steiner (1972; see also Figure 6.3) summarizes the findings as follows. In disjunctive tasks a group's productivity is determined by the resources of its most competent member. However, even when there is a very competent member, process losses may prohibit the group from producing the correct solution. This is the case when the most competent member does not employ his or her resources or when other group members do not adhere to the most competent member's solution. The latter circumstance seems to be very likely (a) when the most competent member has low status in the group; and (b) when the highly competent member is not confident enough to express his or her solution, or fails to persuade the other group members (see further Figure 6.3).

In order to predict the group product from the productivity of individual group members, Laughlin (1980) made use of the general Social Decision Scheme (SDS) model developed by Davis (1973, 1982). SDS offers a mathematically formulated general framework for describing how groups combine individual responses to render a group response. In the following we will introduce SDS in a rather informal way. The model starts with a probability distribution of individual preferences for a number of response alternatives. From this distribution the chances can be estimated of all possible initial response distributions in groups of every size. To illustrate: if there are 2 alternatives and the group size is 3, the possible group distributions are (3,0), (2,1), (1,2) and (0,3). The probability of each group distribution is dependent on the probability distribution of the individual preferences. If the individual preferences are equally divided among the alternatives, the group distributions (2,1) and (1,2) in randomly composed groups are more probable than the distributions (3,0) and (0,3). If a majority of individuals initially prefer the first alternative, then a randomly composed group is likely to have a (3,0) composition, next a (2,1) division, and so on. What will be the distribution of the group responses or group decisions of the groups under study? This depends on the SDS, that is, the 'procedure the groups use' to transform the responses of the individual members into a group decision or group response. If the above-mentioned group follows some kind of majority rule, then a (3,0) and a (2,1) group distribution should result in the choice of the first response alternative, while from a (1,2) and a (0,3) distribution the group is predicted to choose the second alternative. So, starting from a probability distribution of individual preferences and initial group distributions, the SDS model predicts the distribution of group responses by taking into account the SDS of the group. From a theoretical point of view, the SDS is a method of formalizing a set of assumptions about the group process in order to make predictions about group responses. In numerous studies the predicted and obtained group response are then compared statistically. If they differ, then the SDS – the formalized set of assumptions about the group process or, in other words, the theory of the social combination process (Laughlin, 1980) – does not describe the group processes that actually occur. In the following we describe briefly five possible SDSs for group tasks with two response alternatives, for example, the correct and incorrect response to a problem-solving task. The first SDS, Majority, Equiprobability Otherwise (MAEQ), predicts that the group choice should correspond with the initial response of the majority in the group. If there is no majority, then both alternatives have an equal probability of being the group response. Truth-Wins (TWIN): if a single group member proposes the correct alternative, then the group adopts that alternative. Thus, if the group contains at least one correct member, the group is certain to adopt the correct response. Truth-Supported Wins (TSWIN): a correct group member must be supported by at least one other group member for the group to be correct. Strict Equiprobability (STEQ): the group choice is equally likely to be one of the alternatives proposed by one or more members.

The SDSs shown so far concern disjunctive tasks in Steiner's (1972) typology. According to the Error-Wins (EWIN) scheme, the group decision will be incorrect if at least one member is incorrect. Fortunately, EWIN turned out to be a bad predictor of group decisions (Laughlin, 1980). This fifth SDS is theoretically interesting, because it corresponds to a conjunctive task in Steiner's typology.

On a variety of disjunctive tasks, Davis's (1973) SDS model has been investigated in an extensive research programme by Laughlin and others (see, for example, Laughlin, 1980; McGrath, 1984; Stasser, Kerr and Davis 1989). The results of these studies can be summarized as follows:

1 On problem-solving tasks with a strong Eureka character, for which the correctness of an answer is convincingly demonstrable, for example, in the case of simple arithmetic problems, group performance is best described by the SDS Truth-Wins.
2 Other tasks have a correct response which is, however, not so convincingly demonstrable and intuitively compelling when presented. Examples of these tasks are verbal analogies, English vocabulary, general verbal achievement items. On these tasks, group performance is best described by the SDS Truth-Supported Wins. The group will adopt the correct alternative if it is chosen by at least two members.
3 In the case of tasks with even less demonstrable solutions, the Strict Equiprobability SDS best predicts group choices.
4 Laughlin (1980) contrasts intellectual tasks which have an objective criterion or demonstrable solution with tasks wherein the correctness of the solution or decision is a matter of subjective judgement. Examples are judgements on ethical, aesthetic and attitudinal issues, or the risky choice dilemmas of Stoner (1961; see chapter 3). The group response on these judgemental tasks is best described by some version of the SDS Majority, Equiprobability Otherwise. A demonstration of this is Cartwright's (1971) reanalysis of results obtained from three-person groups that had to reach unanimous decisions on risky choice dilemmas. Of all group decisions, 41 per cent could be predicted successfully by a simple 2/3 majority rule. A string of three rules, namely, simple majority, or a coalition between two adjacent responses, or the mean of the three initial responses, could explain 75 per cent of all group decisions correctly. Subsequent studies employing choice dilemma tasks in which eight or more SDSs were compared (e.g. Laughlin and Earley, 1982; Crott, Szilvas and Zuber, 1991; Zuber, Crott and Werner, 1992) show that the group decision is best described as consensus (or unanimity), or majority, or pairwise comparison of neighbouring responses, resulting in the choice of the median position of the response scale as the group decision.

Discretionary tasks and the effects of decision rules

The last task type in the typology of Steiner (1972, 1976) consists of discretionary tasks. In this task type, the group members are completely free to combine their individual responses in any way they wish. The group can explicitly formulate a group decision rule, like majority, unanimity, averaging, weighted averaging, etc., or delegate the decision to one member, or even to an outsider. The decision rule of a group in this case is often prescribed by law, by law within the group or by tradition. The effects of the adoption of different rules are reviewed by Miller (1989). Two characteristics of rules seem to be important. Rules differ in strictness. A strict rule like unanimity requires total agreement on a response in order to become the group choice; a majority rule is less strict because it requires less agreement among members. Rules also differ in the distribution of power in the group. Two extremes are dictatorship, with all outcome control concentrated in one person, and majority, with equal influence exerted by each member. These two characteristics are often, but not necessarily, related; for example, a majority rule is less strict than a unanimity rule, but both are egalitarian. Miller (1989) discusses several effects of the selection of a specific rule:

1 A unanimity rule is more likely than a majority rule to result in failure to reach a group decision at all. A unanimity rule requires a compromise between all group members, while a majority rule does not. There are indications that the quality of group decisions made by a unanimity rule is higher than that of decisions made by a majority rule.
2 A unanimity rule leads to longer discussion time and more conflicts during the discussions, but also to more satisfaction with, and adherence to, the group decision.
3 Outside observers, and even group members themselves, may assume that the group decision reflects the opinion of all group members. This assumption may be right if the rule was strict or egalitarian with a representative decision as a result. If the rule was less strict or less egalitarian, the assumption is likely to be wrong. Therefore, Allison and Messick (1985; 1987) have labelled this phenomenon 'the group attribution error'.

In conclusion: the choice of a group decision rule may have several surprising effects, for example, on the discussion process, the quality of the decision and the satisfaction of group members, which are not easily detected and realized in the daily life of existing groups because they seldom experiment with different rules.

Conjunctive tasks

In conjunctive tasks it is necessary that all members contribute to the task. For tasks like climbing a mountain and marching in file, the criterion is that all group members make the proper response. When conjunctive tasks are unitary, each member must contribute; otherwise the group fails (Steiner, 1972). That is, the group process depends on the competence of the least proficient member, and because the chance of having an incompetent member increases with group size, it is logical that as the number of group members increases, group productivity will diminish.

In daily life, however, many conjunctive tasks are divisible into subtasks, which are then allocated to individual members. For example, climbing a mountain can be divided into several subtasks, like those performed by a rope leader and followers. If the most able climber performs the most difficult subtask, i.e. that of the rope leader, group productivity is higher than the potential productivity of the least able group member. In sum, the performance of unitary conjunctive tasks depends on the least able group member. However, for divisible conjunctive tasks, group performance can exceed the potential productivity of the least able group member if the abilities of the group members match the requirements of specific subtasks.

From the foregoing two conclusions may be drawn. First, Steiner's classification system allows us to make a set of predictions with respect to the types of tasks under consideration. In Figure 6.3 these predictions are summarized. Second, the basic idea that group productivity is equal to the extent to which group members succeed in meeting the demands of the task minus the process losses and gains that may arise appears to offer a deeper understanding of the nature of tasks. Moreover, for some tasks, it has been established that process losses and gains are due to motivation and coordination losses and gains. Lastly, it may be argued that Steiner's task classification system refers not only to tasks but also, as his emphasis on motivation and coordination makes clear, implicitly to reflective and communicative tuning, respectively.

Mixed-motive, cooperative and competitive tasks

In the following we will first deal with problem-solving tasks in which group members are cooperatively independent, competitively interdependent or a mixture of the two. Thereafter we will present situations in which the group is involved not in solving a group task but in the distributing of outcomes *per se*.

The classification scheme and predictions of Steiner pertain mainly to task environments in which group members feel cooperatively interdependent. In chapter 4 (reflective tuning) we explained that the bulk of research findings suggest that cooperative groups outperform competitive groups. Another example is a study by Zander and Wolfe (1964) in which the experimental task consisted of buying, selling and exchanging information within groups that functioned as 'coordinating committees' in a large business firm. There were three experimental conditions. In the cooperative condition, the supervisors of the committee allegedly received information about the sum of the individual group members' scores, that is, one group score was to be provided. In the competitive condition, information about the performance of each of the individual group members was to be provided, and in the mixed condition, both the sum of the group score and individual scores were to be provided to the supervisors. Several dependent measures were taken. It turned out that in the mixed condition as compared with the competitive condition, performance was higher. Moreover, there was more trust of other group members, a greater desire for more information and more exchange of information. Performance and the other measures appeared to be even more favourable in the cooperative condition as compared with the mixed condition.

The difference between the three conditions in the study of Zander and Wolfe is not absolute: even group members in the competitive condition had to act as a group at a group task, so considerable cooperative interdependency was involved. However, since inter-member competition was induced more strongly in the competitive condition, for simplicity's sake this condition is labelled competitive as compared with the cooperative and mixed conditions, in which the inducement of competition was absent or weaker, respectively.

Why are more cooperative groups more productive than more competitive ones? In answering this question Kelley and Thibaut (1969) distinguished between two kinds of communication processes: information processing in groups, which is an aspect of what we have labelled cognitive tuning in groups, and bargaining about the distribution of rewards, which is an instance of what we have referred to as reflective tuning.

As for information processing in groups, in more competitive groups it is quite often to a member's advantage to withhold important information in order to attain a better or earlier solution than the other group members. Moreover, information exchange in more competitive groups is inhibited because one is likely to focus on the distribution of rewards instead of working at the group task. As a consequence, there is less inter-member influence and less acceptance of others' ideas, group members have greater difficulty in communicating to and understanding others, and there is less coordination of efforts, less division of labour, and poorer productivity in more competitive as compared with more cooperative problem-solving groups. Thus, in problem-solving groups in which groups members have to solve the group task and distribute task rewards as well, task performance may be hampered when group members are involved in bargaining about the scarce group rewards, i.e. cognitive tuning may be inhibited by reflective tuning. In cooperative groups the group members' individual interests coincide with the group interest, so that maximum attention may be paid to cognitive tuning – i.e. information exchange aimed at solving the task – whereas in competitive problem-solving groups bargaining about the scarce group resources takes place at the expense of information exchange necessary to solve the group task.

In the foregoing it was shown that in mixed groups problem-solving group members have to resolve two problems simultaneously, namely the task itself and the distribution of group rewards, and that the latter activity is likely to inhibit the solution of the group task itself. In mixed-motive situations like social dilemma situations and coalition formation situations, the task concerns only the distribution of group outcomes, and the communication pertains entirely to the distribution of these outcomes. In the following we will briefly describe these situations and the most relevant research findings.

Social dilemmas

Social dilemmas (see Dawes, 1980) refer to choice situations in which there is a conflict between individual and group interests. Individual preferences dictate that group members pursue their self-interests, whereas the collective preference dictates that members make choices that benefit the group. Examples of this include the social loafing effect we described in chapter 2 and the commons dilemma described earlier in this chapter. Whereas social loafing has been introduced to explain the lower productivity of groups as compared with separate individuals, the commons dilemma metaphor has been applied to many societal problems, including tax evasion, energy waste and pollution: for all of us it is most attractive to evade taxes, to waste energy and to pollute, yet if we all evade taxes, waste energy and pollute we are worse off than if we had not.

Social dilemmas have been investigated by means of experimental games, for example the take-some and give-some games. Take-some games refer to choice situations in which group members are confronted with a common resource from which group members may take as much as they want. There is only one restriction, and that is that one does not receive anything once that resource has been exhausted. This is a social dilemma since the individual group members' rewards are served by taking as much as possible, whereas the group interests are served by collective restraint. Give-some games have a similar reward structure, but here a resource has to be created by volunteer donations or contributions of individual group members. It is announced by the experimenter that all individual contributions will be multiplied, for example by two. This is again a social dilemma, since individual outcomes are higher if other group members do contribute than if the individual personally contributes. Yet, if all group members think and act as free-riders, the common resource will not be created and the individual will be worse off than he or she would have been if all had contributed.

Numerous studies (see Messick and Brewer, 1983; Wilke, Messick and Rutte, 1986) have been performed in this area. One of the most important questions addressed in these studies was how groups can be brought to act in the group's interest in spite of their personal inclination not to do so. In the following, we will report some of the findings. The most noteworthy result is that in social dilemma situations, group members do not exclusively pursue their individual interests but show some (though not sufficient) concern for the group. This is explained by group members' adherence to an implicit rule of fairness, according to which they themselves should contribute (in the case of give-some games) as much as they expect others to contribute, and should take (in take-some games) as much as they expect other group members to take (see Wilke, 1991).

So, confronted with a conflict between personal and group interests, group members seem to apply a rule of fairness based on equal contributions or equal harvests (see further chapter 4 on reflective tuning). Furthermore, in some conditions, further concern for the group is encouraged, to wit (a) when groups are smaller rather than larger; (b) when there is emphasis on the importance of the outcomes for the group because of higher group rewards, as compared with emphasis on personal interest and personal rewards; (c) when group members receive information that other group members are making cooperative (group-centred) choices rather than information that fellow group members are making selfish choices; (d) when group members are identifiable rather than un-identifiable, i.e. when their choices are not anonymous; and (e) when group members are allowed to communicate. These are all circumstances that facilitate cooperative, group-centred choices in small groups.

Kerr has shown that the social dilemma analogy is of relevance for our understanding of task performance (Kerr, 1983; Kerr and Bruun, 1983). He reasoned that if groups increase in size, group members' behaviour is less identifiable, and group members' task efforts usually have less effect on the total group performance. As a consequence, motivation losses in larger groups are greater than in smaller ones. In one of his experiments (experiment 2; Kerr and Bruun, 1983), subjects in two-person or in three-person groups had to perform an additive, a disjunctive or a conjunctive task. Each member of the most productive group would receive a prize.

Before task performance, group members were informed of how much they had to produce in order to be successful. Thereafter, various task instructions were given. In the additive condition, the number of successful members counted. In the conjunctive condition, every member had to succeed for the group to succeed, that is, group performance was dependent on the performance of the least able group member. In the disjunctive condition, the group was successful if at least one member was successful, that is, group performance was dependent on the most able group member. Success or failure in comparison with other groups was established in several trials. For all conditions, the performance of individual group members showed that task performance was higher for two-person than for three-person groups. So, increasing group size elicits motivation losses, an effect which is an example of social loafing.

In another experiment (experiment 1; Kerr and Bruun, 1983), after a first session group members received information about their relative ability and about the size of their group. Each group had one member with a high ability score and one member with a low ability score. Subjects were randomly assigned to one of these ability positions. Two-, four- and eight-person groups were introduced. Besides ability positions and size of the group, task demands also varied. Additive, conjunctive or disjunctive task instructions were provided. Kerr reasoned that in a disjunctive task group, in which only the best member's performance matters, the less able members would become free-riders because their efforts would be dispensable. In contrast, in a conjunctive task group, in which the least able group member's performance matters, he expected that high-ability group members would become free-riders, i.e. would tend to reduce their efforts.

As predicted, the ability of the group members had opposite effects for the conjunctive and disjunctive tasks. When only the best individual score counted (disjunctive task), the low-ability member performed less well, but when the group score was defined by the worst individual score (conjunctive task) the high-ability member worked less hard. The subjects' responses to the question, 'how much did the success of the group depend upon you, personally?' indicated that the effects reported above reflected the extent to which group members considered themselves dispensable. The reduced efforts of low-ability subjects in a disjunctive task setting and of high-ability subjects in a conjunctive task setting were labelled 'free-rider effects'.

Besides social loafing and free-rider effects, Kerr (1983) found evidence for the 'sucker effect'. Being a sucker in a social dilemma situation refers to the circumstance in which people themselves contribute and later on learn that other group members have not contributed but nevertheless profit from the contribution of the sucker(s). Kerr demonstrated that group members with a capable partner who 'free-rode' on their efforts, that is, who was capable of contributing to the group but would not, reduced their efforts in order to escape the role of sucker.

In sum, Kerr's research shows that performing group members take into account forthcoming behavioural outcomes. As a consequence, they reduce their efforts if the group size is larger (the social loafing effect), if their own efforts are considered dispensable (the free-rider effect) and if they fear to become suckers (the sucker effect).

Coalition formation

In informal groups there quite often arises competition for scarce resources: who will have the advantage of being the group's spokesperson, who will have more influence than others, who will receive the greatest share of the outcomes derived from the group product? An area in which such structural tuning has been explicitly investigated is coalition formation or subgroup formation. Within groups coalitions are subgroups consisting of group members who stick together, i.e. cooperate with one another, and as a subgroup compete with other group members who are not part of the coalition. This involves a mixed-motive situation since some group members may make a coalition, i.e. cooperate, whereas they as a subgroup compete with group members who are not part of the coalition and who may eventually receive nothing.

Coalitions are investigated under conditions in which a subset of group members are explicitly forced to make a coalition. Quite often coercion is exerted by the experimenter, who, for example, might announce that two members of a three-person group may form a coalition as soon as they can make an agreement on a division of the coalition outcomes, while excluding the third group member, who will not receive anything.

Given such a situation, where two out of three may have favourable outcomes and the third one will receive nothing, we argue that group members search for *cues* on which to base cooperation between the two and exclusion of the third group member. We provide a summary of the most relevant cues investigated to date in studies employing three-person groups: weights assigned randomly or according to previous efforts and attitudinal similarity.

Weights assigned randomly: revolutionary coalitions

Vinacke and Arkoff (1957) worked with three-person groups consisting of A, B and C, and randomly assigned them the weights 4, 3 and 2, respectively. The groups were asked to play pachisi, an Indian board game, under the following constraints: for each move, an individual player rolled the dice once, and the value of the dice rolled multiplied by the player's assigned weight determined the number of spaces he or she could advance. Players were also told that they could form coalitions, and that a coalition could act as a single player whose weight would be the sum of those of the individual coalition members. But the coalition had to decide in advance how the prize (e.g. 100 points) would be split, and the players were not allowed to form a three-person coalition or to make side-payments to players who were not part of the coalition. Usually this game is played in a series of rounds.

Before we describe the results that are usually obtained, it seems worthwhile to stress that when no coalition is formed, A, with a weight of 4, will automatically be the winner. Moreover, it should be noted that two kinds of predictions can be made. Minimum Power Theory and Minimum Resource Theory (see Gamson, 1964) make different predictions. Minimum Power Theory suggests that players respond to the cue of pivotal power, that is, the number of times a player may be part of a (winning) coalition. For the 4–3–2 case, it is obvious that A can be part of an AB and an AC coalition and that B and C can also be members of two coalitions. Consequently, Minimum Power Theory predicts that the possible coalitions, AB, AC and BC occur equally often. Minimum Resource Theory is based on another type of reasoning, namely that players respond to the mixed-motive situation of coalition formation by adhering to the equity or proportionality norm (see chapter 4) and that weights determine how much a player should profit from a coalition once formed. BC coalitions are predicted since B and C can make a more profitable coalition together, i.e. 3/5 and 2/5 of the coalition outcomes, respectively, than they could in a coalition with A that would yield them 3/7 and 2/6 of the coalition outcomes, respectively. In other words, since B and C ought to prefer 60 per cent and 40 per cent of the coalition outcomes above 43 per cent and 33 per cent respectively, a BC coalition is predicted and the outcomes are to be shared in proportion to their weights, i.e. according to proportionality or equity. The results indicate that BC coalitions are formed most often. However, within a BC coalition the outcomes are shared somewhere between proportionally and equally (see further Komorita and Meek, 1978). For example, where C's proportional share would be 2/5, or 40 per cent, in a coalition with B, he receives 45 per cent of the coalition outcomes, which is halfway between his proportional share and an equal share (50 per cent).

At first glance, the results of the Vinacke and Arkoff experiment seem to corroborate the Minimum Resource Theory, since the two weakest players quite often formed so-called revolutionary coalitions against A and players did not start from the notion of pivotal power as Minimum Power Theory would expect.

Kelley and Arrowood (1960) have argued that it may not be the complicated reasoning of Minimum Resource Theory that is responsible for the higher frequency of BC coalitions. They reasoned that A's misperception may be responsible: since A receives all outcomes (e.g. 100 points) if no coalition is formed, A is inclined to overestimate his share, a supposition that received some support in their study. So another cue besides that proposed by Minimum Resource Theory might be responsible for the coalition between the weakest players. Nevertheless, a large number of other studies in other settings have shown that when weights are randomly assigned to players, quite frequently revolutionary coalitions do occur. An example is a political convention game study (Wilke, Pruyn and de Vries, 1978) in which three players had to assume that they were representatives of three political parties that had 40, 30 and 20 seats in parliament. Only two-party coalitions were permitted. Coalitions were formed by dividing eight cabinet posts. It appeared that revolutionary coalitions (30-20) were formed most often. Moreover, in this situation too, the outcomes of the coalitions were divided halfway between proportionally and equally.

Weights deserved: conservative coalitions

Messé, Vallacher and Phillips (1975) argued that in a pachisi board game revolutionary coalitions are formed because players experience the advantage assigned to '4' as unjust, since it is not deserved but assigned by chance. Consequently, the weak players make a (revolutionary) coalition to correct for that injustice. In a part of their experiment, there were two conditions. In the weights-irrelevant condition, the three subjects were assigned the weights 4, 3 and 2 in a random way. In the weights-relevant condition, the weights 4, 3 and 2 were also assigned, but in that case it was communicated that '4' had worked 2 hours for the experimenter, '3' had worked 1½ hours, and '2' had worked 1 hour, i.e. the weights were deserved. The results indicate that in the weights-irrelevant condition, revolutionary (3–2) coalitions were formed most often, whereas in the weights-relevant condition, the two strongest players (4 and 3) more often entered into a coalition. These conservative coalitions were explained by assuming that when weights are perceived as relevant inputs (see equity theory in chapter 4), the outcomes are divided so that the two strongest players receive most outcomes.

A similar result was obtained in an experiment by Wilke and Pruyn (1981). In the deserved condition, weights were deserved because of previously shown competence: 4 appeared to be more competent than 3, whereas 3 appeared to be more competent than 2. In the not-deserved condition, the assignment of weights occurred by chance. It was found that in the deserved condition, conservative (4–3) coalitions were more often formed, whereas in the not-deserved condition revolutionary (3–2) coalitions were more often formed.

Do these results suggest that when weights are assigned by chance, revolutionary coalitions will always be observed? In a clever experiment Murnighan (1978) assigned weights by chance to members of 5-person groups, and demonstrated that when weights corresponded with pivotal power, conservative coalitions were formed most often, whereas when weights did not correspond with pivotal power, revolutionary coalitions were most often observed.

Attitudinal similarity

In a political convention experiment by Wilke *et al.* (1978) three members A, B and C were randomly assigned 40, 30 and 20 seats, respectively, in parliament. Thus, weight assignment was one factor in the experiment. Another factor was attitudinal distance: a third of the subjects were assigned a Left, a third a Centre and another third a Right political programme. Any two-party coalition could be formed as long as the two parties could come to an agreement about the collective coalition programme and the allocation of eight cabinet posts. Minimal Range Theory (de Swaan, 1973) predicts that those parties will make a coalition whose attitudinal distance or range is minimal. This means that mainly Centre-Left and Right-Centre coalitions were expected. The results indicate that a majority of BC or revolutionary coalitions were formed, as Minimum Resource Theory would expect. The effect of the attitudinal distance inducements was much stronger: it was found that most of the coalitions that were formed included Centre, that Centre realized most of its party programme and that Centre was able to obtain a majority of cabinet posts. In sum, as in political field studies (de Swaan, 1973), Minimal Range Theory predicted rather well, and much better than Minimal Resource Theory (in terms of explained variance).

The results may be explained in terms of reasoning similar to that put forward in our introduction to Expectation States Theory (see chapter 5). As may be recalled, the major factor explaining influence differentials was that group members search for cues on which to base differential expectations of group members. In coalition formation studies, subjects are forced to make decisions about who might be part of the coalition and who will be excluded. We argue that in such a circumstance subjects search for cues that will assist them in making these choices. In political convention games it is attitudinal distance, whereas in simple majority games involving weights much depends on the convincingness of the cue. When weights stand for, or are associated with, previous effort expenditure or competence, conservative coalitions are formed, i.e. 'strength is strength', meaning that the most competent group members who have exerted the most effort in the past become members of the coalition. When weights are assigned randomly, revolutionary coalitions ('weakness is strength') are formed. In pachisi board games revolutionary coalitions may be ascribed to 4's tendency to wait too long to enter the bargaining process. However, in political convention games minimal winning or revolutionary coalitions are formed because a coalition with 4 is too expensive for 3 and 2, who are better off together. A second observation is that in mixed-motive groups coalition outcomes seem partly to be divided according to group members' positions on the cue that is made relevant, i.e. the allocation of coalition rewards is based partly on proportionality, the latter referring to differential positions in terms of weights, competence, pivotal power and attitudinal similarity. However, the results indicate that the coalition outcomes are usually divided halfway between proportionality and equality. Theoretically, equality has not received much attention to date. A cognitive basis for the tendency towards equal outcomes allocation may be that members of a coalition form a unit, and being in one unit may lead to an amelioration of differences in outcomes between the members of the coalition. A reflective and communicative basis for the tendency towards equal allocations may be that a division according to proportionality makes the weaker member highly sensitive to counter-offers made by the third group member, who fears being excluded from the coalition. Conversely, an equal share for the stronger member makes the stronger member highly sensitive to counter-offers from the group member who might be excluded. That is to say, a division between proportionality and equality may serve as a tacit bargaining point.

EMPHASIS ON INTERPERSONAL RELATIONS

The moment group members meet they may have feelings about each other, for example they may like or dislike one another at first sight. Feelings may also develop and change in the course of the interaction as a result of cognitive, reflective and communicative processes. These feelings are reflected in a wide variety of verbal and non-verbal behaviours which are perceptible. Perceptions of these behaviours are assumed to lead to cognitive representations of the actual interpersonal relationships in the group. When forming these representations, people make use of cognitive schemes, representations that have accumulated in the past. The process of learning actual interpersonal relations on the basis of schemes formed in the past was discussed at the beginning of this chapter, where we described De Soto's (1960) experiment on the learning of social structures.

Balance theory

De Soto's study was inspired by Heider's 'balance theory of social perception' (Heider, 1946, 1958). In the most simple case, Heider discerns three elements which form a system or structure: a perceiver (p), another person (o), and an entity (x, which may be an object or a third person). He also discerns two kinds of relations which may exist between two elements: sentiment relations and unit relations. Sentiment relations are assumed to involve positive or negative feelings, such as like (L+) or dislike (L−). Unit relations are perceptions that two elements in some way belong together (U+) or are disconnected (U−). Examples of relations between two elements are: p and o like each other (pL+o, oL+p) and p likes o, but o dislikes p (pL+o, oL−p). Examples of relations between three elements are: p and his friend both like jazz music (pL+o, pL+x, oL+x); or p likes jazz but his friend hates it (pL+x, pL+o, oL−x).

According to Heider's analysis, the first and third examples differ in an important aspect from the second and fourth examples. The elements in the first

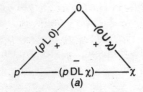

(a)

The given situation is unbalanced:
two position relations and one
negative relation.

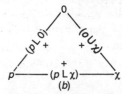

(b)

Change in sentiment relation
resulting in a balance of
three positive relations.

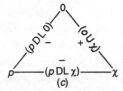

(c)

Change in sentiment relation
resulting in a balance of two
negative relations and one
positive relation.

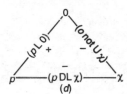

(d)

Change in unit relation resulting in
a balance of two negative relations
and one positive relation.

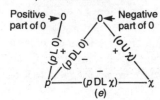

(e)

Change in unit relation through
differentiation resulting in a
balance of two negative relations
and one positive relation.

Figure 6.4 Change towards balance within unbalanced triads (Heider, 1958)

and third examples form a balanced system, while in the second and fourth examples the elements are in a state of imbalance. If a system is in balance the relations fit together; if a system is not in balance there exists some kind of incongruency between the relations. Generally Heider describes a dyad as balanced if the two relations between elements have the same sign, positive or negative, while in an imbalanced dyad the signs are different. A triad is in balance if all three relations are positive or if one relation is positive and two relations are negative. A triad is not in balance when two relations have a positive sign and the third is negative, so that the product of the three signs (++−) is negative. The main postulate of Heider's theory is that cognitive representations of systems in a state of imbalance are unsteady, and he assumes a tendency in the perceiver to change these structures in such a way that the new structures represent systems or structures in balance. Balanced presentations are assumed to have a steady state.

Balance can be achieved or restored by changing sentiment relations or unit relations in the representation as shown in Figure 6.4.

The tendency to change an imbalanced system into a balanced one, the balance principle, may be conceived as a set of cognitive inference rules, that is, a set of rules which predicts the inferences people draw from information they receive. By definition, unit relations are symmetric: pUo implies oUp. Unit relations can have two values: present ('on') and absent ('off'). Sentiment relations need not be symmetric: p may like o, but p may be disliked by o. Possible values of sentiment relations are: like, dislike and no relations. Besides the set of rules constituted by the balance principle, other more simple inference rules may be conceived (see, for example, Crockett, 1982). One of these is the positivity rule. If perceivers are presented with one or two positive sentiment relations in a triad, employment of the positivity rule will lead them to infer that all sentiment relations are positive.

The reverse of the positivity rule is the negative rule of inference. It says that if one sentiment relation is negative all other sentiment relations will be inferred to be negative too. Other competing rules discerned by Crockett are the source agreement and target agreement rules. The source agreement rule implies that if one relation from p, the source, is positive, it will be inferred that the other one is also positive; if one relation is negative, the inference is that the other one will also be negative. Examples are: if pL+o, then pL+x; if pL–x, then pL–o); in this case no relation is inferred as to the third relation in the triad. The target (which may be o or x) agreement rule implies that the two relations to o should have the same sign, whilst no relation is inferred as to the third relation (e.g. if oL+p, then oL+x).

The set of rules comprising the balance principle consists of the following: (1) sentiment relations and unit relations are symmetric; (2) these relations are usually transitive (e.g. if pL+o and oL+x, then pL+x); (3) negative sentiment relations are anti-transitive, i.e. when p has a negative relation to o and o has a negative relation to x, then p has the opposite relation with x (pL+x); (4) present unit relations induce positive sentiment relations and vice versa; and (5) negative sentiment relations induce non-unit relations (Crockett, 1982).

A number of experiments have been performed to establish to what extent the balance principle or the more simple alternative rules affect subjects' cognitive representations. This was arranged by providing subjects with incomplete information about the relations in a given structure (e.g. a triad) and asking them to draw inferences about the relations that were not presented.

An example is: if p likes o and o likes x, what is the probability that p likes x? Crockett (1982) reviewed about fifty experiments using this approach. The results showed strong evidence for the balance principle. In addition, he found a much weaker tendency towards use of the positivity rule and the two agreement rules. A second test of the balance principle is the study of De Soto (1960), which we discussed earlier. In this experiment and in six comparable experiments, balanced social structures were learned more easily than unbalanced structures. A third way to test the balance principle is to have subjects study balanced and unbalanced structures and measure which structures are recalled more correctly. In his review Crockett (1982) again found strong evidence that balanced structures are recalled more accurately than unbalanced systems. Taken together, these results offer strong evidence for the proposition that cognitive representations tend to be organized in the direction of balance. Heider (1946, 1958) describes this tendency as a cognitive phenomenon, which is comparable to the grouping of physical stimuli according to the rules of Gestalt psychology.

A generalization of the balance principle is that people prefer balanced structures over unbalanced ones. This implication was tested for the first time in an experiment by Jordan (1953). He presented subjects with hypothetical triads in which they themselves were an element. Subjects were asked to indicate the degree of pleasantness or unpleasantness of each structure. Jordan found evidence for a balance effect: balanced systems were rated as more pleasant than unbalanced systems. A reanalysis of these results (Jordan, 1966, in Zajonc, 1968) showed that the pleasantness of the situations could be predicted if the balance principle was combined with three additional assumptions. These assumptions are: (1) a liking relation is more important than a unit relation; (2) a p–o relation is more important than a p–x relation; and (3) a p–x relation is more important than an o–x relation. The pattern of results in this experiment and subsequent studies appears to be complicated and sometimes contradictory; these results are discussed by Zajonc (1968) and Insko (1984).

Socio-emotional structures

Whereas Heider (1958) proposes that imbalance will always be corrected by cognitive reconstruction, Newcomb (1953, 1961, 1968), paying more attention to real behaviours, proposes that imbalance may be corrected through p's attempts to modify his or her own and others' behaviour. Newcomb assumes that existing imbalance leads to psychological tension and pressure towards balance. This tension may be so strong that it instigates verbal behaviours, communicative acts, and other overt behaviours aimed at restoring or achieving balance. In other words, where Heider emphasizes the cognitive consequences of imbalance, Newcomb is more inclined to stress the communicative tuning consequences.

In an extensive field study, Newcomb (1961) followed seventeen male students in a college house during an academic term. The subjects responded weekly to questionnaires and interviews and attended regular house meetings. At the beginning of the study, the relation between similarity in attitudes and values and interpersonal attraction was rather weak, but this relation became steadily stronger during the term, while attitudes remained the same. So, as the students became acquainted with one another's attitudes, attraction increased between those students who had similar attitudes.

The balance principle also appears relevant to the question of why people with a similar work attitude stick together. This was shown in an experimental study by E.G. French (1956). In that study, subjects were categorized by means of a projective test (see chapter 1) as either placing high value on achievement and competence with little concern for affiliative activities or as placing high value on affiliations with little concern for achievement and competence. During the experiment they had to make a choice between either a partner who was very competitive but not especially liked, or a friend who was not very competitive. It was found that people who valued achievement selected partners who were competent, but not very likeable. People who valued affiliation selected partners who fulfilled their affiliative needs, but who were short on competence.

Another way of looking at the development of group structure is proposed by Byrne (1971), who emphasizes that people strive for positively evaluated relations and tend to eschew negatively evaluated others; that is, more than Heider, Byrne starts with the notion of reflective tuning, while emphasizing the reinforcing consequences of positive rewards. Agreement with one's own attitude is experienced as rewarding, and this reward is associated with the provider of the reward. Conversely, disagreement with one's own attitude is experienced as punishment, and this negative incentive is associated with the provider of the negative incentive. As a consequence, Byrne reasons, a group member develops stronger liking relations with some group members and weaker ones with others.

Byrne's reflective view on group structure proposes that individual group members are responding in accordance with their own views on the differential rewards and punishments provided by specific group members, that is, group members form relations in which they are directly involved. Moreover, the reflective view may explain why interpersonal relations may be strengthened and weakened during interaction. For example, suppose that a group member A has been rewarded in the past by B. In that case, for A group member B is associated with rewards. Suppose further that B subsequently starts to deliver negative incentives. In that case the once positive relation from A to B is weakened. In the same vein, a positive relation between A and B may be strengthened if B provides A with further positive incentives.

How subsequent rewards may instigate cooperative exchanges between two group members has been described extensively in the literature (for a review, see Burnstein, 1969). For example, Sidowski, Wyckoff and Tabory (1956) and Sidowski (1957) let subjects repeatedly play a game with rewards (e.g. +10) and punishments (e.g. −10) as shown in Figure 6.5. For example, if p chooses Right and o chooses Left, p receives −10 and o receives +10 cents.

A particular aspect of the original Sidowski et al. study (1956) was that p was unaware that he or she was actually working with o. Moreover, p could only make two choices, without complete knowledge of the matrix in Figure 6.5. P could turn on a right or a left switch. So p presumably thought that this was an individual experiment. In reality there was another subject. The results indicated that cooperative interdependence (Right p, Right o) developed in the absence of any awareness by p or o that their respective outcomes were contingent on the behaviour of another: after repeated trials p and o 'learned' to make a cooperative choice (+10, +10; see Figure 6.5).

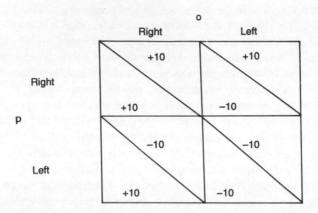

Figure 6.5 Game matrix employed in the Sidowski (1957) study

Kelley, Thibaut, Radloff and Mundy (1962) viewed the Sidowski *et al.* experiment from the perspective of what they called the 'win–stay, lose–change' rule, implying that a person tends to repeat the response following a positive (+10) outcome and to change to the alternative following a negative outcome (–10, see Figure 6.5). In their study p was aware that o was responding. In the condition in which p and o had to make a choice simultaneously, they found that mutual cooperation increased over trials.

Although in the experiment by Kelley *et al.* (1962) subjects were directly receiving positive or negative rewards, by implication their research findings are of relevance to the effect of attitudinal agreement on the formation of interpersonal relations. This is because, assuming that agreement with our own attitude is rewarding, it may be expected that we will build up strong ties with group members who agree with us. Conversely, weak ties will be built up with group members who disagree with us. If it subsequently turns out that strong ties are associated with attitudinal disagreement, this will affect the strength of the interpersonal relation in that the disagreers will be less liked than before.

EMPHASIS ON ROLE STRUCTURE

Earlier, we defined structure as a cognitive and normative social representation of how parts (group members and tasks) are interrelated. This is nearly identical to the idea that group members are expected to fulfil and in fact do fulfil various roles. In the language of role theory (e.g. Biddle, 1979; Sarbin and Allen, 1968), groups are described as systems of interdependent roles. As a starting point for our discussion of groups as role structures, we offer the definition of a role provided by Jones and

Gerard: 'behavior that is characteristic and expected of a person or persons who occupy a position in the group' (Jones and Gerard, 1967, p. 718). A key concept in this definition is position. If the group task is divisible, positions are dictated by the various subtasks which have to be performed. For example, in a group of mountain climbers there are the positions of rope leader and followers. A plane cockpit crew includes the positions of pilot, co-pilot and flight engineer. Any position implies several sets of behaviours: behaviours that concern the task and various behaviours directed to the other group members, who occupy their own positions as well. In addition, each group member occupies many positions at the same time. For example, the pilot is the boss as well as a member of the crew, and he or she may also be a friend of the co-pilot. The other key concept in the definition is expected behaviour. Expectations vary greatly in formality, detail and explicitness. For example, a plane crew has to follow a detailed step-by-step flight manual, while a secretary at a fairly informal meeting would be expected to take the minutes in one way or another. The expectations of plane crew members are spelled out in a manual and are totally independent of the particular person who holds the position during a particular flight. For example, at a given moment during a flight it is specified who will actually fly the plane and at a later moment the same person may act as the co-pilot.

Other expectations are more informal and idiosyncratic. In this respect Bales described a joker as, 'ascendant and expressive, non-task oriented, perhaps unconventional or even deviant. He seems neither clearly friendly nor unfriendly, but entertaining, joking, dramatic, relativistic, free in his associations, taking pleasure in play, activity, novelty and creativity' (Bales, 1970, p. 245).

Katz and Kahn (1978) define role behaviour as a sequence of behavioural units or role episodes. Each unit is 'construed' in several stages. First, expectations must be formed and communicated to the role player (or role occupant). The sources of these communications, the role senders, may be people outside the group, the other group members, the role occupants themselves or any combination of these sources. In the next stage, these communications, or role messages, are received and interpreted by the role occupant. The resulting mental representation is transformed into behaviours directed towards others inside and, depending on task demands, perhaps outside the group. The behaviours are observed, interpreted and evaluated by the role senders. Finally, group members may give evaluative feedback about the fit or match between the observed role behaviours and their expectations concerning the role. In this view, group interaction and task performance are ongoing sequences of role episodes in which each member is simultaneously role sender to one or more others and the target of communications sent by one or more others. The expectations discussed thus far are normative: they prescribe desirable behaviours. However, members differ in their involvement in the group and in the task. As a consequence, they tend to differ in the amount and nature of their contributions to the group process. Very early in the group process, and sometimes right from the start, as we have seen in chapter 5, group members develop representations of themselves and of each other, which in turn lead to expectations and prescriptions. These expectations are also called 'role anticipation'. They steer the interaction at later moments and finally result in role differentiation between members. Therefore, role structures in a group may be considered both cause and consequence of the ongoing interaction.

Role theorists (e.g. Biddle, 1979; Katz and Kahn, 1978; Sarbin and Allen, 1968) have devoted much attention to the sources of stress in a role system. They make a distinction between three broad sources of role stress: ambiguity, conflict and overload. In the following we will briefly discuss these problems.

Role ambiguity may arise for several reasons. A role sender may communicate unclear expectations or the expectation that different behaviours should be performed at the same moment. This makes it difficult for the role occupant to form a clear and stable cognitive representation of the received role messages, especially if new or rapidly changing situations are involved. Even if the representation is clear, it may be difficult to transform it into consistent role episodes. Especially difficult in this respect is the role of newcomer in an existing group (Moreland and Levine, 1989).

Role conflict may arise if several role senders communicate incompatible expectations to a role taker. This is especially likely to occur if the role position serves as a link between two or more groups and these groups impose conflicting demands on the role occupant. Another kind of conflict may arise if the level of ability of the role occupant is below the level required for role performance. A third form of conflict may arise if the role requires behaviour that is in disagreement with personal beliefs and values of the role occupant.

Role overload may result when too many role demands are incorporated in a single role or when there is competition between different roles, especially if the priorities between conflicting expectations are not specified.

How serious are these three forms of role stress? In a review of nearly sixty studies Fisher and Gitelson (1983) compared the consequences of role ambiguity, role conflict and role overload. They found strong negative relations between the amount of expected role conflict in organizations, on the one hand, and reported satisfaction with co-workers, supervisor, salary and job, on the other. For role ambiguity and role overload these relations were weaker, suggesting that role conflict has more serious consequences than role ambiguity and role overload.

It is obvious that removal of the above-listed sources of role stress requires cognitive, reflective and communicative tuning, processes that should lead to a new and less demanding role structure in the group. Such a change in role structure will undoubtedly have consequences for all the other structures that have been discussed in this chapter.

CONCLUSIONS AND SUMMARY

Structure is a consensual representation that is developed through cognitive, reflective and communicative tuning processes. Consensual representation refers to how group members and their tasks actually relate. This is the descriptive part of social structure. A consensual representation implies prescriptions of the interrelatedness of group members and their connections with the task, that is, social structure also pertains to how group members should act.

Following four examples – of (a) interdependent structures in a task group; (b) interdependent structures in an organization; (c) the emergence and change of structures; and (d) the interrelatedness of influence, outcomes and task structure – this chapter outlined the consequences of three tuning processes. In cognitive tuning the emphasis is on how a social structure is learned. With regard to reflective tuning, it was shown that the exchange of rewards is partly responsible for the emergence of social structures. In the section on communicative tuning we described how influence differentials may arise due to approving and disapproving communication. In the remainder of this chapter it was argued that these three tuning processes are of relevance to an understanding of both the organization of a task and the structure of group relations.

Steiner's system of task classification has been described, and it has been shown that the properties of a task, the way in which outcomes are to be distributed among group members and social decision schemes strongly affect group performance. One of the consequences of divisible tasks is that the task can be partitioned in such a way that each group member is assigned a part of the task and can play a particular role. It has been shown that roles are distributed through cognitive, reflective and communicative tuning. It has been stressed that interpersonal relations are cognitively organized and that the motivation to strive for balance plays a major role. In addition, it has been emphasized that exchanging rewards through communication also has a strong impact on the way interpersonal relations are organized.

Chapter 7

Influence and leadership

In the introduction to the previous chapter we showed that influence structures within groups are learned, built up by pairwise comparison of who controls the behaviour of whom (De Soto, 1960), that is, influence structure refers to a shared cognitive representation.

Moreover, in chapter 5 on communicative tuning, we explained Expectation States Theory, or EST (Berger *et al.*, 1980), a theory which emphasizes that influence differentials are a consequence of expectations group members hold about group members' potential contributions to group success, and it seems logical to derive from this theory that the influence structure within a group may be based on differential expectations about the extent to which individual members will contribute to group success. In addition, Blau's ideas about exchange between group members (Blau, 1955) make it clear that when one group member is contributing more effort and ability than other group members, he or she is compensated for it by the right to lead the group.

Lastly, as one might remember, EST offers an explanation of how there emerges an influence structure in free-communicating groups (Bales, 1950) that is featured by distinct task and socio-emotional leadership differentials. These studies suggest not only that influence differentials in small groups are a consequence of cognitive and reflective processing about who is contributing more to group success, but that it is by communication that group members form cognitions and are able to reflect on the group members' potential contributions.

Having more or less influence may pertain to the organization of the task or to the organization of the group, and usually a combination of both is involved. Regarding the organization of the group members, in a learning experiment by De Soto (1960) subjects exposed to stimulus materials learned that A had more influence than B, whereas B had greater control over C, and so on. This means that, for example, C had less influence than A, but more than D, suggesting that influence has a relative significance: although A has more control than C, this does not mean that C does not have any control over group members lower in the pecking order. Thus, an influence structure departing from a definition of influence over people implies that there is no member who has absolute influence, but that influence is shared, with members higher in the pecking order exerting more influence. Moreover, the concept of influence is not as simple as it seems. In De Soto's experiment subjects had to learn who controlled whose behaviour. However, one may imagine that in groups members lower in the pecking order may also resist influence attempts by group members higher in the pecking order. Usually, group members higher in the pecking order can better resist influence exercised by lower group members than the reverse, and in this respect influence over people in the learning experiment of De Soto refers to the net influence exercised: the influence attempts by group members higher in the pecking order minus the influence resisted by group members lower in the pecking order.

With regard to the organization of the task, influence also concerns who in the group is allowed to perform certain tasks, so influence via specific task behaviour is involved. Following our analysis of tasks this means that group members higher in the pecking order are more responsible for higher hierarchical sensing-testing-effecting minisystems than lower-placed individuals, who are responsible for lower hierarchical sensing-testing-effecting minisystems.

In sum, influence structure may be described as a covariation of influence over, influence to and influence from. Members higher in an organization usually have more influence over people, have more freedom to set organizational goals and are more able to resist influence attempts than members lower in the organization. What this description of influence structure implies is that influence is not absolute, but relative: higher-placed group members may have more influence than other members, but it does not follow that group members higher in the organization are active and the workers or followers passive. On the contrary, (a) followers may also influence people above them, although this occurs to a lesser extent than the reverse; (b) followers may resist influence attempts by their supervisors; and (c) within their own task realm followers have a certain task autonomy: whereas top managers in an organization are more responsible for hierarchically higher sensing-testing-effecting minisystems (i.e. for planning), and supervisors for intermediate minisystems, workers are responsible for hierarchically lower minisystems involving the final effecting of the task, i.e. task exertion.

Leadership is based on influence, and it usually implies greater influence on the part of leaders over followers than the reverse, and a greater degree of influence exerted by leaders on the organization of the task than by followers. In the present chapter it will be argued that leadership involves task, cognitive, reflective and communicative tuning by leaders and followers with respect to each other and the group task. Before we explicitly examine these tuning processes, we will present a short review of some of the previous approaches to leadership.

HISTORICAL DEVELOPMENTS

Early studies focused on leadership as a role distinguished from the role of followers. These studies were mainly data-driven and did not give much attention to the underlying processes.

The leadership role is a position which may be occupied by any of the members of a group. Why is it, then, that a certain person becomes the leader? In the following we will deal with several answers to this question, namely: (1) the leader is born to leadership; (2) the leader exhibits certain behaviours; and (3) the leader exhibits certain behaviours in specific situations.

The great man theory of leadership

What are the characteristics of a successful leader? Until 1950 what is referred to as the trait approach was very popular. Reviewing studies in which characteristics of leaders were compared with those of non-leaders, Stogdill (1948) found that leaders are more intelligent, have more education, are more inclined to take on responsibilities, are more active and have higher socio-economic status.

He concluded that the personality approach yields interesting data, but that dependency on situational factors seems to be of major importance in determining who will become a leader.

The behavioural approach

Another approach to leadership focuses on the behaviour of leaders. Several methods of investigation were used to establish how leaders behave. In Chapter 5 we already saw that Bales and Slater (1955), employing observation methods (Bales's Interaction Process Analysis: Bales, 1950), discovered that leaders score higher than their followers on task and socio-emotional activities and that consequently two kinds of leaders can be distinguished: the Best-liked person or socio-emotional leader, who ensures a harmonious group atmosphere; and the Best-idea person or a task-leader, who, more than any other member, contributes to task achievement.

The questionnaire method was employed in the Ohio State University leadership studies. The following steps were taken. First, researchers developed a list of nine key types of behaviour that seemed to characterize military and organizational leaders. Second, a questionnaire that asked subordinates to rate leaders was constructed and submitted in all kinds of organizational settings. Third, correlations between these ratings were calculated and then compared via factor analysis, a method for tracing salient patterns of correlations. Two factors explained 83 per cent of the variation in the followers' evaluation of their leaders (Halpin and Winer, 1957). The factors were *consideration* and *initiating structure*. Consideration pertains to the degree to which the leader responds to group members in a warm and friendly fashion and involves mutual trust, openness and willingness to explain decisions. Initiating structure is defined as the degree to which the leader organizes, directs and defines the group's structure and goals, regulates group behaviour, monitors communication and reduces goal ambiguities (Halpin and Winer, 1957; Lord, 1977).

Other questionnaire studies also revealed two broad categories of leader behaviour. Most notable are the investigations performed at the University of Michigan. Likert (1967) employed steps that were similar to those taken in the Ohio State University leadership studies. His results also revealed two factors, namely *employee centered* and *production centered* behaviour, factors which seem to match the aforementioned Ohio State leadership factors, i.e. consideration and initiating structure, respectively.

Thus in a group there seems to be a need for two kinds of leadership styles, each having its own impact on group productivity. Steiner (1976, p. 418) summarizes these findings as follows:

actual productivity = potential productivity − unrealized productivity

In his view, task leaders bolster a group's potential productivity. They ensure that as many as possible of the group's social resources are mobilized. Socioemotional leaders serve to minimize unrealized productivity. They prevent the accumulation of tensions that might undermine harmonious group relations and be detrimental to actual group productivity.

At present, the behavioural approach does not seem to be popular any more. The main reason is that quite often little support for the consideration factor has been found in observational studies (e.g. Lord, 1977). In an observational investigation Couch and Carter (1953) report a low correlation between ratings of leadership and the consideration factor. They even found that consideration and initiating structure together explained less variation than a third factor, *individual prominence*, which refers to the leader's assumption of the leadership role by declaring himself or herself as the leader.

From the above-reported studies it may be concluded that the results of questionnaire studies partially contradict findings collected by means of observational methods. Ilgen and Fujii (1976) have pointed out that the main weakness of the questionnaire studies is that researchers ask respondents for desirable images of their leaders, instead of for realistic ones. Observational studies, on the other hand, are performed by trained outsiders who are less likely to exhibit such bias.

In sum, research representing the behavioural approach has clearly demonstrated that leaders take care of task success: observational studies indicate that leaders contribute more than their followers to the task process, while questionnaire results indicate that leaders should behave in a task-oriented way. The second factor − consideration or socio-emotional behaviour − has received less support. Questionnaire results indicate that respondents appreciate it if their leader favours a harmonious group atmosphere. Results collected by means of observational methods provide relatively less support for this factor. Individual prominence − the leader's tendency to be assertive and stand out in his or her group − is possibly a much more important characteristic of leaders.

Situational determinants of leadership

The example of Jones's restaurant (chapter 6) demonstrates that in the beginning Jones's leadership was rather implicit, but became more explicit as his restaurant increased in size and complexity. Many groups start without a leader. Committees, clubs, and friendship and study circles quite often start as leaderless groups. However, after a while a leader usually emerges. The question to consider is: when does a group require an explicit leader?

As is suggested in the example of Jones's restaurant, the size of a group can be an important reason to introduce explicit leadership. Large groups seem to have a greater need for explicit leadership than small groups. This was shown in a study by Hemphill (1950). He compared the behaviours of large-group leaders with those of small-group leaders. He observed that large groups rely more often on a leader to make rules clear, keep members informed and make group decisions. In a later review of situational factors affecting the need for leadership, Hemphill (1961) suggests that other factors also facilitate the emergence of explicit leaders in groups, namely, the nature of the task and the availability of a group member who has experience in the leadership role. He specifies the following task circumstances as those which promote the emergence of a leader: (1) groups must have the feeling that task success is possible; (2) group members must attach great value to task success; and (3) the task itself requires co-ordination and communication.

The task requirements mentioned above are clearly involved in what are referred to as social dilemmas (see Dawes, 1980). Social dilemmas are task structures in which it is in anybody's interest to behave selfishly. They pose a dilemma, because if everybody makes a selfish choice, one is worse off than one would be if everyone had made a collective choice. We encountered this dilemma before, when we referred to the free-rider dilemma: all group members are inclined to keep their task expenditure to a minimum; however when all group members do so, the group as a whole fails. Other illustrations may also be given. For example, every student in a hall of residence is inclined to heat his or her room to maximum, because it is known that the price of heating is to be shared anyway; however, if all students behave likewise, the collective bill may be extremely high. Dawes (1980) refers to societal problems such as over-population, energy depletion and pollution as social dilemmas. Rutte and Wilke (1984) considered the circumstances under which group members will opt for a leader in a social dilemma situation. Two factors appeared to be of relevance: (1) whether the group had failed to maintain the collective resource; and (2) whether large differences in outcomes between group members had emerged. The first factor refers to task success: if task success is in danger, one opts for a leader. The second factor pertains to equity: when outcomes have been inequitably allocated, group members prefer a leader who will take decisions on behalf of all group members.

Three additional results seem to be of importance. First, Rutte and Wilke (1985) investigated subjects' preferences for other decision structures as well, to wit: unanimity, large majority, small majority and everyone for him- or herself. It turned out that over all conditions of the experiment, the preference for a leader was lower than the preference for any other decision structure, suggesting that group members have a strong reluctance to opt for a leader who will take away their own decisional freedom. Second, when asked which group member they would like to choose as a leader, most subjects were likely to prefer themselves, indicating that holding such a powerful position is very attractive, and that being powerless is a demotivating factor. Third, when elected leader, subjects acted in the interest of the group and allocated the outcomes in a fair way (Steiner, 1972, 1976).

These findings may be related to Steiner's ideas about group productivity, i.e.

$$\text{group productivity} = \text{potential productivity} \pm \text{coordination losses/gains} \pm \text{motivation losses/gains}$$

The instalment of a leader is a means to increase the coordination of group efforts, which obviously gives rise to coordination gains. In turn, coordination gains may motivate group members to contribute to group success. However, motivational losses may also play a role. The loss of subordinates' decisional freedom to take decisions may induce them to minimize their efforts, and to leave it to the leader to take care of the productivity of the group.

By implication, the results of the experiment of Rutte and Wilke (1985) suggest that group members in a leaderless group have no need to install a leader if the group acts successfully without a leader and if the outcomes of group performance are allocated in a fair way, indicating that in some groups co-ordination by a leader is considered superfluous. That the leadership role is unlikely and unnecessary under certain conditions has been shown more explicitly by Kerr and Jermier (1978).

Figure 7.1 suggests that when a group is composed of (1) competent group members, who have (2) a great need for independence, and (3) a sense of professional identity, task-oriented leadership is unnecessary, since it may be assumed that, without the intervention of a task leader, the group is able to mobilize sufficient potential productivity, to coordinate its efforts and to moti-vate its members.

Properties of the task may also make a leader superfluous. When the task itself automatically controls the behaviour of the group members, for example in an assembly-line, a task or coordinating leader is not necessary (5, 6, 7). In that case there is more need for relationship-oriented leadership which keeps the group members' motivation at a satisfactory level. Lastly, the type of organization also influences whether a task leader is necessary. When an organization is highly formalized (9, 10, 11), task leadership is unnecessary because leadership has been built into formal rules. In that case there is a greater need for relationship-oriented leadership, which humanizes the rigid organizational environment.

Characteristics	Will tend to neutralize	
	Relationship-oriented leadership	Task-oriented leadership
Of the group member		
1. Ability, experience, training, knowledge		X
2. Need for independence	X	X
3. 'Professional' orientation	X	X
4. Indifference towards group rewards	X	X
Of the task		
5. Unambiguous and routine		X
6. Methodologically invariant		X
7. Provides its own feedback concerning accomplishment		X
8. Intrinsically satisfying	X	
Of the organization		
9. Formalization (explicit plans, goals, and areas of responsibility)		X
10. Inflexibility (rigid, unbending rules and procedures)		X
11. Highly specified and active advisory and staff functions		X
12. Closely knit, cohesive work groups	X	X
13. Organizational rewards not within leader's control	X	X
14. Spatial distance between superior and subordinate	X	X

Figure 7.1 Substitutes for leadership (adapted from Kerr and Jermier, 1978)

Figure 7.1 also makes clear that when group members are indifferent to organizational rewards, namely, when the group is very cohesive (12) and when the leader has neither the means (13) nor the faculties (14) to motivate his subordinates, both relationship- and task-oriented leadership seem to be inadequate.

In sum, the above-reported findings suggest that there is a greater need for leadership as groups increase in size. In large groups the coordination and motivation of group members may become a problem, and this problem may be solved by the instalment of a leader. Two other circumstances seem to lead to the introduction of a leader, namely, endangered task success and an unfair allocation of outcomes among group members. By implication, these data suggest that leadership is unlikely when a leaderless group achieves task success and when the group outcomes are allocated in a fair way. Other circumstances pertaining to the persons involved, the task and the type of organization also influence whether a leader is likely to emerge. In the following section we will explain Fiedler's approach, which offers an explicit model of leader effectiveness that takes into account both the behavioural style of the leader, as measured by his attitude towards the least preferred co-worker, and the favourableness of the situation.

Behavioural style and situation

According to Fiedler (1978) studies of leadership have failed to acknowledge that the effect of the behaviour of the leader is contingent on certain characteristics of the situation. His contingency model assumes that group productivity can only be predicted when one knows both the leader's leadership style and his or her situational control; in other words, the specific leadership style involved and the degree of situational control together determine a leader's effectiveness.

Leadership style refers to the extent to which a leader is either relationship- or task-motivated and is based on the leader's ratings of the Least-Preferred Co-worker (LPC). The 'high-LPC leader' or relationship-motivated leader perceives this co-worker in a relatively favourable manner. This type of leader derives considerable satisfaction from successful interpersonal relationships. The 'low-LPC leader' or task-motivated leader rates his or her least preferred co-worker in a very unfavourable way and is described as a person who derives most satisfaction from task performance.

Besides leadership style, situational control is of importance. A leader's situational control has three components, namely, leader/member relations, which may be good or bad; the task, which may be structured or unstructured; and the leader's position power, which may be strong or weak. In the following these three components will be explained.

* *Leader/member relations* can be measured with the 'Group Atmosphere Scale', which has the leader assess his or her work team on a series of scales, such as pleasant/unpleasant, friendly/unfriendly and bad/good. Leader/member relations are conceived of as 'good' if the leader rates his or her team above average in a positive way, and 'bad' if the leader rates the team below average on the scale.
* The *structure of the task* may vary between 'structured' and 'unstructured'. A task is 'structured' to the extent that it has clear-cut requirements and a prescribed method of solution, i.e. when there is a simple goal and one solution that can be realized easily.
* *Position power* refers to the ability of leaders to evaluate the performance of their workers and to give them rewards or punishments. For example, a leader who can increase or decrease a worker's salary or promotion prospects is assumed to have 'strong position power', whereas a leader who does not possess the means to reward is assumed to have 'weak position power'.

The three components of situational control led Fiedler to distinguish eight situations, which may be conceived as the conditions of a 2 (leader/member relations: good, bad) × 2 (task structure: structured, unstructured) × 2 (leader position power: strong, weak) factorial design. In the bottom part of Figure 7.2 these eight situations are depicted and ordered in terms of the extent to which situational control may be conceived of as favourable or unfavourable.

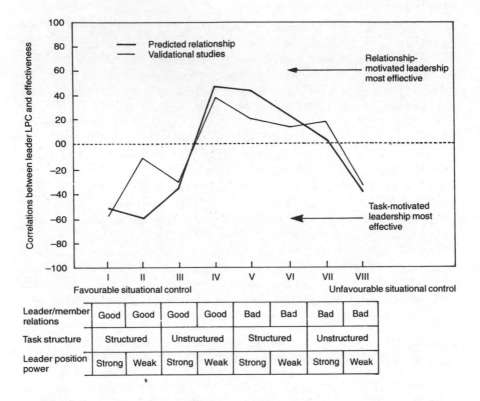

Figure 7.2 The predicted and obtained relationship between LPC score and leadership effectiveness in eight group situations (adapted from Fiedler, 1978)

Thus, according to Fiedler, leadership style and situational control together determine leadership effectiveness as measured by group performance, that is, one has to know how leadership style and situational control interact to be able to predict the effectiveness of a leader. Fiedler's main hypothesis is that low-LPC or task-motivated leaders are most effective when situational control is either very favourable or very unfavourable (see Figure 7.2). In contrast, high-LPC or relationship-motivated leaders are able to elicit good group performance when situational control is good. Thus, in extreme (favourable and unfavourable) situations, task-motivated leaders are most effective, while relationship-motivated leaders are most effective in middle-range situations.

From the upper part of Figure 7.2 it can be seen that the predictions derived from Fiedler's contingency model have received empirical support (see also Chemers, 1983). The model nevertheless possesses certain limitations which should be noted. First, a theoretical problem is the exact meaning of the LPC instrument (Schriesheim and Kerr, 1977), suggesting that no satisfactory interpretation of LPC scores exists. Hosking (1981) has pointed out that not knowing what LPC scores mean implies not knowing why these measures should be expected to correlate with group performance. Second, there are numerous methodological problems associated with Fiedler's contingency model, to wit: (1) the Group Atmosphere Scale is not independent of the leader, yet his situational favourableness is conceptualized as an independent dimension; (2) quite often LPC scores were obtained from persons who did not actually perform the leadership function; (3) LPC scores correlate with group performance, suggesting that LPC is not an independent variable; (4) LPC scores are unstable over time; and (5) a number of statistical problems are involved (for a critical evaluation, see: Hosking, 1981). Third, several investigators, such as Hosking (ibid.), suggest that the weight of evidence does not support Fiedler's model.

Thus, the literature shows that Fiedler's contingency model is rather controversial. Opponents, such as Hosking, as well as supporters, such as Chemers (1983), are of the opinion that considerably more work remains to be done (see further, for example, Fiedler and Garcia, 1987).

Another theory of leadership style has been proposed by Blake and Mouton (1982), who began from the basis of the Ohio State studies. They suggest that leadership style depends on the answers to two basic questions: 'how strong is the leader's concern for production, i.e. for group performance?' and 'how strong is the leader's concern for the feelings of the people involved?' By and large, the following four explicit types of managers may be distinguished:

- the *apathetic leader*, who has concern neither for the task nor for his people, i.e. he has low concern for production and low concern for people;
- the *task master*, who pursues a high level of production with no concern for his people, i.e. he has high concern for production but no concern for his people;
- the *country club leader*, who is concerned with pleasant intra-group relations, but not with the group task, i.e. he has low concern for productivity but high concern for people;
- the *ideal leader*, who values both people and products highly, i.e. he has high concern for production and high concern for people. The ideal leader tackles organizational goals with teamwork involving a high degree of shared responsibility, coupled with high levels of participation and commitment.

Research reported by Blake and Mouton (1982) suggests that only one style is the best: the ideal leader. However, other authors question whether this combination of high production and high concern for people style is best in all situations (e.g. Quinn and McGrath, 1982). A contrasting proposal is presented by Hersey and Blanchard (1982).

According to Hersey and Blanchard, the optimal leadership style depends on the maturity of the group. A group is defined as mature when it has the capacity to set high but attainable goals, when it shows a willingness to take on responsibility, and when individual group members or the group itself possesses education and/or experience. Newly started groups are immature, whereas groups that function as a team when working towards goals are mature. They propose that the best leadership style for a newly formed group is that characterized by high task concern and low concern for people (the task master style). As the group matures and begins working adequately in pursuit of the task, the leader can adopt the 'ideal' (Blake and Mouton, 1982) leadership style, which involves high production and a strong concern for people. Still later in the group's history, the leader can ease off and put less emphasis on task-motivated leadership, i.e. a country club leadership may be adopted. Finally, when the group is functioning very well as a group and maintaining a good level of production, apathetic leadership style involving low concern for production and low concern for people might be best. Of course, Blake and Mouton (1982) question this model. They argue that too much attention is paid to the maturity of the group. Moreover, they emphasize that in all developmental phases of a group a careful balance between emphasis on the task and emphasis on social relations should be maintained.

This short review of leadership and leader effectiveness suggests there is not much consensus among scholars about which types of behaviour a leader should adopt given a certain work situation. This does not come as a surprise since the behaviour of leader and followers is not the only antecedent of group success. Two examples may suffice to clarify this point. Peters and Waterman (1982), having collected data in a large number of highly successful organizations, tried to explain how the success of these excellent organizations could be explained by the behavioural style of their leaders. A year after this 'search for excellence' it appeared that a large number of these organizations had not remained successful. A second example is van der Vlist's (1970) careful study of the antecedents of group success in the case of crews on fishing trawlers; for example, the ability of the skipper, the motivation of the crew, the influence structure, and characteristics of the trawlers like the engine and the technical outfit. Group performance was measured as the number of tons of fish caught. One of the research questions concerned the extent to which the human and technical factors could explain task performance. It turned out that the technical factors were far more important than the human factors in explaining the performance of the trawlers, suggesting that the human factor may be only partially responsible for task success. And among the human factors, the behaviour of the leader is only one of the decisive determinants. So, since group performance cannot be explained exclusively in terms of the behaviour of the leader, it seems much wiser to try to make an inventory of leadership processes, a strategy that has recently been proposed by Hollander and Offerman (1990). In the following we aim to describe leadership processes from four points of view: (a) task-tuned leadership; (b) the cognitive tuning of leadership; (c) the reflective view on leadership; and (d) the communicative tuning of leadership. We do not suggest that these views are exclusive, but argue that together they may shed light on the complex functioning of leadership.

THE TASK APPROACH TO LEADERSHIP

In chapter 1 we focused on tasks. We proposed that complex tasks are more or less hierarchically organized, that is, they consist of coupled sensing-testing-effecting minisystems wherein the hierarchically higher minisystems steer the hierarchically lower minisystems. In his book on the management control function, Anthony also employs the thermostat analogy to describe the role of management (leadership) in organizations. He defines the management control function as, 'the process by which managers influence other members of the organization to implement the organization's strategies' (Anthony, 1988, p. 3). Managers are assumed to influence the members of the organization by making decisions about what to do and by ensuring that desired results are obtained, i.e. after sensing (gathering information) they formulate goals, which serve as a standard for members of the organization. Moreover, they test whether the formulated goals are implemented, i.e. are effected.

He also points out that the thermostat analogy does not imply that managerial control is mechanical:

1 The goal (the temperature) in the case of a thermostat is externally preset, whereas in human functioning persons decide on goals.
2 The thermostat takes action as soon as the actual temperature is lower than the preset temperature. In human functioning persons have to decide whether there is a discrepancy between a preset goal and the actual results.
3 Unlike the thermostat, persons do not act automatically as soon as there is a discrepancy between actual and desired performance (the goal), i.e. persons gather information through their own senses and in coordination with other organization members.
4 As soon as the thermostat 'concludes' that there is a discrepancy between the actual temperature and the desired one, standard procedures (e.g. heating up the furnace) are followed. In human decision making there are only rarely standard procedures that can be followed as soon as a discrepancy between actual results and the desired goals has been established.
5 The thermostat is a simple system, whereas human decision making in organizations requires coordination with other organization members.
6 Testing, or control as it is called by Anthony, is not a result of actions taken by an external regulating device like the thermostat. In contrast, in groups and organizations control is mostly based on self-control: control is based on one's own judgement concerning necessary actions. This judgement is influenced not only by the formal influence structure but also by informal relations among organization members.
7 Effecting of the established goals is not always automatic, because plans are formulated in specific circumstances and change quite easily when the circumstances change.

In sum, although the thermostat analogy may have some advantages as a means of describing a hierarchically organized task group, the sensing of information, the setting of goals and the monitoring of whether the actual actions meet the desired goals do not proceed in an automatic way but are accomplished by persons who make judgements, who reflect upon possible outcomes and who communicate with other people. So task leadership is interwoven with cognitive, reflective and communicative tuning within groups and organizations.

Having made this reservation, Anthony explains that the top of the organization (where 'the' leader is to be found) is mainly responsible for the hierarchically highest sensing-controlling-effecting minisystem. He calls this 'strategic planning': the process of deciding on the supergoals of the organization and the grand strategies. In the case of profit organizations, examples of supergoals include a satisfactory return on investments, employment stability and providing a good work environment. Non-profit organizations like hospitals and universities set other supergoals. For example, in universities, top management may set goals such as good teaching, good research and stable employment.

Grand strategies pertain to the ways supergoals can be reached. In the case of profit organizations, examples include the selection of markets and of marketing, financial, organizational and research strategies. At any point in time an organization has a set of strategies. The selection of these strategies is based on two types of stimuli: threats and opportunities. Examples of external threats are market inroads by competitors, shifts in consumer tastes, and new government regulations. Internal threats, which come from inside the organization, include failing production, research, and output quality. Opportunities may also come from both outside and inside the organization. Opportunities might involve technological innovations, new perceptions of customer behaviour, or ideas for improving the organization.

Grand strategies developed by top managers have to be implemented by senior managers just under the top-management level. Anthony (1988) calls this *management control*: the process by which managers influence other members of the organization to influence the organization's strategies. Senior managers have to find ways to see that the grand strategies are implemented so that the supergoals can be reached as efficiently as possible. Senior management translates the top management's supergoals and grand strategies into more specific goals and more specific strategies that people in the lower echelons can fulfil.

At the lowest management level there is task control: the process of ensuring that specific tasks are carried out in an efficient way, so that the overall goals can be reached, that is, making sure that the detailed tasks are performed by workers (or machines and computers). Task control refers to one of the lowest levels of sensing-controlling-effecting minisystems, whilst the actual performance of tasks occurs at the lowest level of a task organization. In Figure 7.3 a summary is given of the task-tuned organization. Anthony (1988) points out that the assignment of planning and control in organizations is not absolute. Most of the activities of top managers involve the development of general strategies, i.e.

Management	Sensing: information processing	Controlling: goals	Effecting activities
Top: strategic planning	General assessment of outside and inside opportunities and threats	Supergoals: formulation and general implementation	Strategies
Senior: management control	intermediate	Intermediate goals	Implementation of strategies
Lower: task control	More specific assessment of inside opportunity and threats	Lower goals	More specific activities

Figure 7.3 Management levels and sensing, controlling and effecting

planning. But senior managers' jobs also involve some strategic planning, albeit at a more concrete level, whilst at lower levels of task organization strategic planning is even more concrete and more specific. The reverse is the case for 'control': top managers devote more time to strategic planning, but less time to control. Senior managers devote their time as much to strategic planning as to control, whereas lower management pays the most attention to task control and the least to planning.

The task approach to leadership is closely related to several prominent prior perspectives on leadership. In the following we will briefly describe some of the ideas associated with the 'scientific management school' (Taylor, 1911), Weber's (1922, 1957) 'bureaucratic organization', and the 'scientific adminis-tration' movement (Fayol, 1916).

Taylor, the founder of the scientific management school, performed time and motion studies in order to reduce complex tasks to simple tasks that could be performed by workers. Moreover, he was of the opinion that these simple tasks could be assigned to workers in a strict format and based on formulae and rules, so that the worker, would only be responsible for the execution of the task, whereas all planning and control of these activities would be assigned to their supervisors. In short, Taylor was a proponent of both rigid horizontal differen-tiation of the formal structure of the organization, that is, the idea that workers perform very simple tasks, and rigid vertical differentiation, the notion that task execution is to be performed by workers and all 'brain work' (control and planning) by their supervisors.

Weber (1922, 1957) argued that the scientific management school paid too little attention to the organization as a whole. Weber foresaw enormous growth by organizations and proposed that the organization should be organized like a military or bureaucratic organization. In his view, complex task structure should be divided in such a way that concrete tasks are hierarchically organized and assigned to specific persons so that everyone in his or her task position knows exactly who is responsible for which concrete task. Moreover, he proposed that everyone's rights and duties should be standardized by rules and procedures. In such an organization the people being assigned to the various task positions would be connected with one another in an impersonal way through rules and procedures.

Whereas Weber's ideas were inspired mainly by his own thinking and experience (in the military service), the scientific administration movement was inspired more by practice. During the 1930s a number of pragmatic principles were formulated: (1) the scalar principle: authority relations should run from the top to the bottom of an organization; (2) unity of command: every member of an organization should receive commands from only one other person in the organization, his superior; (3) the exception principle: tasks should be divided in such a way that they have a routine character so that they can be standardized through rules and procedures, and exceptional cases for which there are no rules available should be referred to the superior; and (4) span of control: the number of subordinates of each superior should be limited, because of the superior's inability to lead larger groups.

It should be noted that the above-described historical approaches to task leadership, like Anthony's recent proposal, follow from the idea that the organizational task gives rise to a hierarchical structuring of the organization, whereas in a consequent formal organization structure a distinction is made between top, middle and lower management. However, unlike Weber, the scientific management school and the scientific administration movement, Anthony acknowledges that strategic planning, management control and task control are performed by persons who have to grasp what the external threats and opportunities at each level are. Moreover, it is emphasized by Anthony that management implies the influencing of other members of the organization, whereas in the historical approaches it was tacitly assumed that influencing or control could only be exercised by impersonal influence, i.e. by influence over task positions.

THE COGNITIVE APPROACH TO LEADERSHIP

The task approach to leadership suggests that in a formal organization or in groups, formal positions (like president, secretary, followers) are assigned to persons. Formal group relations are organized hierarchically. This agrees with De Soto's (1960) experiment about the learning of influence relations in small groups (see chapter 6). He showed that asymmetrically or hierarchically organized structures are learned faster when the task involves learning influence relations as compared with learning liking relations. Moreover, he suggests that in the learning of influence relations previously learned schemata or cognitive representations play a role. In the following we will explain a recently developed line of thinking which argues (a) that knowledge about leadership at the top of the influence structure is learned by processing certain cues that give rise to the attribution of leadership; and (b) that implicit cognitive representations have an effect on the perception of the leader's and the followers' behaviours.

Attribution

In chapter 5 we explained Berger's Expectation States Theory (Berger *et al.*, 1980). In short, EST focuses on the emergence of influence differentials in interacting groups. It is assumed that group members search for cues (or status characteristics) to supplement their expectations about successful task contribution. As long as group members consider a certain characteristic a valid predictor of task success, group members who are known to score better on that characteristic are given higher status. Consequently, (a) higher-status persons receive more opportunities to influence lower-status group members than the reverse; and (b) higher-status group members are more inclined to reject influence attempts by lower-status group members than the reverse.

Empirical support for EST has been reported by Berger *et al.* (1980) and others. For example, Greenstein and Knottnerus (1980) observed that a person of greater ability was more influential than a person of lower ability; Torrance (1954) reported that in crews working on the horse-trading problem, a person higher in military rank was able to exert more influence than persons lower in rank; Lee and Ofshe (1981) found that someone who showed more assertiveness was more influential than someone whose behaviour was less assertive; Ridgeway (1978) found that a person who showed the strongest group orientation was more able to influence other group members than another person who apparently pursued his own self-interest. A summary of these findings may be found in Figure 7.4 (see further chapter 5). Figure 7.4 demonstrates why in initially leaderless groups, like the ones investigated by Bales and Slater (1955), a group structure may come into existence. By matching each person with the subtask that he or she is most qualified to perform, group structure arises. Because some characteristics, or qualifications, give rise to higher expectations of successful task contribution than others, status and influence differentiation in groups does occur. That status differences do not always lead to better group performance was shown in the aforementioned study by Torrance (1954), who employed pilots, navigators and gunners as subjects. The group discussion data indicate that of the pilots who had reached the correct answer before group discussion, one tenth failed to persuade their associates to accept it, while one fifth of the navigators and one third of the gunners failed to do so. Thus, a correct solution is more likely to prevail when it is offered by a high-status person than when it is offered by someone of lower status. However, Torrance's results suggest that this also holds for higher-status members who advocate the wrong solution, i.e. high-status members appear to be more successful at persuading other group members to accept the wrong solution than low-status members are. Thus, a high-status person who is on the wrong track is a greater obstacle to group success than an equally mistaken low-status person.

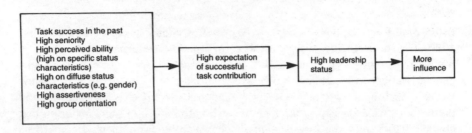

Figure 7.4 Characteristics which give rise to high-status community leadership (adapted from Veen and Wilke, 1984)

EST stresses that, through communication, group members search for cues that will help them to establish the influence structure. A further question is why these cues or attributes give rise to leadership differentials. Calder (1977) and Pfeffer (1977) have argued that attribution theory (see chapter 1) offers a useful framework for understanding group members' perception of leadership. These researchers maintained that leadership is an ascribed disposition that exists only in the eye of the beholder. It is inferred from performance information and from environmental information.

As may be recalled from chapter 1, two types of attribution theories can be distinguished. Kelley (1967) makes use of the covariance principle and causal schemata. Green and Mitchell (1979) have built further on Kelley's ideas in an effort to predict when followers will ascribe the quality of leadership. The second type is Weiner's classification of the causes of behaviour as internal (ability and effort) and external (task difficulty and chance), wherein ability and task difficulty are seen as stable and effort and chance as unstable factors (Weiner and Kukla, 1970). Because most research in this area has been performed by researchers who employed Weiner's classification system (see Phillips and Lord, 1981), we will present one study which shows that the re-election of a leader in an experimental situation is based on the attributions regular group members make.

In a study carried out by Wit, Wilke and van Dijk (1989) regular group members had chosen to have a leader who harvested on behalf of all in a take-some situation. Subsequently, they were informed either that the size of the collective resource ('the pool') was very predictable or that the size was rather uncertain and thus unpredictable. Thereafter they saw how their leader performed, i.e. harvested. Half of the group saw that their leader was successful in that the leader was able to prevent the collective pool from becoming exhausted. This was, of course, arranged by means of bogus feedback about the leader's behaviour. Likewise, the other half of the group saw that the leader was unsuccessful, i.e. failed to maintain the collective pool. So there were four conditions: success or failure of a leader in either a predictable or an unpredictable environment.

After the leader had either performed successfully or not, regular group members were requested to express whether they wanted their leader back or not. Moreover, subjects had to indicate separately whether the leader's results had something to do with ability, with effort, with task difficulty, or with chance. It appeared that subjects wanted the leader back more often if the leader had succeeded than if he had failed. Moreover, a successful leader was re-elected more often in a predictable environment (when he could foresee the consequences of his choices) than when he had succeeded in an unpredictable environment. Another result was that the effects of the independent factors (success or failure of a leader in a predictable or unpredictable environment) on re-election or endorsement appeared to be largely mediated by attribution of ability and chance. A leader's endorsement or re-election depended on whether it was inferred that he or she possessed the quality of a leader. Leadership refers to the attribution of an internal factor, namely ability, that is discounted when success has been achieved in an unpredictable environment.

Implicit leadership theories

As we argued before when we dealt with De Soto's (1960) experiment in which subjects had to learn influence relations, followers confronted with leaders do not start from nothing, since over time they have built up expectations or cognitive representations about how leaders should act. Or, to put this in line with recent theorizing about leadership, in the past followers have built up 'implicit leadership theories' (ILT), preconceptions or 'prototypes' with respect to the attributes a leader should have and how a leader should perform (Lord, De Vader and Alliger, 1986). If someone in a group acts in a way that matches the group members' ILTs, that person is more likely to emerge as a leader (Lord, Foti and De Vader, 1984).

ILTs of group members, being learned cognitive representations, are responsible for subsequent selective information processing: it has been shown that when group members believe that dominance is viewed as a central indication of leadership, they may mistakenly remember their leader acting in a dominant way and forget instances in which their leader engaged in submissive behaviour (see Cronshaw and Lord, 1987).

Interesting in this respect are the results of studies in which raters had to judge supervisors with the help of the Ohio State scales, i.e. initiating structure and consideration. Rush, Thomas and Lord (1977) found that when undergraduate students received a minimum of information about supervisors, the two-factor structure was replicated, suggesting that the ILTs adopted by lay people do match the explicit leadership theories developed by students in the Ohio State research. This does not mean that followers are entirely insensitive to the actual behaviour of a leader. For example, Mitchell, Larson and Green (1977), using an audio recording as stimulus material, found that a leader was rated higher on initiating structure in a high-performance condition than in a low-performance condition. However, all in all, these studies suggest that previously acquired cognitive representations or preconceptions have a strong effect on how leaders are selected and judged.

Gender role theory

Eagly and Karau (1991) have investigated why male leaders tend to emerge in small groups more often than female leaders do. The theoretical background of their study is gender role theory. In contrast with the above-explained Expectation States Theory, which emphasizes that status differentials are based on expectation differentials, gender role theory reflects a broader perspective in that it is assumed that roles are formed during early child-rearing and reinforced in the economy and society. As a consequence, men are more inclined to specialize in task behaviours related to occupational roles, and women in social behaviours related to domestic roles. In small natural groups as well as in small laboratory groups, it has been observed that men do indeed specialize more in task activities and women more in social activities. In terms of Bales's (1950) observation scheme (IPA or Interaction Process Analysis) this boils down to the circumstance that males score higher on problem-solving attempts, whereas females score higher on positive reactions. A further consideration is that females and males tend to behave in a consistent way, that is, to act according to their socially assigned role.

But why then do males often emerge as leaders? Eagly and Karau (1991) propose two reasons. First, leadership is quite often perceived as strongly connected with task competence, and second, quite often – especially in laboratory groups – the main task concerns task performance. Thus, since males specialize more in task behaviours, and since more prominent contributions to task behaviour lead to the attribution of leadership qualities, males are more often perceived as leaders.

Eagly and Karau's comparison of a number of studies in a meta-analysis indeed indicated that males emerged as leaders more often than did females. Moreover, male leadership was particularly likely in short-term groups and in groups carrying out simple tasks, i.e. male leadership was less pronounced in groups having to perform complex tasks, because complex tasks apparently imply social task activities. Male leadership was less likely in groups with a longer interaction history because in such groups characteristics other than gender may become conspicuous. Lastly, women emerged slightly more as socio-emotional leaders than men.

The main difference between gender role theory and EST is the idea in gender role theory that role differentiation (males engaging in task activities and females engaging in social activities) is due to education, a circumstance that EST takes for granted. In a sense, gender role theory corresponds with the idea that people maintain preconceptions about what a leader should be like. However, more than implicit leadership theories, gender role theory seems to stress that these cognitive representations are culturally mediated.

In the foregoing we started with the EST proposition that group members search for cues that are valid predictors of group success. Task success in the past, seniority, gender, assertiveness, and so on are cues that are more or less associated with ability differentials and expectations of future success. Thereafter it was shown that leadership is inferred from the attribution of ability, a dispositional or internal cue. Lastly, it was shown that group members maintain 'implicit leadership theories' or prototypes. Prototypes lead one to expect that leaders are intelligent, extroverted, masculine, dominant and interpersonally sensitive (Lord et al., 1986). One might agree that these prototypes bear a strong resemblance to the cues group members employ in constructing influence differentials, as EST proposes. Assuming that there is a strong resemblance, it might be suggested that in undifferentiated groups, group members make use of their prototypes to establish who should have more influence or occupy a higher leadership position.

THE REFLECTIVE APPROACH TO LEADERSHIP

In the following we will present two approaches to leadership which suggest that leaders and followers reflect upon outcomes in their exchanges with one another and with the task environment. Contingency approaches to leadership deal with the effectiveness of a leader under certain social and task circumstances. The exchange approaches to leadership, which will subsequently be presented, are more explicit than the contingency approaches in the sense that they focus on the process of the exchange of behavioural outcomes between leaders and followers.

Further contingency approaches

Fiedler's least preferred co-worker model (Fiedler, 1967) is an example of a contingency model since it assumes that the effectiveness of a leader depends on three factors: (a) leader–membership relations; (b) task structure; and (c) leader-position power. This model suggests the prediction that when these factors are either all favourable or all unfavourable, task-oriented leaders (or low-LPC leaders) perform best. When these factors are mixed or intermediate, relationship-oriented leaders (or high-LPC leaders) should perform best. Thus, according to Fiedler, leadership effectiveness is a joint function of leader qualities and situational demands such as contingencies, which interact to make qualities variously appropriate to the three factors at hand. Two other prominent contingency models are path-goal theory (House and Mitchell, 1974) and the normative contingency model (Vroom and Yetton, 1973). To give an insight into what an alternative route to contingency implies, in the following we will briefly describe the path-goal model.

Path-goal theory (House and Mitchell, 1974) builds further on the idea that there are two leadership styles: the well-known consideration or people-orientation and task-orientation or initiating structure. It is assumed that the leader's function is to motivate followers and to show them how they might reach their goals, i.e. the leader is responsible for increasing the probability of goal attainment. It is a contingency model based on the idea that the leader's effectiveness increases subordinates' motivation to pursue a goal. The three contingencies are (a) task circumstances; (b) characteristics of the subordinates; and (c) the nature of the subordinates' group. Some of the predictions of the theory are: (1) people-orientation on the part of a leader is most effective when the subordinates' tasks are highly structured; task orientation on the part of a leader will be more effective when the task is complex and when the subordinates experience great uncertainty about what they should do (role ambiguity); (2) subordinates respond better to the leader's directiveness when the task is unstructured than when the task is structured (see further for a critique Schriesheim and Kerr, 1977).

The above-described contingency approaches are alike in that both start from the notion that the probability of a leader's success is contingent on certain task and inter-group factors. However, with regard to the exchange processes that are responsible for the probability of a leader's success, these approaches are rather implicit. In the following we will present some ideas about exchange processes within groups and organizations.

Exchange

Regular group members as well as leaders reflect upon the outcomes of their behaviour. Group members form groups when they are better off together than acting alone or in another group. In other words, since their comparison level of outcomes in a specific group is better than the alternative comparative level of behavioural outcomes for acting alone or in another group, they form a group. Being part of a group does not end reflection, since group members are then also inclined to strive for higher behavioural outcomes. Blau's study of the influence relations in a group consisting of federal agents (see chapter 6) showed that less competent agents wanted to improve their reports by asking for advice from a more com- petent agent. In doing so they had to acknowledge the superior competence of their more competent colleague. Conversely, the more competent agent had to interrupt his own work, but in return received the respect of less competent colleagues (see Blau, 1964). This example fits with what is known as the 'transactional approach to leadership' (Hollander and Offerman, 1990), which emphasizes the social exchange or transaction between leader and followers: the leader renders positive outcomes to followers, such as a definition of the situation and direction, or may withhold negative sanctions, which followers reciprocate with heightened esteem for, and responsiveness to, the leader.

When two people offer each other something that they cannot acquire as profitably outside as inside their relationship, they may engage in an exchange relation in which the investments made by one actor may mean a profit to the other actor, and the reverse. In Blau's field study the competent agent invested his time and expertise in return for prestige, whereas less competent agents had to acknowledge their inferiority in return for better task performance. It also appeared that some of the other competent agents were not willing to engage in an exchange relation: they were not willing to share their time and expertise with less competent agents, and therefore they did not receive higher prestige in return. So for more competent agents it was not enough to be more competent; time and expertise had to be invested in the exchange relation in order to receive prestige in return for help. It was the less competent agents' ambition to improve their reports that made it possible for (some of) the more competent agents to offer advice in return for something else, i.e. prestige and compliance with recommendations. So exchange relations emerge in situations in which at least one of the actors is dependent on a resource or commodity that the other actor possesses.

Dependency and power

Emerson (1972) has analysed the circumstances in which a person P is more dependent on another person O, to wit: (1) if O has resources available that have a greater value to P, P is more dependent on O than when O has resources available that are of lesser value to P; (2) P is also more dependent on O when P cannot satisfy his goals outside the P–O exchange relation than when P's goals can be satisfied in alternative exchange relations; and (3) when O has multiple resources available that are of value to P, P is more dependent on O than when O has only one kind of resource available. In Blau's example this means that a less competent agent is less dependent on good advice from the more competent agent when turning out well-prepared reports is not that important to less competent agents.

Dependency on the specific competent agent is also lessened if there are other competent agents available who are willing to engage in an exchange. Dependency on the part of less competent agents is also reduced when less competent agents are only dependent on good advice and not in other respects as well, for example, when they are not subject to sanctions imposed by more competent agents.

Emerson (1972), making a connection between dependency and power, maintains that in an exchange relation actor P's dependency is equal to actor O's power. Power refers then to O's resources in so far as they are valuable to P. From the foregoing it follows that O's power is greater (1) when O's resources are of greater value to P; (2) when O's resources are more precious to P, i.e. cannot be acquired in an alternative exchange relation; and (3) when O has several kinds of commodities or resources available to invest in his or her exchange relation with P.

Power bases

French and Raven (1959) have distinguished several bases of power, which refer to the resources O can invest in an exchange so that P can be induced to comply with O's wishes. These bases of power are: (1) sanctioning power: the power holder may reward and/or punish if the dependent other does not comply; (2) legitimate power: the power holder may make an appeal to the other by stressing his or her legitimate right to require and demand compliance; (3) reference power: the power holder may induce the other to comply because of the other's identification with and attraction to the power holder; and (4) expert power: power may be derived from the other's assumption that the power holder possesses superior skills and/or abilities.

It may be noted that this description of power bases is inferred from the common definition of power, namely that the power of an actor O over actor P is greater to the extent that O can induce P to engage in behaviours that P otherwise would not engage in. This implies that, in the eyes of P, the actor O may possess one or more bases of power that are attractive to P and make P willing to comply with O's wishes. This definition of power is also proposed by Emerson (1972). In addition, he argues that the dependency of P on O is a function of (a) the attractiveness of the resources (or power bases) O is perceived to have in the eyes of P; (b) whether these resources are perceived by P as available in alternative relationships; and (c) whether O is perceived to possess only one or more bases of power. Moreover, Emerson considers an exchange relation to be impossible when P does not possess something that is of value to O. So the tacit assumption in French and Raven's (1959) description of power bases is that it is P's compliance with O's wishes that is of value to O. Lastly, it might be argued that in an exchange relation, the power and the dependency of the actors O and P are balanced. To give an example: in Blau's field study, on the one hand the very competent federal agent apparently needed prestige, that is, he was dependent on the less competent agents who could give him their respect, and in that sense the less competent agent had power over the very competent agent and the more competent agent was dependent; on the other hand, the less competent agents needed additional expertise, and in that respect the less competent agents were dependent and the more competent agent had power over the less competent agents.

According to the transactional approach to leadership, leader and followers are involved in exchange: leaders have to fulfil the needs of followers, and followers have to satisfy the needs of leaders, so that an equitable relationship is established. In the case of the exchange between the most competent and the less competent agents, an equitable exchange boils down to:

$$\frac{\text{investment most competent agent}}{\text{outcomes most competent agent}} = \frac{\text{investment less competent agents}}{\text{outcomes less competent agents}}$$

or:

$$\frac{\text{time and expertise invested}}{\text{prestige in return}} = \frac{\text{acknowledgement of own inferiority}}{\text{better reports}}$$

In this view the leader (e.g. the most competent agent in Blau's field study) is perceived as a group resource and has to meet the expectations of followers (e.g. contribute to better reports), and followers have to meet the expectations of the leader (e.g. conform with advice and confer prestige), suggesting that influence over others is acquired in return for being influenced by others. Hollander (1978) has proposed that leaders provide group success and an equitable allocation of outcomes among group members in return for esteem and responsiveness. In sum, leaders and followers are involved in an exchange where both parties have their own rights and duties. In the following we briefly describe some implications of this by focusing on follower effects on leaders, and the reverse.

Leader–member transactions

Several experimental studies (see Wilke, 1991) show that, in informal groups, group members opt for a leader when the group as a whole is not able to achieve group success and when outcomes have been distributed in an inequitable way. Moreover, it was established that elected leaders who were achieving group success and who were distributing the group outcomes in an equitable way were more endorsed by followers on a later occasion than leaders who did not live up to the expectations of their constituency. These results suggest that followers support their leader when the leader is achieving group success and when he behaves in an equitable way, indicating that while the leader's chief external task is to be successful, his chief internal task is to be fair (Katz and Kahn, 1978).

In a related vein, Hollander's credit model (see Hollander, 1985) assumes that a leader is usually judged with respect to competence and probably conformity to group norms as well. Hollander found in problem-solving groups that early non-conformity by an otherwise competent group member blocked the acceptance of that person's influence, while later non-conformity produced changes in the group's norms. Accordingly, his credit model proposes that leaders should first build up some idiosyncratic credit in the eyes of followers, and as soon as they have collected that credit they may deviate from the existing group norms. The credit model makes a distinction between norms to which regular group members are expected to conform, but from which leaders may deviate, and particular expectancies associated with the leader's role. For example, leaders may arrive late at meetings or take independent stands with relatively little loss of prestige. However, they are not allowed to act in an unfair way by behaving in their own interests.

Tactics

An exchange between leader and follower may be enacted with few problems. However, that is not always the case. The question is, then, what happens when one or both parties view their returns on investment as unsatisfactory?

Several researchers have explored that question by asking people to describe the methods that they use to influence others in business (e.g. Falbo and Peplau,

1980; Kipnis, 1984). Quite often people mention tactics like promises, rewards, threats, punishment and expertise. Other tactics mentioned supplemented those suggested by French and Raven (1959), namely discussion, making requests and demands, persistence, ingratiation, disengagement, bargaining, manipulation, *faits accomplis*, persuasion, etc. These tactics differ from one another in strength, rationality and laterality.

1 *Strength*: strong tactics are explicit overt methods of influence, such as threats, demands and *faits accomplis*. Dropping hints, ingratiation and evading the issue are examples of weak or indirect methods of influence.
2 *Rationality*: some tactics are based on the idea that a rational discourse is appropriate. Examples are persuasion and bargaining. Other tactics rely on misinformation and emotionality, such as evasion and ingratiation.
3 *Laterality*: some tactics are bilateral and based on reciprocity, such as persuasion, discussion and negotiation. Other tactics are referred to as unilateral, since one of the parties involved engages in influence attempts without much concern for the other party. Such tactics include demands, *faits accomplis*, evasion and disengagement.

Kipnis (1984) has shown that managers use various and strong tactics to influence their followers. However, while dealing with their own superiors, these managers appear to employ primarily tactics such as persuasion and bargaining. Managers of higher status more often used strong tactics to influence their subordinates, whereas lower-status managers more often used weak tactics. It also appeared that when subordinates showed more resistance, managers were more likely to shift from weak to strong tactics.

In an investigation of people's reactions to various tactics, Falbo (1977) arranged for people using such tactics as discussion, negotiation, persistence, threat and evasion to meet in same-sex groups to discuss the topic, 'what I plan to get out of college'. After the discussion participants were requested to rate one another on friendliness, consideration, desirability as a group, and willingness to join in another discussion. It was found that evaluation of liking and willingness to join was more closely related with reported rational tactics than with strong tactics. Group members who reported having used discussion, persuasion and expertise were more favourably rated than group members who claimed to have used tactics such as manipulation, evasion and threat. Group members who said they used weak/rational tactics such as ingratiation and persuasion, were rated as more friendly than group members who said they used strong/non-rational tactics, such as threat and *faits accomplis*.

In sum, we made it clear in the foregoing that the leaders and followers of a given group do balance their costs and benefits. Power is based on the attractiveness and the number of resources an actor possesses that the other actors can only obtain in that specific exchange relation. Several resources or power bases may be distinguished. To signal that one has a specific power basis and/or to prevent an inequitable exchange from occurring, group members employ power tactics.

THE COMMUNICATIVE APPROACH TO LEADERSHIP

In groups and organizations, leaders and followers work at their task and exchange cognitions and reflections through communication. That is to say, communication is the medium through which tasks and groups become organized. Communication consists of purposeful actions that influence group members as well as the group task. This implies that communication has consequences for group members and task performance. Communication in groups may be vertical, i.e. between higher- and lower-placed members in an organization, as well as horizontal, i.e. between personnel positioned at the same hierarchical level.

From field research by Porter and Roberts (1975) it appears that two thirds of the total communication in groups involves vertical communication. More specifically, less powerful members communicate upwards, and the most powerful members communicate more with one another, that is, in a horizontal way (Cartwright, 1968). According to Porter and Roberts, less powerful organization members or subordinates communicate more upwards than sideways and downwards. So the picture that emerges from spontaneous communication in groups is that higher-placed individuals communicate more with one another, whereas subordinates communicate more upwards, i.e. show upward communication. In the following we will present two models of the relations between leaders and followers in groups.

Mulder's power distance theory

According to Mulder (1977) group members may be rank-ordered as to their power distance from the leader of the group. Mulder makes a distinction between two power tendencies. The followers' power distance reduction tendency concerns the motivation of less powerful members to reduce their distance from the leader. His main prediction from the followers' power reduction tendency is that members whose power distance from the leader is smaller will be more inclined to identify with the leader than group members farther away in power distance from the leader. Moreover, if the leader has to be succeeded, those members who are at a smaller power distance will be more inclined to take over a vacant leadership position than group members at a larger power distance.

The second tendency is the leader's power distance enlargement tendency: leaders try to keep their followers at a distance, and the more so when the power distance between leader and followers is larger. In several experimental studies Mulder (1977) has provided evidence for the two tendencies. Recently, Bruins and Wilke (1992) showed that in a hierarchically structured mock investment forum, the leader (A) indeed identifies less with his followers (B, C, D, E and F) the further away in power distance these followers are, i.e. support for the leader's power distance enlargement tendency was found. In a subsequent study, Bruins and Wilke (1993) investigated the followers' power reduction tendency in a simulated hierarchically organized investment agency with five positions,

(A–E). The real subjects occupied the position B, C and D. This was possible because communication took place by desk computers. Several measures were taken, to assess the amount of identification with each position and the preference to take over the position of A when it became vacant. Two contrasting predictions were made. Whereas Mulder's followers' power reduction tendency would predict that B would be inclined to have a stronger preference than C, with C showing a stronger preference than D to take over A's position, Ng (1977, 1980) makes a slightly different prediction. Ng proposes that in a hierarchically organized group, group members apply the so-called bureaucratic rule, implying that the person right below A, i.e. B, will feel more entitled to take over A's vacant position than C or D, who will not differ in their preference to take over A's vacant position. The results were in accordance with Ng's prediction, which means that the followers' power reduction tendency may be explained by considerations of entitlement due to the bureaucratic rule.

The leader-member-exchange (LMX) model

This model has been proposed by Graen (1976). It assumes that leaders make a distinction between their subordinates, or conversely it is assumed that a leader's attitudes and behaviour towards his subordinates are not identical. The LMX model distinguishes between followers who are quite close (in power distance) to the leader and those who are at a greater power distance. The first have a better-quality relationship with the leader, but the leader also has higher expectations for their performance and loyalty. For the others, the leader makes fewer personal demands and gives fewer benefits. Liden and Graen (1980) found that subordinates who reported a high-quality relationship with their superiors assumed more job responsibility, contributed more, and were rated as higher performers than those with low-quality relationships with the leader.

Vecchio and Gobdal (1984) investigated leader-followers relationships in banks. They found that subordinates who had a more personal exchange relation with their boss were more productive, and were also more content than subordinates who maintained a 'supervisory exchange' with their boss. Lastly, in a Japanese study, Wakabayashy and Graen (1984) found that subordinates who had a closer relationship with their superiors achieved faster promotions, regardless of how competent they were.

Regarding vertical communication in groups, Mulder's power distance theory and Graen's LMX model suggest that leaders do not communicate with their followers in the same way, and the reverse: some followers (at a smaller power distance) maintain a closer exchange relation with the leader than do other followers, who are presumably at a larger power distance. Whereas the LMX model is mainly descriptive, Mulder's power distance theory may provide the explanation: leaders prefer communication with subordinates at a smaller power distance, and followers at a smaller power distance from the leader have a stronger tendency to decrease the power distance than do those further away from the leader.

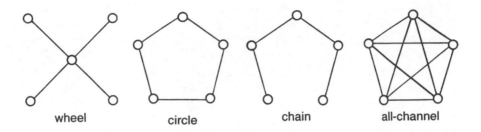

wheel   circle   chain   all-channel

Figure 7.5 Some communication networks

Communication networks

Elements – persons and positions – of the group structure are linked by communication networks, which may be viewed as coordination devices. In the following we describe several kinds of communication networks, and the question will be, which communication network leads to better group performance? In many organizations all communications have to go through formal channels, while other organizations are less restrictive and permit anyone to communicate freely with anyone else.

Leavitt (1951) asked whether communication patterns in groups affect their efficiency. In his experiments subjects were seated around a circular table, separated by vertical partitions. Slots which could be opened and closed by the experimenter allowed the subjects to pass certain messages to certain other group members. Figure 7.5 shows a number of communication networks. The networks become increasingly centralized from right to left; the 'wheel' is most centralized since any group member in the periphery must send his messages through the single central person. In contrast, in the 'all-channel' network no one controls the distribution of messages, and any person may communicate to any other person without having to rely on someone else.

The task used was relatively simple. From a set of six symbols (a circle, a triangle, a diamond, a square, a plus-sign and an asterisk), each subject was given a list of five symbols. These lists were constructed in such a way that there was only one collective symbol, and the group task was to discover this common symbol.

This so-called symbol identification task requires that information be collected by one position. In terms of Steiner (1972, 1976), a centralized network implies more coordination of the group members' efforts than a less centralized network. In the following we will see how the degree of coordination affects both actual group productivity and the motivation of the group members. Quite consistent with Steiner's views, the nature of the task tends to play an important intervening role.

Group performance

Leavitt (1951) found that the most centralized network was most efficient for problem solving. The circle network was least efficient: it took more time, showed more errors and needed more messages. Shaw (1964), however, who used more difficult tasks, found the reverse: circles were more efficient than wheels. Shaw (1981) concluded that when the task is relatively simple, requiring only the gathering of information, a centralized network is more efficient, but when the task is more complex, requiring operations to be performed upon the information (for example, mathematical manipulations), decentralized networks are more efficient in terms of time and errors.

Several explanations for these results may be offered. Shaw (1981) points out that in groups facing a more complex task, the central person is confronted with a heavy task load. He has to collect the information and perform the mathematical operations. This task load easily leads to saturation of the network. Moreover, since these operations require a rather competent person, the centralized network is highly vulnerable since the central position may be occupied by a less competent group member.

Mulder (1963) argues that wheel groups facing complex tasks need more time to find out how the task should be done, and how the network channels should be used, that is, he stresses the discretionary aspect of the task (Steiner, 1972, 1976). In an experiment in which complex tasks were employed, he demonstrated that, for the first problem in a series, circle groups were indeed superior to the more centralized wheel groups. Thus, after some time, more centralized networks perform better on complex tasks than less centralized networks. Centralized network groups just need more time to attune to their network setting and their task. Research data collected by Mackenzie support this interpretation: 'on both simple as well as on complex tasks centralized networks perform better than less centralized networks' (Mackenzie, 1976, p. 300). A centralized network needs time for development, but as soon as the group has adapted to its network, centralized networks are superior.

Steiner's ideas may also be applied here; Steiner (1972, 1976) suggests:

$$\begin{array}{ccccc} \text{group} & & \text{potential} & & \text{coordination} & & \text{motivation} \\ \text{productivity} & = & \text{productivity} & \pm & \text{losses/gains} & \pm & \text{losses/gains} \end{array}$$

Both simple and complex tasks require coordination. For both types of tasks it is necessary that groups coordinate information. For simple tasks groups merely have to gather information. This is also necessary in complex tasks. However, groups performing complex tasks also have to perform rather complex operations upon this information. Thus, complex tasks are relatively more discretionary than simple tasks, that is, complex tasks leave it more to the group to decide how to perform the task. Since simple and complex tasks require coordination, it is not surprising that, in the long run, centralized networks are superior to decentralized networks, and given the rather indiscretionary nature of the simple task, it is not surprising that simple task groups immediately profit from the introduction of a coordinating, centralized network of relations. For complex task groups these coordination gains only become visible after a while, since initially the group has to pay attention to the complex operations of the task itself. It is even possible that initially the introduction of a centralized network may impair group productivity, because coordination losses are involved. Being confronted with the double task of how to solve a problem and how to organize the group may be too heavy a task. However, as soon as these groups have discovered the necessary operations for performing the task, complex task groups may also profit from the advantages a centralized network offers.

Group motivation

Thus, it appears that with regard to performance, centralized networks are superior to decentralized networks in the long run. This is not true with regard to satisfaction. In many network studies (see Shaw, 1981), subjects are requested to indicate their satisfaction, i.e. how much they enjoyed the task. Two related research findings may be noted. First, satisfaction in decentralized networks is greater than in centralized networks. Second, in centralized networks the person in the central position is more satisfied than the subjects on the periphery. The explanation of the latter finding is that the central group member is more able to determine the behaviour of the peripheral group members than the peripheral group members are able to determine the behaviour of the central group member, that is, the central group member has more power, and according to Mulder (1963), having more power leads to more satisfaction.

In a decentralized network subjects have equal power, and the satisfaction of its members is greater than the satisfaction of the peripheral group members in a centralized network. As a consequence of the sheer numbers, the total satisfaction or group morale in decentralized networks is greater than in centralized networks.

The above findings suggest that having a centralized network in the long run elicits coordination gains; however, simultaneously the danger of motivation losses arises. This conclusion comes close to what has been noticed about the introduction of a leader in a social dilemma situation (see Wilke, 1991). Having a leader may increase group productivity, since coordination gains are at stake; however, the introduction of a leader has the disadvantage that the motivation of the subordinate group members may decrease. Thus, it seems that having a centralized network (implying a leader) is a solution for discretionary tasks, as long as coordination gains outweigh motivational losses. Thus, leaders in successful groups are able to provide coordination and motivation gains, but having a leader as such may elicit serious motivational losses. In several circum-stances the instalment of a leader is therefore neither preferred by regular group members, nor necessary given the characteristics of the group members, the task and the type of organization. Furthermore, Steiner's model of group performance may be applied to explain productivity and satisfaction in so-called communication networks. For group performance in the long run, centralized networks are superior. However, besides coordination gains, motivational losses may be incurred. In the following we will describe some recent attempts to overcome motivational losses by introducing participative decision making.

Participative decision making

The research on communication networks suggests that group performance may increase when leaders make all the decisions, but that subordinates' motivation to execute their task may decrease, and may, in turn, negatively affect group performance. An important attempt to overcome the drawbacks of centralized decision making is participative decision making. Participative decision making (PDM) allows subordinates to share the leader's power to take decisions. Several forms of participation may be distinguished that embody the idea that subordinates should be permitted, or even encouraged, to influence their work environment. Tannenbaum and Schmidt (1958) distinguish the following possibilities: (1) autocratic decisions are made by managers; (2) managers sell their decisions; (3) managers present their considerations and decisions and invite their subordinates to pose questions, which may allow the managers to provide further information; (4) managers suggest what decision might be taken, but point out that another decision could be taken by themselves after discussion with subordinates; (5) managers sketch the problem, they invite subordinates to make suggestions about desirable decisions, however, managers decide; (6) managers sketch the problem, and the group is invited to make the decision, with the manager included in the decision making group; and (7) managers leave the decision to the group of subordinates. Tannenbaum and Schmidt (1958) suggest that in practice most PDM programmes involve versions of (5) and (6).

Evidence of a positive relationship between participative decision making and outcomes concerning performance and satisfaction is mixed. In a field experiment that was run for one-and-a-half years, Morse and Reimer (1956) investigated four departments within an insurance company. In two departments the authority to make decisions was delegated to lower echelons. This was the 'autonomy programme'. In two other departments the authority to make decisions was delegated to higher echelons than had previously been the case. This was the 'hierarchically controlled programme'. It appeared that an increased role in decision making for rank-and-file groups indeed increased their satisfaction, whereas a decreased role for these organization members decreased their satisfaction. However, with regard to productivity, it appeared that performance increased for both programmes. Letwin and Stringer (1968) even reported a decrease in performance in more democratic groups.

In a review of studies, Miller and Monge (1986) came to the conclusion that there is a notable correlation between participation and satisfaction (.34), but only a small, although significant, correlation (.15) was found between participation and performance. In an analysis, Wagner and Gooding (1987) argued that the small correlation between participation and performance may be ascribed to methodo-logical artifacts, its relation with group performance being doubtful. This conclusion is supported by Locke and Schweiger (1979), who took the results of laboratory studies, correlational field studies and field studies into account.

Schweiger and Leana (1986) concluded that context variables are important in moderating the relationship between PDM and performance, and that no degree of participation – from autocratic decisions through various levels of consultive decisions to truly joint decision making -- can be employed effectively in all situations. Several proposals have been made to explain why participation might not work in every situation. These proposals concern, for example: (a) the nature of the decision: when subordinates who are involved in PDM do not have the competence (see Mulder, 1977) to continue and/or when the decisions are of minor importance to them, the PDM may become a show designed to give them a sense of involvement without giving them real influence; (b) rising expecta-tions: subordinates may expect higher influence, but routine failure to accept subordinate influence may demotivate them; and (c) PDM requires that leaders have certain skills to manage cognitive conflicts and conflicts of interest. That PDM does not work in all situations is a conclusion that contingency theories such as Vroom and Yetton (1973) have long maintained.

Similar to Tannenbaum and Schmidt (1958), Vroom and Yetton (1973) intro-duced a PDM continuum of 'autocratic leadership', 'consultive leadership' and 'group leadership'. Vroom and Jago (1988) proposed several rules of thumb to be employed by leaders, such as (1) the leader–information rule: when the decision is important and the leader does not have enough information or expertise, the leader should not show autocratic leadership; (2) the goal-congruence rule: when the decision is important, but the leader does not expect the subordinates to pursue the goals of the organization, the leader should not rely on group leader-ship; and (3) the acceptance rule: the leader should not use autocratic methods if acceptance of the decision by subordinates is critical to effective implementation of the decisions. This is especially important when the leader expects dis-agreement among subordinates.

CONCLUSIONS AND SUMMARY

In the introduction to this chapter it was explained that leadership is closely connected with influence. A distinction was made between influence over people, influence to and influence from: members higher in a group or organ-ization usually have more influence over people, have more freedom to set organizational goals and are more able to resist influence attempts than members lower in the pecking order.

After tackling the problematic relation between influence and leadership, we presented a sketch of how leadership has historically been ascribed to something in the person ('the great man theory of leadership'), to something in the situation ('situational determinants of leadership') and to something in the person combined with something in the situation ('behavioural style and situation'), suggesting that in the past students of leadership have been searching for the causes of leadership in a way that is predicted by attribution theory (see chapter 1). Apart from this, there has been a tendency merely to describe the behaviour of leaders with respect to their two main tasks: the accomplishment of the task and the maintenance of optimal interpersonal relations, goals which correspond respectively to task and socio-emotional leadership.

In the remainder of the chapter we explained that leadership may be approached nowadays from the perspective of the interplay of the task and cognitive, reflective and communicative processes in task groups and organizations.

Departing from Anthony's (1988) book on the management control function, which sets forth ideas about task performance that closely resemble the ideas described in the section in chapter 1 on the 'task approach', it was explained that higher members in organizations ('leaders') are more responsible for the setting, testing and effecting of hierarchical goals, whereas subordinates are more responsible for lower levels of the organization of the task.

The *cognitive approach* to leadership emphasizes that leadership is attributed, i.e. in the 'eye of the beholder'. In ascribing leadership one makes use of implicit pre-existing ideas about how leaders should behave.

In the section on the *reflective approach* to leadership, it was stressed that leadership is a consequence of the exchange of rewards and costs between leader and followers.

Lastly, it was argued that leaders occupy a more central position in the *communication* network. Consequences of the centrality of communication networks on group performance and on group motivation were described. Participative decision making as a way to increase workers' motivation was also discussed.

In conclusion, this chapter too has shown that behaviour in task groups and organizations can only be understood if cognitive, reflective and communicative processes are taken into account.

References

Adams, J.S. (1965). Inequity in social exchange. In L. Berkowitz (ed.), *Advances in experimental social psychology*, vol. 2. New York: Academic Press.

Alexander, C.N., Jr, Zucker, L.G., and Brody, C.L. (1970). Experimental expectations and autokinetic experiences: Consistency theories and judgmental convergence. *Sociometry, 33*, 108–122.

Allen, V.L. (1965). Situational factors in conformity. In L. Berkowitz (ed.), *Advances in experimental social psychology*, vol. 2. New York: Academic Press.

Allen, V.L. (1975). Social support for nonconformity. In L. Berkowitz (ed.), *Advances in experimental social psychology*, vol. 8. New York: Academic Press.

Allison, S.T., and Messick, D.M. (1985). The group attribution error. *Journal of Experimental Social Psychology, 21*, 563–579.

Allison, S.T., and Messick, D.M. (1987). From individual inputs to group outputs, and back again: Group processes and inferences about group members. In C. Hendrick (ed.), *Group processes: Review of personality and social psychology*, vol. 8. Newbury Park, Cal.: Sage.

Anthony, R.N. (1988). *The management control function*. Boston: Harvard Business School Press.

Asch, S.E. (1951). Effects of group pressure upon the modification and distortion of judgments. In H. Guetzkow (ed.), *Groups, leadership and men*. Pittsburg, Pa.: Carnegie Press.

Asch, S.E. (1952). *Social psychology*. Englewood Cliffs, N.J.: Prentice Hall.

Asch, S.E. (1956). Studies of independence and conformity: I. A minority of one against a unanimous majority. *Psychological Monographs, 70*, no. 416.

Atkinson, J.W., and Feather, N.T. (eds) (1966). *A theory of achievement motivation*. New York: Wiley.

Bales, R.F. (1950). *Interaction Process Analysis: A method for the study of small groups*. Cambridge, Mass.: Addison-Wesley.

Bales, R.F. (1958). Task roles and social roles in problem-solving groups. In E.E. Maccoby, T.M. Newcomb and E.I. Hartley (eds), *Readings in social psychology*. New York: Holt, Rinehart and Winston.

Bales, R.F. (1970). *Personality and interpersonal behavior*. New York: Holt, Rinehart and Winston.

Bales, R.F., and Slater, P.E. (1955). Role differentiation in small decision-making groups. In T. Parsons and R.F. Bales (eds), *Family, socialization and interaction process*. New York: Free Press.

Bales, R.F., and Strodtbeck, F.L. (1951). Phases in group problem-solving. *Journal of Abnormal and Social Psychology, 46*, 485–495.

Bandura, A. (1986). *Social foundations of thought and action: A social cognitive theory.* Englewood Cliffs, N.J.: Prentice Hall.

Bar-Tal, D., and Frieze, J.H. (1976). Attributions of success and failure for actors and observers. *Journal of Research in Personality, 10,* 256–265.

Bass, B.M. (1965). *A program of exercises in management and organizational psychology.* Pittsburg: Management Development Associates.

Bechterew, V.M., and de Lange, M. (1924). Die Ergebnisse des Experiments auf dem Gebiet der kollektiven Reflexologie. *Zeitschrift für angewandte Psychologie, 24,* 305–344.

Bem, D.J. (1972). Self-perception theory. In L. Berkowitz (ed.), *Advances in experimental social psychology,* vol. 6. New York: Academic Press.

Berger, J., Rosenholtz, S.J., and Zelditch, M., Jr (1980). Status organizing processes. *Annual Review of Sociology, 6,* 479–508.

Berger, J., Webster, M., Ridgeway, C., and Rosenholtz, S.J. (1986). Status cues, expectations and behavior. In E.J. Lawler (ed.), *Advances in group processes, 3.* Greenwich, Conn.: JAI Press.

Biddle, B.J. (1979). *Role theory.* New York: Academic Press.

Biddle, B.J., and Thomas, E.J. (eds) (1966). *Role theory: Concepts and research.* New York: Wiley.

Blake, R.R., and Mouton, J.S. (1982). How to choose a leadership style. *Training and Development Journal, 36,* 39–46.

Blau, P.M. (1955). *The dynamics of bureaucracy.* Chicago: University of Chicago Press.

Blau, P.M. (1964). *Exchange and power in social life.* New York: Wiley.

Bond, C.F., and Van Leeuwen, M.D. (1991). Can a part be greater than the whole? On the relationship between primary and meta-analytic evidence. *Basic and Applied Social Psychology, 12,* 33–40.

Brehmer, B. (1976). Social judgment theory and the analysis of interpersonal conflict. *Psychological Bulletin, 83,* 985–1003.

Brehmer, B. (1988). The development of Social Judgment Theory. In B. Brehmer and C.R.B. Joyce (eds), *Human judgment. The SJT view.* Amsterdam: North-Holland.

Brehmer, B., and Joyce, C.R.B. (eds), (1988). *Human judgment. The SJT view.* Amsterdam: North-Holland.

Brown, R. (1965). *Social psychology.* New York: Macmillan.

Brown, R. (1974). Further comment on the risky shift. *American Psychologist, 29,* 468–470.

Brown, R. (1986). *Social psychology* (second edition). New York: Free Press.

Brown, R. (1988). *Group processes: Dynamics within and between groups.* Oxford: Blackwell.

Bruins, J.J., and Wilke, H.A.M. (1992). Cognitions and behavior in a hierarchy: Mulder's power theory revisited. *European Journal of Social Psychology, 22,* 21–39.

Bruins, J.J., and Wilke, H.A.M. (1993) Upward power tendencies in a hierarchy: Power distance theory versus bureaucratic rule. *European Journal of Social Psychology, 23,* 239–254.

Brunswik, E. (1952). *The conceptual framework of psychology.* Chicago: University of Chicago Press.

Burnstein, E. (1969). Interdependence in groups. In J. Mills (ed.), *Experimental social psychology.* London: Macmillan.

Burnstein, E. (1982). Persuasion as argument processing. In H. Brandstätter, J.H. Davis and G. Stocker-Kreichgauer (eds), *Group decision making.* London: Academic Press.

Burnstein, E., and Vinokur, A. (1975). What a person thinks upon learning he has chosen differently from others: Nice evidence for the persuasive-arguments explanation of choice shifts. *Journal of Experimental Social Psychology, 11,* 412–426.

Burnstein, E., and Vinokur, A. (1977). Persuasive arguments and social comparison as determinants of attitude polarization. *Journal of Experimental Social Psychology, 13,* 315–332.

Burnstein, E., Vinokur, A., and Trope, Y. (1973). Interpersonal comparison versus persuasive argumentation: A more direct test of alternative explanations for group induced shifts in individual choice. *Journal of Experimental Social Psychology, 9*, 236–245.

Butler, R. (1992). What young people want to know when: Effects of mastery and ability goals on interest in different kinds of social comparison. *Journal of Personality and Social Psychology, 62*, 934–943.

Byrne, D. (1971). *The attraction paradigm.* New York: Academic Press.

Calder, B.J. (1977). An attribution theory of leadership. In B.M. Staw and G.R. Salancik (eds), *New directions in organizational behavior.* Chicago: St Clair Press.

Campbell, D.T. (1961). Conformity in psychology's theories of acquired behavioral dispositions. In I.A. Berg and B.M. Bass (eds), *Conformity and deviation.* New York: Harper.

Campbell, R., and Snowden, L. (eds) (1985). *Paradoxes of rationality and cooperation.* Vancouver: University of British Columbia Press.

Cartwright, D. (1968). The nature of group cohesiveness. In D. Cartwright and A. Zander (eds), *Group dynamics: Research and theory.* New York: Harper and Row.

Cartwright, D. (1971). Risk taking by individuals and groups: An assessment of research employing choice dilemmas. *Journal of Personality and Social Psychology, 20*, 361–378.

Carver, C.S., and Scheier, M.F. (1990). Origin and functions of positive and negative affect: A control-process view. *Psychological Review, 97*, 19–35.

Chaiken, S. (1986). Physical appearance and social influence. In C.P. Herman, M.P. Zanna and E.T. Higgins (eds), *Physical appearance, stigma, and social behavior. The Ontario symposium*, vol. 3. Hillsdale, N.J.: Erlbaum.

Chaiken, S., and Stangor, S. (1987). Attitudes and attitude change. *Annual Review of Psychology, 38*, 575–630.

Chemers, M.M. (1983). Leadership theory and research: A systems-process integration. In P.B. Paulus (ed.), *Basic group processes.* New York: Springer Verlag.

Christensen-Szalanski, J.J. (1978). Problem solving strategies: A selection mechanism, some implications, and some data. *Organizational Behavior and Human Performance, 22*, 307–323.

Christensen-Szalanski, J.J. (1980). A further examination of the selection of problem-solving strategies: The effects of deadlines and analytic aptitudes. *Organizational Behavior and Human Performance, 25*, 107–122.

Cialdini, R.B. (1986). Compliance principles of compliance professionals: Psychologists of necessity. In M.P. Zanna, J.M. Olson and C.P. Herman (eds), *Social influence: The Ontario symposium*, vol. 5. Hillsdale, N.J.: Erlbaum.

Codol, J.P. (1975). On the so-called 'superior conformity of the self' behavior: Twenty experimental investigations. *European Journal of Social Psychology, 5*, 457–501.

Connor, T.L. (1977). Performance expectations and the initiating of problem solving attempts. *Journal of Mathematical Sociology, 5*, 178–198.

Cook, K., and Yamagishi, (1983). Social determinants of equity judgments: The problem of multidimensional input. In D.M. Messick and K. Cook (eds), *Equity Theory.* New York: Praeger.

Cook, R.L., and Hammond, K.R. (1982). Interpersonal learning and interpersonal conflict reduction in decision-making groups. In R.A. Guzzo (ed.), *Improving group decision making in organizations: Approaches from theory and research.* New York: Academic Press.

Cooley, C.H. (1902). *Human nature and the social order.* New York: Scribner's.

Cottrell, N.B. (1968). Performance in the presence of other human beings: mere presence, audience and affiliation effects. In. E.C. Simmel, R.A. Hoppe and G.A. Milton (eds), *Social facilitation and imitative behavior.* Boston: Allyn and Bacon.

Cottrell, N.B. (1972). Social facilitation. In C.G. McClintock (ed.), *Experimental social psychology.* New York: Holt, Rinehart and Winston.

Couch, A.S., and Carter, L.F. (1953). A factorial study of the rated behavior of group members. *American Psychologist, 8*, 333.

Crockett, W.H. (1982). Balance, agreement, and positivity in the cognition of small social structures. In L. Berkowitz (ed.), *Advances in experimental social psychology*, vol. 15. New York: Academic Press.

Cronshaw, S.F., and Lord, R.G. (1987). Effects of categorization, attribution and encoding processes on leadership perceptions. *Journal of Applied Psychology, 72*, 97–106.

Crott, H.W., Szilvas, K., and Zuber, J.A. (1991). Group decision, choice shift, and polarization in consulting, political and local political scenarios: An experimental investigation and theoretical analysis. *Organizational Behavior and Human Decision Processes, 49*, 22–41.

Crutchfield, R.S. (1955). Conformity and character. *American Psychologist, 10*, 191–198.

Davis, J.H. (1973). Group decision and social interaction: A theory of social decision schemes. *Psychological Review, 80*, 97–125.

Davis, J.H. (1982). Social interaction as a combinatorial process in group decision. In H. Brandstätter, J.H. Davis and G. Stocker-Kreichgauer (eds), *Group decision making*. London: Academic Press.

Dawes, R.M. (1980). Social dilemmas. *Annual Review of Psychology, 31*, 169–193.

de Gilder, D. (1991). *Expectation states theory*. Unpublished Doctoral dissertation, University of Groningen.

Delbecq, A.L., Van de Ven, A.H., and Gustafson, D.H. (1975). *Group technique for program planning*. Glenview, Ill.: Scott, Foresman.

De Soto, C.B. (1960). Learning a social structure. *Journal of Abnormal and Social Psychology, 60*, 417–421.

de Swaan, A. (1973). *Coalition theories and cabinet formations*. San Francisco: Jossey Bass.

Deutsch, M. (1949a). A theory of cooperation and competition. *Human Relations, 2*, 129–152.

Deutsch, M. (1949b). An experimental study of the effects of cooperation and competition upon group process. *Human Relations, 2*, 199–231.

Deutsch, M., and Gerard, H.B. (1955). A study of normative and informational social influences upon individual judgment. *Journal of Abnormal and Social Psychology, 51*, 629–636.

de Vries, N.K. (1988) Gelijkheid en Complementariteit. Unpublished Doctoral dissertation, University of Groningen.

Diehl, M., and Stroebe, W. (1987). Productivity loss in brainstorming groups: Towards the solution of a riddle. *Journal of Personality and Social Psychology, 53*, 497–509.

Doise, W. (1969). Inter-group relations and polarization of individual and collective judgments. *Journal of Personality and Social Psychology, 12*, 136–143.

Eagly, A.H. and Karau, S.J. (1991). Gender and the emergence of leaders: A meta-analysis. *Journal of Personality and Social Psychology, 60*, 685–710.

Ellemers, N. (1991). *Identity management strategies*. Unpublished Doctoral dissertation, University of Groningen.

Ellemers, N., van Knippenberg, A.F.M., and Wilke, H.A.M. (1990). The influence of permeability of group boundaries and stability of group status on strategies of individual mobility and change. *British Journal of Social Psychology, 29*, 233–246.

Emerson, R.M. (1972). Exchange theory, Part II: Exchange relations and network structures. In J. Berger, M. Zelditch and B. Anderson (eds), *Sociological studies in progress*, II, 58–87. Boston: Houghton Mifflin.

Falbo, T. (1977). The multidimensional scaling of power strategies. *Journal of Personality and Social Psychology, 35*, 537–548.

Falbo, T., and Peplau, L.A. (1980). Power strategies in intimate relationships. *Journal of Personality and Social Psychology, 38*, 612–628.

Farkas, A.J., and Anderson, N.H. (1979). Multidimensional input in equity theory. *Journal of Personality and Social Psychology, 37*, 879–896.

Fayol, H. (1916). *Adminstration industrielle et générale.* Paris: Dunod.

Festinger, L. (1950). Informal social communication. *Psychological Review, 57*, 271–282.

Festinger, L. (1954). A theory of social comparison processes. *Human Relations, 7*, 117–140.

Festinger, L., Schachter, S., and Back, K. (1950). *Social pressures in informal groups: A study of human factors in housing.* New York: Harper.

Fiedler, F.E. (1967). *A theory of leadership effectiveness.* New York: McGraw-Hill.

Fiedler, F.E. (1978). The contingency model and the dynamics of the leadership process. In L. Berkowitz (ed.), *Advances in experimental social psychology*, vol. 11. New York: Academic Press.

Fiedler, F.E., and Garcia, J.E. (1987). *New approaches to effective leadership: cognitive resources and organizational performance.* New York: Wiley.

Fishbein, M., and Ajzen, I. (1975). *Belief, attitude, intention and behavior: An introduction to theory and research.* Reading, Mass.: Addison-Wesley.

Fisher, C.D., and Gitelson, R. (1983). A meta-analysis of the correlates of role conflict and ambiguity. *Journal of Applied Psychology, 68*, 320–333.

Fiske, S.T., and Taylor, S.E. (1991). *Social cognition* (second edition). New York: McGraw-Hill.

Flowers, M.L. (1977). A laboratory test of some implications of Janis' groupthink hypothesis. *Journal of Personality and Social Psychology, 35*, 888–896.

Forsyth, D.R. (1983). *An introduction to group dynamics.* Belmont, Cal.: Brooks/Cole.

Fraser, C., and Foster, D. (1984). Social groups, nonsense groups and group polarization. In H. Tajfel (ed.), *The social dimension: European developments in social psychology*, vol. 2. Cambridge: Cambridge University Press.

French, E.G. (1956). Motivation as a variable in work-partner selection. *Journal of Abnormal and Social Psychology, 53*, 96–99.

French, J.R.P. (1956). A formal theory of social power. *Psychological Review, 63*, 181–194.

French, J.R.P., and Raven, B. (1959). The bases of social power. In D. Cartwright (ed.), *Studies in social power.* Ann Arbor, Mich.: Institute for Social Research.

Gamson, W.A. (1964). Experimental studies of coalition formation. In L. Berkowitz (ed.), *Advances in experimental social psychology*, vol. 1. New York: Academic Press.

Gastorf, J.W., Suls, J.M., and Lawhon, J. (1978). Opponent choices of below average performers. *Bulletin of The Psychonomic Society, 12*, 217–220.

Gates, M.F., and Allee, W.C. (1933). Conditioned behavior of isolated and grouped cockroaches on a simple maze. *Journal of Comparative Psychology, 15*, 331–358.

Geen, R.G. (1983). Evaluation apprehension and the social facilitation/inhibition of learning. *Motivation and Emotion. 7*, 203–212.

Geen, R.G., and Bushman, B.J. (1989). The arousing effects of social presence. In H. Wagner and A. Manstead (eds), *Handbook of social psychophysiology.* Chichester: Wiley.

Gerard, H.B., Wilhelmy, R.A., and Conolley, E.S. (1968). Conformity and group size. *Journal of Personality and Social Psychology, 8*, 79–82.

Glaser, A.N. (1982). Drive theory of social facilitation: A critical reappraisal. *British Journal of Social Psychology, 21*, 265–282.

Gordon, K.H. (1924). Group judgments in the field of lifted weights. *Journal of Experimental Psychology, 7*, 398–400.

Graen, G. (1976). Role-making processes within complex organizations. In M.D. Dunnette (ed.), *Handbook of industrial and organizational psychology.* Chicago: Rand McNally.

Green, S.G., and Mitchell, T.R. (1979). Attributional processes of leaders in leader–member interactions. *Organizational Behavior and Human Performance, 23*, 429–458.

Greenberg, J. (1987). Using diaries to promote procedural justice in performance appraisals. *Social Justice Research, 1*, 219–234.

Greenstein, T.N., and Knottnerus, J.D. (1980). The effects of differential evaluations on status generalization. *Social Psychology Quarterly, 43*, 147–154.

Griffith, T.L., Fichman, M., and Moreland, R.L. (1989). Social loafing and social facilitation: an empirical test of the cognitive-motivational model of performance. *Basic and Applied Social Psychology, 10*, 253–271.

Guerin, B., and Innes, J.M. (1989). Cognitive tuning sets: Anticipating the consequences of communication. *Current Psychology: Research and Reviews, 8*, 234–249.

Halpin, A.W., and Winer, B.J. (1957). A factorial study of the leader behavior descriptions. In R.M. Stogdill and A.E. Coons (eds), *Leader behavior: Its description and measurement*. Columbus: Ohio State University.

Hamilton, J.O. (1974). Motivation and risk taking behavior: A test of Atkinson's theory. *Journal of Personality and Social Psychology, 29*, 856–874.

Hammond, K.R. (1955). Probabilistic functioning and the clinical method. *Psychological Review, 62*, 255–262.

Hammond, K.R. (1965). New directions in research on conflict resolution. *Journal of Social Issues, 21*, 44–66.

Hammond, K.R., Rohrbaugh, J., Mumpower, J., and Adelman, L. (1977). Social Judgment Theory: Applications in policy formation. In M. Kaplan and S. Schwartz (eds), *Human judgment and decision processes in applied settings*. New York: Academic Press.

Hammond, K.R., Stewart, T.R., Brehmer, B., and Steinmann, D.O. (1975). Social Judgment Theory. In M.F. Kaplan and S. Schwartz (eds), *Human judgment and decision processes*. New York: Academic Press.

Hammond, K.R., Todd, F.J., Wilkins, M., and Mitchell, T.O. (1966). Cognitive conflict between persons: Application of the 'lens model' paradigm. *Journal of Experimental Social Psychology, 2*, 343–360.

Hardin, G.J. (1968). The tragedy of the commons. *Science, 162*, 1243–1248.

Harkins, S.G., and Petty, R.E. (1982). Social loafing: allocation of effort or taking it easy. *Journal of Experimental Social Psychology, 16*, 457–465.

Heider, F. (1946). Attitudes and cognitive organization. *Journal of Psychology, 21*, 107–112.

Heider, F. (1958). *The psychology of interpersonal relations*. New York: Wiley.

Hemphill, J.K. (1950). Relations between the size of the group and the behavior of 'superior' leaders. *Journal of Social Psychology, 32*, 11–22.

Hemphill, J.K. (1961). Why people attempt to lead. In L. Petrullo and B.M. Bass (eds), *Leadership and interpersonal behavior*. New York: Holt.

Henchy, T., and Glass, D.C. (1968). Evaluation apprehension and the social facilitation of dominant and subordinate responses. *Journal of Personality and Social Psychology, 10*, 446–454.

Hersey, P., and Blanchard, K.H. (1982). *Management of organizational behavior* (fourth edition). Englewood Cliffs, N.J.: Prentice Hall.

Hewstone, M. (1989). *Causal attribution: From cognitive processes to collective beliefs*. Oxford: Blackwell.

Hewstone, M., and Jaspars, J.M.F. (1987). Covariation and causal attribution: A logical model of the intuitive analysis of variance. *Journal of Personality and Social Psychology, 53*, 663–672.

Higgins, E.T. (1981). The 'communication game': Implications for social cognition and persuasion. In E.T. Higgins, C.P. Herman and M.P. Zanna (eds), *Social cognition: The Ontario symposium*, vol. 1. Hillsdale, N.J.: Erlbaum.

Hinsz, V.B., and Davis, J.H. (1984). Persuasive arguments theory, group polarization, and choice shifts. *Personality and Social Psychology Bulletin, 10*, 260–268.

Hoekstra, M.H.R., and Wilke, H.A.M. (1972). Wage recommendations in groups, a cross-cultural study. *Nederlands Tijdschrift voor de Psychologie, 27*, 266–272.

Hollander, E.P. (1978). *Leadership dynamics: A practical guide to effective relationships.* New York: Free Press/Macmillan.

Hollander, E.P. (1985). Leadership and power. In G. Lindzey and E. Aronson (eds), *The handbook of social psychology* (third edition), vol. 2. New York: Random House.

Hollander, E.P., and Offerman, L.R. (1990). Power and leadership in organizations. *American Psychologist, 45*, 179–189.

Holzkamp, K. (1972). Soziale Kognition. In C.F. Graumann (ed.), *Handbuch der Psychologie, 7. Band, Sozialpsychologie, 2. Halbband: Forschungsberichte*. Göttingen: Hogrefe.

Homans, G.C. (1974). *Social behavior. Its elementary forms* (revised edition). New York: Harcourt, Brace, Jovanovich.

Hosking, D.M. (1981). A critical evaluation of Fiedler's contingency hypothesis. In G.M. Stephenson and J.M. Davis (eds), *Progress in applied social psychology*. Chichester: Wiley.

House, R.J., and Mitchell, T.R. (1974). Path-goal theory of leadership. *Journal of Contemporary Business, 3*, 81–97.

Ilgen, D.R., and Fujii, D.S. (1976). An investigation of the validity of leader behavior descriptions obtained from subordinates. *Journal of Applied Psychology, 61*, 642–651.

Ingham, A.G., Levinger, G., Graves, J., and Peckham, V. (1974). The Ringelmann effect: Studies of group size and group performance. *Journal of Personality and Social Psychology, 10*, 371–384.

Insko, C.A. (1984). Balance theory, the Jordan paradigm, and the Wiest tetrahedron. In L. Berkowitz (ed.), *Advances in experimental social psychology*, vol. 18. Orlando: Academic Press.

Isenberg, D.J. (1986). Group polarization: A critical review and meta-analysis. *Journal of Personality and Social Psychology, 50*, 1141–1151.

Jackson, J.M., and Harkins, S.G. (1985). Equity in effort: An explanation of the social loafing effect. *Journal of Personality and Social Psychology, 49*, 1199–1206.

Jacobs, R.C., and Campbell, D.T. (1961). The perpetuation of an arbitrary tradition through several generations of a laboratory microculture. *Journal of Abnormal and Social Psychology, 62*, 649–658.

Janis, I.L. (1972). *Victims of groupthink*. Boston: Houghton Mifflin.

Janis, I.L. (1982). *Victims of groupthink* (second edition). Boston: Houghton Mifflin.

Janis, I.L., and Mann, L. (1977). *Decision making. A psychological analysis of conflict, choice, and commitment*. New York: Free Press.

Jasso, G., and Rossi, P.H. (1977). Distributive justice and earned income. *American Sociological Review, 42*, 639–651.

Jellison, J.M., and Arkin, R. (1977). Social comparison of abilities: A self-presentation approach to decision-making in groups. In J.M. Suls and R.L. Miller (eds), *Social comparison processes*. Washington, D.C.: Hemisphere.

Jellison, J.M., and Riskind, J. (1970). A social comparison of abilities interpretation of risk-taking behavior. *Journal of Personality and Social Psychology, 15*, 375–390.

Johnson, D.W., Maruyama, G., Johnson, R., Nelson, D., and Skon, L. (1981). Effects of cooperative, competitive and individualistic goal structures on achievement: a meta-analysis. *Psychological Bulletin, 89*, 47–62.

Johnson, H., and Johnson, P. (1991). Task knowledge structures: Psychological basis and integration into system design. *Acta Psychologica, 78*, 3–26.

Johnston, L., Jr. (1968). The immediate and short-term effects of group discusssions and individual study on risk-levels. Unpublished Doctoral dissertation, Florida State University.

Jones, E.E., and Davis, K.E. (1965). From acts to dispositions: The attribution process in person perception. In L. Berkowitz (ed.), *Advances in experimental social psychology*, vol. 2. New York: Academic Press.

Jones, E.E., and Gerard, H.B. (1967). *Foundations of social psychology*. New York: Wiley.

Jones, E.E., and Nisbett, R.E. (1972). The actor and the observer: divergent perceptions of the causes of behaviour. In E.E. Jones, D.E. Kanouse, H.H. Kelley, R.E. Nisbett, S. Valins and B. Weiner (eds), *Attribution: Perceiving the cause of behavior*. Morristown, N.J.: General Learning Press.

Jordan, N. (1953). Behavioral forces that are a function of attitudes and of cognitive organization. *Human Relations, 6*, 273–287.

Kahneman, D. (1973). *Attention and effort*. Englewood Cliffs, N.J.: Prentice Hall.

Kaplan, M.F. (1987). The influence process in group decision making. In C. Hendrick (ed.), *Group processes. Review of personality and social psychology*, vol. 8. Newbury Park, Cal.: Sage.

Katz, D., and Kahn, R.L. (1978). *The social psychology of organizations* (second edition). New York: Wiley.

Keers, C., and Wilke, H. (1987). *Oriëntatie in de sociale psychologie*. Alphen aan de Rijn: Samsom.

Kelley, H.H. (1967). Attribution theory in social psychology. In D. Levine (ed.), *Nebraska symposium on motivation*, vol. 15. Lincoln, Neb.: University of Nebraska Press.

Kelley, H.H., and Arrowood, A.J. (1960). Coalitions in the triad: critique and experiment. *Sociometry, 23*, 231–244.

Kelley, H.H., and Thibaut, J.W. (1969). Group problem solving. In G. Lindzey and E. Aronson (eds), *The handbook of social psychology* (second edition) vol. 4. Reading, Mass.: Addison-Wesley.

Kelley, H.H., and Thibaut, J.W. (1978). *Interpersonal relations: A theory of interdependence*. New York: Wiley.

Kelley, H.H., Thibaut, J.W., Radloff, R., and Mundy, D. (1962). The development of cooperation in the 'minimal social situation.' *Psychological Monographs, 76*, no. 538.

Kerr N.L. (1983) Motivation losses in small groups: A social dilemma analysis. *Journal of Personality and Social Psychology, 45*, 819–828.

Kerr, N.L., and Bruun, S.E. (1981). Ringelmann revisited: Alternative explanations for the social loafing effect. *Personality and Social Psychology Bulletin, 7*, 224–231.

Kerr, N.L., and Bruun, S.E. (1983) Dispensability of member effort and group motivation losses: Free-rider effects. *Journal of Personality and Social Psychology, 44*, 78–94.

Kerr, S., and Jermier, J.M. (1978). Substitutes for leadership: Their meaning and measurement. *Organizational Behavior and Human Performance, 22*, 375–403.

Kervin, J.B. (1977). An information-combining model for expectation status theory: Derivation and tests. *Journal of Mathematical Sociology, 5*, 199–214.

Kiesler, C.A., and Kiesler, S.B. (1969). *Conformity*. Reading, Mass.: Addison-Wesley.

Kipnis, D. (1984). The use of power in organizations and in interpersonal settings. In S. Oskamp (ed.), *Applied social psychology annual*, vol. 5. Newbury Park, Cal.; Sage.

Klugman, S.F. (1947). Group and individual judgments for anticipated events. *Journal of Social Psychology, 26*, 21–33.

Knight, H.C. (1921). A comparison of the reliability of group and individual judgment. Unpublished master's thesis, Columbia University.

Knottnerus, J.D., and Greenstein, T.N. (1981). Status and performance characteristics in social interaction: a theory of status validation. *Social Psychology Quarterly, 44*, 338–349.

Kok, G.J. (1983). *Attitudeverandering binnen groepen*. Unpublished Doctoral dissertation, University of Groningen.

Komorita, S.S., and Meek, D.D. (1978). Generality and validity of some theories of coalition formation. *Journal of Personality and Social Psychology, 36*, 392–404.

Kravitz, D.A., and Martin, B. (1986). Ringelmann rediscovered: The original article. *Journal of Personality and Social Psychology, 50*, 936–941.

Krech, D., Crutchfield, R.S., and Ballachey, E.L. (1962). *Individual in society: A textbook of social psychology.* New York: McGraw-Hill.

Kruglanski, A.W., and Mackie, D.M. (1990). Majority and minority influence: A judgmental process analysis. In W. Stroebe and M. Hewstone (eds), *European review of social psychology*, vol. 1. Chichester: Wiley.

Lamm, H., and Myers, D.G. (1978). Group-induced polarization of attitudes and behaviour. In L. Berkowitz (ed.), *Advances in experimental social psychology*, vol. II. New York: Academic Press.

Latané, B., Williams, K., and Harkins, S. (1979). Many hands make light the work: The causes and consequences of social loafing. *Journal of Personality and Social Psychology, 37*, 822–832.

Latané, B., and Wolf, S. (1981). The social impact of majorities and minorities. *Psychological Review, 88*, 438–453.

Latham, G.P., and Wexley, K.N. (1981). *Increasing productivity through performance appraisal.* Reading, Mass.: Addison-Wesley.

Laughlin, P.R. (1980). Social combination processes of cooperative problem-solving groups on verbal intellective tasks. In M. Fishbein (ed.), *Progress in social psychology*, vol. 1. Hillsdale, N.J.: Erlbaum.

Laughlin, P.R., and Earley, P.C. (1982). Social combination models, persuasive arguments theory, social comparison theory, and choice shift. *Journal of Personality and Social Psychology, 42*, 273–280.

Leavitt, H.J. (1951). Some effects of certain communication patterns on group performance. *Journal of Abnormal and Social Psychology, 46*, 38–50.

Lee, M.T., and Ofshe, R. (1981). The impact of behavioral style and status characteristics on social influence: A test of two competing theories. *Social Psychology Quarterly, 44*, 73–82.

Lerner, M.J., Miller, D.T., and Holmes, J.G. (1976). Deserving and the emergence of forms of justice. In L. Berkowitz and E. Walster (eds), *Advances in experimental social psychology*, vol. 9. New York: Academic Press.

Letwin, G.H., and Stringer, R.H. (1968). *Motivation and organizational climates.* Boston: Harvard Press.

Leventhal, G.S., Michaels, J.W., and Sanford, C. (1972). Inequity and interpersonal conflict: Reward allocation and secrecy about rewards as methods of preventing conflict. *Journal of Personality and Social Psychology, 23*, 88–102.

Leventhal, G.S., and Whiteside, H.S. (1973). Equity and the use of reward to elicit high performance. *Journal of Personality and Social Psychology, 25*, 75–83.

Levinger, G. (1959). The development of perceptions and behavior in newly formed social power relationships. In D. Cartwright (ed.), *Studies in social power.* Ann Arbor, Mich.: Institute for Social Research.

Liden, R.C., and Graen, G. (1980). Generalizability of the vertical dyad linkage model of leadership. *Academy of Management Journal, 23*, 451–465.

Likert, R. (1967). *The human organization.* New York: McGraw-Hill.

Locke, E.A., and Schweiger, D.M. (1979). Participation in decision-making: One more look. In B.M. Staw (ed.), *Research in organizational behavior.* Greenwich, Conn.: JAI Press.

Lockheed, M.E. (1985). Sex and influence: A meta-analysis guided by theory. In J. Berger and M. Zelditch, Jr (eds), *Status rewards and influence.* San Francisco: Jossey-Bass.

Longley, J., and Pruitt, D.G. (1980). Groupthink: A critique of Janis' theory. In L. Wheeler (ed.), *Review of personality and social psychology*, vol. 1. Beverly Hills: Sage.

Lord, R.G. (1977). Functional leadership behavior: Measurement and relation to social power and leadership perception. *Administrative Science Quarterly, 22*, 114–133.

Lord, R.G., Foti, R.J., and De Vader, C.L. (1984). A test of leadership categorization theory: Internal structure, information processing and leadership perceptions. *Organizational Behavior and Human Performance, 34*, 343–378.

Lord, R.G., De Vader, C.L., and Alliger, G.M. (1986). A meta-analysis of the relation between personality traits and leadership perceptions: An application of validity generalization procedures. *Journal of Applied Psychology, 71*, 402–410.

Maass, A., and Clark, R.D. (1984). Hidden impact of minorities: Fifteen years of minority influence research. *Psychological Bulletin, 95*, 428–450.

Maass, A., West, S.G., and Cialdini, R.B. (1987). Minority influence and conversion. In C. Hendrick (ed.), *Group processes. Review of personality and social psychology*, vol. 8. Newbury Park, Cal.: Sage.

McCauley, C.R. (1972). Extremity shifts, risk shifts and attitude shifts after group discussion. *European Journal of Social Psychology, 2*, 417–436.

McClelland, D.C. (1961). *The achieving society*. New York: Van Nostrand.

McGrath, J.E. (1984) *Groups: Interaction and performance*. Englewood Cliffs, N.J.: Prentice Hall.

Mackenzie, K.D. (1976). *A theory of group structures*, vols 1 and 2. New York: Gordon and Beach.

MacNeil, M.K., and Sherif, M. (1976). Norm change over subject generations as a function of arbitrariness of prescribed norms. *Journal of Personality and Social Psychology, 34*, 762–773.

Manstead, A.S.R., and Semin, G.R. (1980). Social facilitation effects: mere enhancement of dominant responses? *British Journal of Social and Clinical Psychology, 19*, 119–136.

Marlowe, D., Gergen, K.J., and Doob, A.N. (1966). Opponent's personality, expectation of social interaction and interpersonal bargaining. *Journal of Personality and Social Psychology, 3*, 206–213.

Martin, M.W., and Sell, J. (1980). The marginal utility of information: Its effects upon decision-making. *Social Psychology Quarterly, 21*, 233–242.

Mazur, A. (1985). A biosocial model of status in face-to-face primate groups. *Social Forces, 64*, 307–402.

Mead, G.H. (1934). *Mind, self and society*. Chicago: University of Chicago Press.

Meertens, R.W. (1980). *Groepspolarisatie*. Deventer: Van Loghum Slaterus.

Messé, L.A., Vallacher, R.R., and Phillips, J.L. (1975). Equity and the formation of revolutionary and conservative coalitions in triads. *Journal of Personality and Social Psychology, 31*, 1141–1146.

Messick, D.M., and Brewer, M.B. (1983). Solving social dilemmas: A review. In L. Wheeler and P. Shaver (eds), *Review of Personality and Social Psychology*, vol. 4. Newbury Park, Cal.: Sage.

Messick, D.M., and Sentis, K.P. (1979). Fairness and preference. *Journal of Experimental Social Psychology, 15*, 418–434.

Messick, D.M., and Sentis, K. (1983). Fairness, preference and fairness biases. In D.M. Messick and K.S. Cook (eds), *Equity theory*. New York: Praeger.

Mikula, G. (1984). Justice and fairness in interpersonal relations: Thoughts and suggestions. In H. Tajfel (ed.), *The social dimension: European developments in social psychology*, vol. 1. Cambridge: Cambridge University Press.

Miller, C.E. (1989). The social psychological effects of group decision rules. In P.B. Paulus (ed.), *Psychology of group influence* (second edition). Hillsdale, N.J.: Erlbaum.

Miller, G.A., Galanter, E., and Pribram, K.H. (1960). *Plans and the structure of behavior*. New York: Holt, Rinehart and Winston.

Miller, K.I., and Monge, P.R. (1986). Participation, satisfaction and productivity: A meta-analytic review. *Academy of Management Journal, 29*, 727–753.

Miller, R.L., and Suls, J.M. (1977) Affiliation preferences as a function of attitude and ability similarity. In J.M. Suls and R.L. Miller (eds), *Social comparison processes*. Washington, D.C.: Hemisphere.

Mintzberg, H. (1979). *The structuring of organizations*. Englewood Cliffs: Prentice Hall.

Mitchell, T.R., and Beach, L.R. (1990). ' . . . Do I Love Thee? Let Me Count . . .': Towards an understanding of intuitive and automatic decision making. *Organizational Behavior and Human Decision Processes, 47*, 1–20.

Mitchell, T.R., Larson, J.R. and Green, S.G. (1977). Leader behavior, situational moderators, and group performance: An attributional analysis. *Organizational Behavior and Human Performance, 18*, 254–268.

Montgomery, R.L., Hinkle, S.W., and Enzie, R.F. (1976). Arbitrary norms and social change in high and low authoritarian societies. *Journal of Personality and Social Psychology, 33*, 698–708.

Moreland, R.L., and Levine, J.M. (1989). Newcomers and oldtimers in small groups. In P.B. Paulus (ed.), *Psychology of group influence* (second edition). Hillsdale, N.J.: Erlbaum.

Morse, N.C., and Reimer, E. (1956). The experimental change of a major organizational variable. *Journal of Abnormal and Social Psychology, 52*, 120–130.

Moscovici, S. (1976). *Social influence and social change*. London: Academic Press.

Moscovici, S. (1980). Toward a theory of conversion behavior. In L. Berkowitz (ed.), *Advances in experimental social psychology*, vol. 13. New York: Academic Press.

Moscovici, S. (1985). Social influence and conformity. In G. Lindzey and E. Aronson (eds), *The handbook of social psychology* (third edition), vol. 2. New York: Random House.

Moscovici, S., and Doise, W. (1974). Decision making in groups. In C. Nemeth (ed.), *Social psychology: Classic and contemporary integrations*. Chicago: Rand McNally.

Moscovici, S., and Zavalloni, M. (1969). The group as a polarizer of attitudes. *Journal of Personality and Social Psychology, 12*, 125–135.

Moscovici, S., Lage, E., and Naffrechoux, M. (1969). Influence of a consistent minority on the responses of a majority in a color perception task. *Sociometry, 32*, 365–380.

Moulton, R.W. (1965). Effects of success and failure on level of aspiration as related to achievement motives. *Journal of Personality and Social Psychology, 1*, 399–406.

Mucchi-Faina, A., Maass, A., and Volpato, C. (1991). Social influence: The role of originality. *European Journal of Social Psychology, 17*, 183–197.

Mugny, G., and Perez, J.A. (eds) (1991). *The social psychology of minority influence*. Cambridge: Cambridge University Press.

Mulder, M. (1963) *Group structure, motivation and group performance*. The Hague and Paris: Mouton.

Mulder, M. (1977). *The daily power game*. Leiden: Martinus Nijhoff.

Mullen, B., Johnson, C., and Salas, E. (1991). Productivity loss in brainstorming groups: A meta-analytic integration. *Basic and Applied Social Psychology, 12*, 3–33.

Murnighan, J.K. (1978). Strength and weakness in four coalition situations. *Behavioral Science, 23*, 195–209.

Murray, H.A. (1943). *Thematic apperception test manual*. Cambridge, Mass.: Harvard University Press.

Myers, D.G., and Lamm, H. (1976). The group polarization phenomenon. *Psychological Bulletin, 83*, 602–627.

Nemeth, C.J. (1986). Differential contributions of majority and minority influence. *Psychological Review, 93*, 23–32.

Nemeth, C.J. (1992). Minority dissent as a stimulant to group performance. In S. Worchel, W. Wood and J.A. Simpson (eds), *Group processes and productivity*. Newbury Park, Cal.: Sage.

Nemeth, C.J., and Kwan, J.L. (1985). Originality of word associations as a function of majority vs. minority influence. *Social Psychology Quarterly, 48*, 277–282.

Nemeth, C.J., and Kwan, J.L. (1987). Minority influence, divergent thinking and detection of correct solutions. *Journal of Applied Social Psychology, 17*, 786–797.

Newcomb, T.M. (1953). An approach to the study of communicative acts. *Psychological Review, 60*, 393–404.

Newcomb, T.M. (1961). *The acquaintance process.* New York: Holt, Rinehart and Winston.

Newcomb, T.M. (1968). Interpersonal balance. In R.P. Abelson, E. Aronson, W.J. McGuire, T.M. Newcomb, M.J. Rosenberg and P.H. Tannenbaum (eds), *Theories of cognitive consistency: A sourcebook.* Chicago: Rand McNally.

Ng, S. (1977). Structural and non-structural aspects of power distance reduction tendencies. *European Journal of Social Psychology, 7*, 317–345.

Ng, S. (1980). *The social psychology of power.* London: Academic Press.

Norman, D.A., and Bobrow, D.G. (1979). Descriptions: An intermediate stage in memory retrieval. *Cognitive Psychology, 11*, 107–123.

Oeser, O.A., and Harary, F. (1962). A mathematical model for structural role theory: I. *Human Relations, 15*, 89–109.

Oeser, O.A., and Harary, F. (1964). A mathematical model for structural role theory: II. *Human Relations, 17*, 3–17.

Ono, K., and Davis, J.H. (1988). Individual judgment and group interaction: A variable perspective approach. *Organizational Behavior and Human Decision Processes, 41*, 211–232.

Osborn, A.F. (1957) *Applied imagination.* New York: Scribner's.

Paulus, P.B. (1983). Group influence on task performance and informational processing. In P.B. Paulus (ed.), *Basic group processes.* New York: Springer.

Paulus, P.B., and Murdoch, P. (1971). Anticipated evaluation and audience presence in the enhancement of dominant responses. *Journal of Experimental Social Psychology, 7*, 280–291.

Pence, E.C., Pendleton, W.C., Dobbins, G.H., and Sgro, J.A. (1982). Effects of causal explanations and sex variables on recommendations for corrective action following employee failure. *Organizational Behavior and Human Performance, 29*, 227–240.

Pepinski, P.N., Hemphill, J.K., and Shevitz, R.N. (1958). Attempts to lead, group productivity and morale under conditions of acceptance and rejection. *Journal of Abnormal and Social Psychology, 57*, 47–54.

Pessin, J. (1933). The comparative effects of social and mechanical stimulation on memorizing. *American Journal of Psychology, 45*, 263–270.

Peters, T.J., and Waterman, R.H. (1982). *In search of excellence.* New York: Harper and Row.

Pfeffer, J. (1977). The ambiguity of leadership. *Academy of Management Review, 2*, 104–112.

Phillips, J.S. and Lord, R.G. (1981). Causal attributions and perception of leadership. *Organizational Behavior and Human Performance, 28*, 143–163.

Porter, L.W., and Roberts, K.H. (1976). Communication in organizations. In M.D. Dunnette (ed.), *Handbook of industrial and organizational psychology.* Chicago: Rand McNally.

Pruitt, D.G. (1971). Choice shifts in group discussion. An introductory review. *Journal of Personality and Social Psychology, 20*, 339–360.

Pruitt, D.G. (1972). Methods for resolving differences of interest: A theoretical analysis. *Journal of Social Issues, 28*, 133–154.

Quinn, R.E., and McGrath, M.R. (1982). Moving beyond the single solution perspective. *Journal of Applied Behavioral Science, 18*, 463–472.

Riches, P., and Foddy, M. (1989). Ethnic accent as a status cue. *Social Psychology Quarterly, 52*, 197–206.

Ridgeway, C.L. (1978). Conformity, group-oriented motivation, and status attainment in small groups. *Social Psychology Quarterly, 41*, 175–188.

Ridgeway, C.L., Berger, J., and Smith, L. (1985). Non-verbal cues and status: an expectation states approach. *American Journal of Sociology, 90*, 955–978.

Rijsman, J.B. (1983). The dynamics of social competition in personal and categorical comparison-situations. In W. Doise and S. Moscovici (eds), *Current Issues in European Social Psychology*, vol. 1. Cambridge: Cambridge University Press.

Riordan, C., and Ruggiero, J. (1980). Producing equal-status interracial interaction: A replication. *Social Psychology Quarterly, 43*, 131–136.

Roethlisberger, F.J., and Dickson, W.J. (1939). *Management and the worker*. Cambridge, Mass.: Harvard University Press.

Rommetveit, R. (1974). *On message structure*. London: Wiley.

Rosch, E. (1978). Principles of categorization. In E. Rosch and B.B. Lloyd (eds), *Cognition and categorization*. Hillsdale, N.J.: Erlbaum.

Rosenbaum, M.E., Moore, D.L., Cotton, J.L., Cook, M.S., Hieser, R.A., Shovar, M.N., and Gray, M.J. (1980). Group productivity and process: Pure and mixed reward structures and task interdependence. *Journal of Personality and Social Psychology, 39*, 626–642.

Ross, M., and Sicoly, F. (1979). Egocentric biases in availability and attribution. *Journal of Personality and Social Psychology, 37*, 322–336.

Rush, M.C., Thomas, J.C., and Lord, R.G. (1977). Implicit leadership theory: A potential threat to the internal validity of the leader behavior questionnaires. *Organizational Behavioral and Human Performance, 20*, 93–110.

Rutte, C.G., and Wilke, H.A.M. (1984). Social dilemmas and leadership. *European Journal of Social Psychology, 14*, 105–121.

Rutte, C.G., and Wilke, H.A.M. (1985). Preference for decision structures in a social dilemma situation. *European Journal of Social Psychology, 15*, 367–370.

Sanders, G.S. (1981). Driven by distraction: an integrate review of social facilitation theory and research. *Journal of Experimental Social Psychology, 17*, 227–251.

Sanders, G.S., Baron, R.S., and Moore, D.L. (1978). Distraction and social comparison as mediators of social facilitation effects. *Journal of Experimental Social Psychology, 14*, 291–303.

Sanna, L.J. (1992). Self-efficacy theory: Implications for social facilitation and social loafing. *Journal of Personality and Social Psychology, 62*, 774–786.

Sarbin, T.R., and Allen, V.L. (1968). Role theory. In G. Lindzey and E. Aronson (eds), *The handbook of social psychology* (second edition), vol. 1. Reading, Mass.: Addison-Wesley.

Schachter, S. (1951). Deviation, rejection and communication. *Journal of Abnormal and Social Psychology, 46*, 190–207.

Schachter, S., Ellertson, N., McBride, D., and Gregory, D. (1951). An experimental study of cohesiveness and productivity. *Human Relations, 4*, 229–238.

Schank, R. (1982). *Dynamic memory: A theory of reminding and learning in computers and people*. New York: Cambridge University Press.

Scheier, M.F., and Carver, C.S. (1988). A model of behavioral self-regulation: Translating intention into action. In L. Berkowitz (ed.), *Advances in experimental social psychology*, vol. 21. San Diego: Academic Press.

Schriesheim, C.A., and Kerr, S. (1977). R.I.P. L.P.C.: A response to Fiedler. In J.G. Hunt and L.L. Larson (eds), *Leadership: The cutting edge*. Carbondale: Southern Illinois University Press.

Schweiger, D.M., and Leana, C.R. (1986). Participation in decision making. In E.A. Locke (ed.), *Generalizing from laboratory to field settings*. Lexington, Mass.: Heath.

Shaw, M. (1932). A comparison of individuals and small groups in the rational solution of complex problems. *American Journal of Psychology, 44*, 491–504.

Shaw, M.E. (1964). Communication networks. In L. Berkowitz (ed.), *Advances in experimental social psychology*, vol. 1. New York: Academic Press.

Shaw, M.E. (1981). *Group dynamics: The psychology of small group behavior* (third edition). New York: McGraw-Hill.

Sherif, M. (1936). *The psychology of social norms*. New York: Harper and Row.

Sherif, M., and Sherif, C.W. (1969). *Social psychology*. New York: Harper and Row.

Sherman, S.J. (1983). Expectation-based and automatic behavior: A comment on Lee and Ofshe and Berger and Zelditch. *Social Psychology Quarterly, 46*, 66–70.

Shiffrin, R.M. (1975). Short-term-store: The basis for a memory system. In F. Restle, R.M. Shriffin, N.J. Castellan, H. Lindman and D.B. Pisoni (eds), *Cognitive theory*, vol. 1. Hillsdale, N.J.: Erlbaum.

Shiffrin, R.M., and Schneider, W. (1977). Controlled and automatic human information processing, II: Perceptual learning, automatic atttending, and a general theory. *Psychological Review, 84*, 127–190.

Sidowski, J.B. (1957). Reward and punishment in a minimal social situation. *Journal of Experimental Psychology, 54*, 318–326.

Sidowski, J.B., Wycoff, L.B., and Tabory, L. (1956). The influence of reinforcement and punishment in a minimal social situation. *Journal of Abnormal and Social Psychology, 52*, 115–119.

Siero, F.W. (1987). *Feedback en motivatie in de klas*. Unpublished Doctoral dissertation. University of Groningen.

Spence, K.W. (1956). *Behavior theory and conditioning*. New Haven, Conn.: Yale University Press.

Stasser, G. (1988). Computer simulation as a research tool: The DISCUSS model of group decision making. *Journal of Experimental Social Psychology, 24*, 393–422.

Stasser, G. (1992). Pooling of unshared information during group discussion. In S. Worchel, W. Wood and J.A. Simpson (eds), *Group process and productivity*. Newsbury Park Cal.: Sage.

Stasser, G., Kerr, N.L., and Davis, J.H. (1989). Influence processes and consensus models in decision-making groups. In P.B. Paulus (ed.), *Psychology of group influence* (second edition). Hillsdale, N.J.: Erlbaum.

Stasser, G., and Stewart, D. (1992). Discovery of hidden profiles by decision-making groups: Solving a problem versus making a judgment. *Journal of Personality and Social Psychology, 63*, 426–434.

Stasser. G., Taylor, L.A., and Hanna, C. (1989). Information sampling in structured and unstructured discussions of three- and six-person groups. *Journal of Personality and Social Psychology, 57*, 67–78.

Stasser, G., and Titus, W. (1985). Pooling of unshared information in group decision making: Biased information sampling during group discussion. *Journal of Personality and Social Psychology, 48*, 1467–1478.

Steiner, I.D. (1972). *Group processes and productivity*. New York: Academic Press.

Steiner, I.D. (1976). Task-performing groups. In J.W. Thibaut, J.T. Spence and R.C. Carson (eds), *Contemporary topics in social psychology*. Morristown, N.J.: General Learning Press.

Steiner, I.D. (1982). Heuristic models of groupthink. In H. Brandstätter, J.H. Davis and G. Stocker-Kreichgauer (eds), *Group decision making*. London: Academic Press.

Stevens, L., and Jones, E.E. (1976). Defensive attribution and the Kelley cube. *Journal of Personality and Social Psychology, 34*, 809–820.

Stogdill, R.M. (1948). Personal factors associated with leadership: A survey of the literature. *Journal of Psychology, 25*, 35–71.

Stoner, J.A.F. (1961). A comparison of individual and group decisions involving risk. Unpublished Master's thesis, Massachusetts Institute of Technology.

Stroebe, W., and Diehl, M. (1991). You can't beat good experiments with correlational evidence: Mullen, Johnson, and Solas's meta-analytic misinterpretations. *Basic and Applied Social Psychology, 12*, 25–32.

Stroebe, W., and Frey, B.S. (1982). Self-interest and collective action: the economics and psychology of public goods. *British Journal of Social Psychology, 21*, 121–137.

Strube, M.J., Miles, M.E., and Finch, W.H. (1981). The social facilitation of a simple task: Field tests of alternative explanations. *Personality and Social Psychology Bulletin, 7*, 701–707.

Tajfel, H. (ed.) (1978). Differentiation between social groups. London: Academic Press.

Tanford, S., and Penrod, S. (1984). Social influence model: A formal integration of research on majority and minority influence processes. *Psychological Bulletin, 95*, 189–225.

Tannenbaum, R., and Schmidt, W.H. (1958). How to choose a leadership pattern. *Harvard Business Review, 36*, 95–101.

Taylor, F.W. (1911). *The principles of scientific management*. New York: Harper.

Tetlock, P.E., Peterson, R.S., McGuire, C., Chang, S., and Feld, P. (1992). Assessing political group dynamics: A test of the groupthink model. *Journal of Personality and Social Psychology, 63*, 403–425.

Thibaut, J.W., and Kelley, H.H. (1959). *The social psychology of groups*. New York: Wiley.

Thibaut, J.W., and Strickland, L.H. (1956) Psychological set and social conformity. *Journal of Personality, 25*, 115–129.

Thibaut, J.W., and Walker, L. (1975). *Procedural justice: a psychological analysis*. Hillsdale, N.J.: Erlbaum.

Thomas, E.J., and Fink, C.F. (1961). Models of group problem solving. *Journal of Abnormal and Social Psychology, 63*, 53–63.

Torrance, A.P. (1954). The behavior of small groups under the stress of conditions of 'survival'. *American Sociological Review, 19*, 751–755.

Travis, L.E. (1925). The effect of a small audience upon eye-hand coordination. *Journal of Abnormal and Social Psychology, 20*, 142–146.

Triplett, N. (1897). The dynamogenic factors in pacemaking and competition. *American Journal of Psychology, 9*, 507–533.

Turner, J.C. (1980). Fairness or discrimination in inter-group behaviour? A reply to Branthwaite, Doyle and Lightbown. *European Journal of Social Psychology, 10*, 131–147.

Turner, J.C. (1991). *Social influence*. Buckingham: Open University Press.

Turner, J.C., and Oakes, P.J. (1989). Self-categorization theory and social influence. In P.B. Paulus (ed.), *The psychology of group influence* (second edition). Hillsdale, N.J.: Erlbaum.

Turner, J.C., Hogg, M.A., Oakes, P.J., Reicher, S.D., and Wetherell, M.S. (1987). *Rediscovering the social group: A self-categorization theory*. Oxford: Blackwell.

Turner, J.C., Wetherell, M.S., and Hogg, M.A. (1989). Referent informational influence and group polarization. *British Journal of Social Psychology, 28*, 135–147.

Tyler, T.R., and McGraw, K.M. (1986). Ideology and the interpretation of personal experience: Procedural justice and political quiescence. *Journal of Social Issues, 42*, 115–128.

Valacich, J.S., Dennis, A.R. and Connolly, T. (forthcoming). Idea generation in computer-based groups: A new ending to an old story. *Organizational Behavior and Human Decision Processes*.

Van de Ven, A.H. (1974). *Group decision-making effectiveness*. Kent, Ohio: Center for Business and Economic Research Press.

van der Vlist, R. (1970). *Verschillen in groepsprestaties in de Nederlandse zeevisserij.* Alphen aan de Rijn: Samsom.

Vecchio, R.P., and Gobdal, B.C. (1984). The vertical-dyad linkage model of leadership: Problems and prospects. *Organizational Behavior and Human Performance, 34*, 5–20.

Veen, P., and Wilke, H.A.M. (1984). *De kern van de sociale psychologie.* Deventer: Van Loghum Slaterus.

Vinacke, W.E., and Arkoff, A. (1957). An experimental study of coalitions in the triad. *American Sociological Review, 22*, 406–414.

Vinokur, A., and Burnstein, E. (1974). The effects of partially shared persuasive arguments on group induced shifts: A group problem solving approach. *Journal of Personality and Social Psychology, 29*, 305–315.

Vinokur, A., and Burnstein, E. (1978). Novel argumentation and attitude change: The case of polarization following group discussion. *European Journal of Social Psychology, 8*, 335–348.

Vinokur, A., Burnstein, E., Sechrest, L., and Wortman, P. (1985). Group decision making by experts: Field study of panels evaluating medical technologies. *Journal of Personality and Social Psychology, 49*, 70–84.

Vinokur, A., Trope, Y., and Burnstein, E. (1975). A decision-making analysis of persuasive argumentation and the choice-shift effect. *Journal of Experimental Social Psychology, 11*, 127–148.

von Grumbkow, J. (1980). *Sociale vergelijkingen van salarissen.* Unpublished Doctoral dissertation, University of Groningen.

von Grumbkow, J., Deen, E., Steensma, H., and Wilke, H.A.M. (1976). The effect of future interaction on the distribution of rewards. *European Journal of Social Psychology, 6*, 119–123.

von Grumbkow, J. Steensma, H., and Wilke, H.A.M. (1977) Toewijzen van beloningen in aanwezigheid van de proefleider. *Nederlands Tijdschrift voor de Psychologie, 32*, 495–500.

von Grumbkow, J., Steensma, H., and Wilke, H.A.M. (1980) Vergelijking van twee methoden om het verdelen van belongingen te onderzoeken. *Nederlands Tijdschrift voor de Psychologie, 35*, 407–416.

von Grumbkow, J., and Wilke, H.A.M. (1974). Sociale witwisseling en billijkheid: Toetsing en evaluatie van billijkheidstheorie. *Nederlands Tijdschrift voor de Psychologie, 29*, 281–316.

Vroom, V.H., and Jago, A.G. (1988). *The new leadership: Managing participation in organizations.* Englewood Cliffs, N.J.: Prentice Hall.

Vroom, V.H., and Yetton, P.W. (1973). *Leadership and decision-making.* Pittsburgh, Pa.: University of Pittsburgh Press.

Wagner, D.G., Ford, R.S., and Ford, T.W. (1986). Can gender inequalities be reduced? *American Sociological Review, 51*, 47–61.

Wagner, J.A., and Gooding, R.Z. (1987). Shared influence and organizational behavior: A meta-analysis of situational variables expected to moderate participation-outcome relationships. *Academy of Management Journal, 30*, 524–541.

Wakabayashy, M., and Graen, G. (1984). The Japanese career progress study: A seven year follow-up. *Journal of Applied Psychology, 69*, 603–614.

Wallach, M.A., Kogan, N., and Bem, D.J. (1962). Group influence on individual risk taking. *Journal of Abnormal and Social Psychology, 65*, 75–86.

Walster, E., Walster, G.W., and Berscheid, E. (eds) (1978). *Equity: Theory and research.* Boston: Allyn and Bacon.

Weary, G., and Arkin, R.M. (1981). Attributional self-presentation. In J.H. Harvey, W.J. Ickes and R.F. Kidd (eds), New directions in attribution research, vol. 3. Hillsdale, N.J.: Erlbaum.

Weber, M. (1922) *Wirtschaft und Gesellschaft: Grundriss der verstehenden Soziologie.* Tübingen: Mohr.

Weber, M. (1957). *The theory of social and economic organizations.* Glencoe, Ill.: Free Press.
Weiner, B. (1986). *An attributional theory of motivation and emotion.* New York: Springer Verlag.
Weiner, B., and Kukla, A. (1970). An attributional analysis of achievement motivation. *Journal of Personality and Social Psychology, 15,* 1–20.
West, S.S., and Wicklund, R.A. (1980). *A primer of social psychological theories.* Monterey, Cal.: Brooks/Cole.
Wheeler, L. (1966). Motivation as a determinant of upward comparison. *Journal of Experimental Social Psychology,* 2 (suppl. 1), 27–31.
Wheeler, L. (1991). A brief history of social comparison theory. In J. Suls and T.A. Wills (eds), *Social comparison: Contemporary theory and research.* Hillsdale, N.J.: Erlbaum.
Whyte, W.F. (1948). *Human relations in the restaurant industry.* New York: McGraw-Hill.
Wilke, H.A.M. (1983). Equity: information and effect dependency. In D.M. Messick and K.S. Cook (eds), *Equity theory.* New York: Praeger.
Wilke, H.A.M. (ed.) (1985). *Coalition formation.* Amsterdam: North-Holland.
Wilke, H.A.M. (1987). *Organisatie-psychologie.* Assen: Van Gorcum.
Wilke, H.A.M. (1991). Greed, efficiency and fairness in resource management situations. In W. Stroebe and M. Hewstone (eds), *European Review of Social Psychology,* vol. 2. Chichester: Wiley.
Wilke, H.A.M., and Pruyn, J. (1981). Billijkheidstheorie en coalitieformatie. *Gedrag, 9, 3,* 159–170.
Wilke, H.A.M., Kuyper, H.M., and Lewis, C. (1983). Aspired partnership. In R. Tietz, (ed.), *Aspiration levels in bargaining and economic decision making.* Berlin: Springer-Verlag.
Wilke, H.A.M., Messick, D.M., and Rutte, C.G. (eds) (1986). *Experimental social dilemmas.* Frankfurt a/Main: Lang.
Wilke, H.A.M., Pruyn, J., and de Vries, G.J. (1978). Coalition formation: political attitudes and power. *European Journal of Social Psychology, 8,* 245–261.
Williams, K.D., Nida, S.A., Baca, L.D., and Latané, B. (1989). Social loafing and swimming: effects of identifiability on individual and relay performance of intercollegate swimmers. *Basic and Applied Social Psychology, 10,* 73–81.
Wit, A.P., Wilke, H.A.M., and van Dijk, E. (1989). Attribution of leadership in a resource management situation. *European Journal of Social Psychology, 19,* 327–338.
Wolters, G. (1988). Ontwikkelingen in het geheugenonderzoek. *Nederlands Tijdschrift voor de Psychologie, 43,* 347–362.
Wood, W., and Karten, S.J. (1986). Sex differences in interaction style as a product of perceived sex differences in competence. *Journal of Personality and Social Psychology, 50,* 341–347.
Zaccaro, S.J. (1984). Social loafing: The role of task attractiveness. *Personality and Social Psychology Bulletin, 10,* 99–106.
Zajonc, R.B. (1960). The process of cognitive tuning in communication. *Journal of Abnormal and Social Psychology, 61,* 159–167.
Zajonc, R.B. (1965). Social facilitation. *Science, 149,* 269–274.
Zajonc, R.B. (1968). Cognitive theories in social psychology. In G. Lindzey and E. Aronson (eds), *The handbook of social psychology* (second edition), vol. 1. Reading, Mass.: Addison-Wesley.
Zajonc, R.B. (1980). Compresence. In P.B. Paulus (ed.), *Psychology of group influence.* Hillsdale, N.J.: Erlbaum.
Zajonc, R.B., and Nieuwenhuyse, B. (1964). Relationship between word frequency and recognition: Perceptual process or response bias? *Journal of Experimental Psychology, 67,* 276–285.

Zajonc, R.B., and Sales, S.M. (1966). Social facilitation of dominant and subordinate responses. *Journal of Experimental Social Psychology, 2*, 160–168.

Zander, A.F. (1968). Group aspirations. In D. Cartwright and A.F. Zander (eds), *Group dynamics: Research and theory* (third edn). New York: Harper and Row.

Zander, A.F. (1971). *Motives and goals in groups*. New York: Academic Press.

Zander, A.F. (1982). *Making groups effective*. San Francisco: Jossey-Bass.

Zander, A.F. (1983). Team spirit vs. the individual achiever. In H.H. Blumberg, A. Hare and M. Davies (eds), *Small groups and social interactions*, vol. 1. New York: Wiley.

Zander, A.F., and Wolfe, D. (1964). Administrative rewards and coordination among committee members. *Administrative Science Quarterly, 9*, 50–69.

Zuber, J.A., Crott, H.W., and Werner, J. (1992). Choice shift and group polarization: An analysis of the status of arguments and social decision schemes. *Journal of Personality and Social Psychology, 62*, 50–61.

Zucker, L.G. (1977). The role of institutionalization in cultural persistence. *American Sociological Review, 42*, 726–743.

Name index

Subject index

LIBRARY, UNIVERSITY COLLEGE CHESTER